MarketPsych

MarketPsych

HOW TO MANAGE FEAR AND BUILD YOUR INVESTOR IDENTITY

Richard L. Peterson
Frank F. Murtha

WILEY

John Wiley & Sons, Inc.

Published by John Wiley & Sons, Inc., Hoboken, New Jersey.
Published simultaneously in Canada.

For general information on our other products and services or for technical support, please contact our Customer Care Department within the United States at (800) 762-2974, outside the United States at (317) 572-3993 or fax (317) 572-4002.

Wiley also publishes its books in a variety of electronic formats. Some content that appears in print may not be available in electronic books. For more information about Wiley products, visit our web site at www.wiley.com.

Library of Congress Cataloging-in-Publication Data:
Peterson, Richard L., 1972-
    MarketPsych : how to manage fear and build your investor identity/Richard L. Peterson, Frank F. Murtha.
        p. cm.
    Includes index.
    ISBN 978-0-470-54358-0 (cloth); 978-0-470-88677-9 (ebk); 978-0-470-88664-9 (ebk)
    1. Investment advisors—Psychology.   2. Investments—Psychological aspects.   3. Stockbrokers—Psychology.   4. Financial planners—Psychology.   I. Murtha, Frank F., 1970-   II. Title.
    HG4621.P468 2010
    332.601'9—dc22   2010013523

Printed in the United States of America
10 9 8 7 6 5 4 3 2

For Sarah, Lucia, and Aurora.
You are such a joy!
—Richard

For Lillian. Thanks for keeping me on the path.
—Frank

Contents

Preface

You may not realize it, but you are on a dangerous journey—the life-long process of wealth accumulation. Your destination is to establish financial freedom and security so that you (and your loved ones) can enjoy the *quality of life* you have always wanted. But make no mistake, you have an enemy that doesn't want you to get there. The enemy is "the market," and it is engaged in a covert psychological war designed to subvert you at every opportunity. The market probes for emotional weak spots and exploits them, scaring you out when the worst is over, luring you in when the gains have been made, baiting you into chasing fool's gold, or convincing you to it's okay to perpetually "start tomorrow."

Sure, the journey seems easy enough. Buy low, sell high, and all that. The market goes up over time. Just put your money away, and you'll get to where you want to go. If only it were that easy. Investing in the market more closely resembles a crooked carnival game in which you throw a softball at a stack of milk bottles for a dollar. "It's so easy! So simple, a child could do it. Step right up!" The deception is the simplicity. The game is designed for you to lose.

Don't believe us? From 1989 through 2008, the S&P 500 Index had a 5.51 percent average annual return after inflation. Looks fine, you say. But what did the average *equities investor* get as an average annual return, postinflation, during that same 20-year period? *Negative 0.97 percent* per year. (We told you the market was out to get you.) Those are percentages. What about real-life dollars?

A "market" return on $100,000 invested in the U.S. stock market in January of 1989 would yield a postinflation total of $292,329 20 years later—nearly three times as much. Yet the average equities investor would have a total of $82,288 after the same time period. These two returns represent the difference between Ivy League universities for your kids or state schools, between a down payment on a house or not, between vacationing or staying home. In short, this is the difference between leading the life you want to live, and leading the life you're forced to live.

Losses are not only possible, they're predictable. It's the way the game is designed. At the carnival, they get you with physics—the milk bottles are spread out so that it is virtually impossible for a softball to knock them all down with one throw. The market gets you with psychology, baiting you into a reactive paradigm that turns your own fear, greed, hope, and even pride against you. After several go-rounds we find ourselves asking, where's my 9 percent average annual return? And how come I never knock down all the milk bottles?

The investing process even preys on our own biology. The rational, reasoning part of our brain—the prefrontal cortex—evolved about 100,000 years ago. It grew *on top of* the deep brain centers that manage emotion and motivation (the limbic system). In general, the evolution of the prefrontal cortex is an excellent thing—it's essentially what makes us "human." The problem is that the prefrontal cortex evolved *after* the limbic system, and thus while it sits on top of the limbic system and manages and directs our impulses, it can be knocked offline by surges of emotion courtesy of you-know-who.

That is why we wrote this book: to destroy this myth, reset the rules of the game, and to arm and train you for the psychological battle. It all starts with the recognition of a truth that we call the fundamental premise: Investing success appears to be about "the market," but it's not; it's about *you*. The market will do what it has always done—go up, go down, and try to throw you off like a rider on a mechanical bull. The only question that matters is, what will *you* do? Here is where our focus needs to be, on what we can control. And this book outlines what those things are and what it takes to master them.

We know that some of the concepts along the way may be counterintuitive. That's why everything in this book is backed up by scientific research in the fields of neuroscience, behavioral finance, and clinical psychology.

Who is this book for? It's for you. You have hopes and desires for a better life for you and the people you care about. And you invest your money—or should—so that you can achieve this better life. Whether you are a first-time investor who is just beginning the process or a seasoned professional looking to optimize performance, the key to success remains the same—managing emotions and establishing what we call an investor identity. This book serves as a guide for doing just that. It uses a number of different techniques including case studies, exercises, and questionnaires/self-assessments along the way so you can relate these concepts specifically to yourself and begin building the skills to use them.

Chapter 1 gives an overview of the relationship between psychology and investing and provides a context for the book. It also introduces the concept of an investor identity and why it is crucial for long-term investing success.

Chapter 2 lays out the fundamentals of an investor identity. It addresses where to start (what we call frames), and the five questions to ask before investing. Unfortunately, in taking these "first steps" many investors start out on the wrong foot, ensuring problems ahead. The chapter goes on to uncover the real and hidden motivations that underlie our investing decisions, another crucial component of your investor identity. The chapter concludes with a section on goal-setting, outlining a technique we call the Slide Show Method that keeps investors focused on what they want their investing to achieve.

Chapter 3 digs into the concept of your investor personality. It breaks your particular personality down into the "Big Five" traits associated with both investing success and vulnerability. It details how you can identify these traits in yourself and work with them. This chapter also addresses the genetic components that contribute to your investing style.

Chapter 4 is about recognizing the role emotions play in your investing decisions. Most people recognize that investing is an emotional process. What they often fail to appreciate is the extent to which these emotions are hidden, even from ourselves. This chapter addresses how these unconscious emotions often subvert our attempts to make good choices with our money—and what we can do to gain control over them.

Chapter 5 addresses your investing values. In particular, it goes into the root causes of the what, how, and why of your biggest investment beliefs and the ways they affect your choices—for good or ill. This chapter also helps you identify ways you can play to your investing strengths by investing in a way that is in keeping with your values and interests. Last, it addresses financial traumas and what they do to our investing identity going forward.

Chapter 6 addresses your blind spots. It details a number of the most common (and nastiest) traps and how and why investors fall into them. This chapter also contains checklists so you can evaluate your personal susceptibility to these problems and outlines steps you can use to free yourself and avoid them in the future. It concludes with a set of investing archetypes based on recognizable characters.

Chapter 7 addresses the ways in which investing stress takes its toll on your decisions and what you can do to prevent its negative consequences. In particular, it focuses on biological and psychological elements, detailing specific techniques you can use to ameliorate the effects of stress. Subjects include breaking out of slumps, cultivating resilience, and creating internal dialogues to improve performance. The chapter concludes with a method we call the Financial Stress Management Plan and a guide of how you can create one for your investing process.

Chapter 8 pulls it all together. Now that you have a stronger sense of your investor identity, this chapter details how you can preserve that identity, operate as your "best self," and create the optimal environment for success. This chapter details a holistic approach to keep you up and running at maximum efficiency.

Lastly, we strongly encourage all readers to complete a free Investor's Personality Test at www.marketpsych.com/personality_test .php. This test identifies strengths and vulnerabilities in personal investing.

It may feel like the market doesn't want you to reach your rightful destination. Well, we do. Consider *MarketPsych: How to Manage Fear and Build Your Investor Identity* to be your personal travel guide on your investing journey. And while we can't guarantee that you will become rich from reading this book, we can guarantee this— if you read this book and do the work contained herein, you will be part of a select group of investors equipped with the essential psychological tools that lead to great performance.

And the next time the market tries to wage psychological war on your future—it'll be a fair fight.

Acknowledgments

Thomas Samuels—your insights, laughs, and keen observations are woven throughout this book. Thank you for being a mentor and friend.

Richard Friesen (MarketPsych Director of Trader Training), we appreciate your wit, wisdom, and enthusiasm. Mark Harbour, wealth advisor extraordinaire and president of the Applied Behavioral Finance Group of the Los Angeles CFA Society, thank you for your invaluable assistance and inspiration in this project (no doubt entirely instigated by Bernadette).

We are indebted to the work of Joe Jabaly and Susie Gharib at *Nightly Business Report* and Bob Frick at *Kiplinger's* for their help in publicizing recent advances in the science of investment psychology. Thank you for providing this invaluable service to the public. We're grateful for the formative insights of Fred Pinto with the Toronto CFA Society and Steve Horan with the CFA Institute. They have provided excellent feedback and encouragement as we've developed applied tools for financial advisors.

We appreciate the enjoyable conversations with Doug Lennick at Lennick Aberman Group and his wonderful insights into the psychological pressures of wealth management.

We'd like to acknowledge the wonderful people at Guardian Investor Services with whom we've worked closely throughout the years. In particular, the crew who coordinate the events, namely Mr. Kim Boriin, Brian Brown, and Jodi Ieva. They are true pros, and we will always owe them a debt of gratitude (and in the case of Brian, a pint of Guinness). Also a special thank you to the many professionals with whom we have worked, including, but not limited to, Peter Kalianosis, Brian Kravitzski, Clint Kruse, Jim Lake, Marco Molea, Mike Rowe, Greg Rusteberg, and many others. Many of them are Red Sox fans, but they're still good people. A special thanks to Sarah Awan Johnson and Frank Marino, who gave us our first chance to put these ideas into action. Their ability to see the value in this work long before others and take a chance on it will always be appreciated.

We'd also like to acknowledge the fine folks at Brandes Investment Partners, in particular Leah Brock, Pascal Boisvert, Matt Brundage, and CEO Oliver Murray. They are always involved in creative and cutting-edge ways of applying behavioral finance. In addition to wonderful business partners, they are simply delightful company, and you couldn't ask for a better bunch to go to a Blue Jays game with.

We appreciate the assistance of Bob Seaberg at Morgan Stanley Smith Barney, who provided invaluable opportunities to interact and share insights with his global network of wealth advisors. Jennifer Gabriele at Morgan Stanley Smith Barney shared her insight into the daily challenges of advisors. We're grateful to Jan Sparrow and Scott Asalone for their perceptive and enriching thoughts on working with emotional investors. They continue their wonderful work through the Greatness Project at greatnessproject .com. We are greatly appreciative of the opportunity to work with some of the top financial advisors in the country at Merrill Lynch Global Wealth Management. Thank you Anna Callori and Rosanna Innes!

We're indebted to the encouragement and good cheer of Alexis Zonfrilli and the kindness and support of Alison Hill at Goldman Sachs. Alison and Alexis went out of their way to support our creative efforts.

We're grateful to Aishwarya Shan and Sharon Liew at Marcus Evans Kuala Lumpur for the opportunities to interact with and learn from private bankers and wealth managers in Asia. We've greatly enjoyed the relationships and friendships that have developed from these annual workshops in Seoul, Singapore, Mumbai, and Sydney. It goes without saying that the past decade has been incredibly tumultuous for investors. We thank those who generously shared their stories, their struggles, and their successes with us, including hundreds of financial advisors and portfolio managers around the world. You are too numerous to name, but without your stories and inspiration this book could not have been written.

We owe a debt to the many scientists and researchers who have advanced the sciences of psychology, experimental economics, behavior change, and neuroscience (all together we will call them neuroeconomics or neurofinance). In particular, we are indebted to the work of Paul Zak, James Montier, Michael Mauboussin, Brian Knutson, Camelia Kuhnen, Colin Camerer, Greg Berns, and John Coates.

And on a personal note, Frank would like to thank his wife, Lillian, for being a major source of support and encouragement during the process; his brother, Loring, for selflessly offering logistical support; and his mom for driving down from New Hampshire to clear up time for him to write, even if it was largely an excuse to see her baby grandson. Frank would also like to thank Rob Crystal and David Berdon, two insightful investing professionals, but more importantly two good friends willing to endure geeky conversations about the market so that he could write a better book. He is grateful to you all.

Richard adores his wife, Sarah, who is his inspiration. Frank sends thanks to the guys (and Georgia!) at Shoreline Trading for putting up with his endless questions and observations about the markets and his intractable accounting illiteracy. Also thanks to the endurance of his colleagues at MarketPsy Capital—Yury Shatz, Thomas Hartman, Jacob Sisk, Ali Arik, and Justin Chan who have traded and profited from market panic with him. They are good friends and co-creators of the novel and quite profitable way of forecasting investor and market behavior.

CHAPTER 1

Your Investor Identity: And Why You Need One

The unexplored area is the emotional area. All the charts and breadth indicators and technical palaver are statisticians' attempts to describe an emotional state.
　　—Edward Johnson, founder of Fidelity Investments

These words were spoken by Edward Johnson more than 40 years ago, and they ring every bit as true today. So why, after so much time, is the psychological understanding of investing decisions still so widely misunderstood? Given the volatility of the past decade, it stands to reason that merging the lessons of psychology and finance could be wonderfully beneficial to investors.

Psychology and Finance: Failure to Communicate

It's not that I can't help these people. It's just I don't want to.
　　—Tom Hanks, *Volunteers*

The movie *Volunteers* is an immensely underrated comedy starring Tom Hanks and the late John Candy. In an effort to avoid a gambling debt, Hanks's character poses as a Peace Corps volunteer and boards a plane to a developing country. Shortly after arriving, he seeks to return home. When an incredulous Peace Corps organizer pleads with him to stay by entreating him, "But you can *help* these people!", Hanks responds with the classic line quoted above.

This quote is also a fair way to think of the relationship between psychology and finance. These two fields have lived side by side in the same neighborhood for more than a hundred years and have never been properly introduced.

Traditionally the world of psychology has not only been uninterested in finance, but often disdainful of it. There are a number of possible reasons for this disconnection, but one may stem from the fact that the world of finance is full of guys who played on the football team and the world of psychology is made up largely of kids from the drama/science/glee clubs. Of course the primary goals for each profession are different, and that contributes to the problem. But the jock/nerd dynamic is still there.

This is unfortunate because the field of psychology has much to offer the investing world. Few things are as emotional (or stressful) to people as their money. Money is the number one issue mentioned both as a cause of divorce and an instigator of sleepless nights. It is at the heart of what we call "quality of life." Simply to help individuals invest more effectively and build greater wealth is to make a huge positive impact on their lives.

It has long been accepted that psychology affects investing decisions. Yet scientific inquiries into how it does so are a recent phenomenon. Part of the reason for this inability to connect may be due to the complicated nature of the task; quantifying human thought and behavior is notoriously messy.

But that's no excuse. The field of psychology has done a poor job of presenting its insights to the financial community in a way it can relate to. Much of the misunderstanding between psychology and finance is due to the language barrier. "Psychobabble"—which has led to such dreadful sentences as "I want to process your affect" and "Let's reframe your cognitive schema"—not only puts up a wall to financial professionals, it annoys them.

To this day in the work we do, we encounter antiquated stereotypes freely voiced or lying just below the surface. For some reason, there is a popular image of psychologists as being older gentlemen who wear earth-tone sweaters, smoke pipes, and periodically stroke their beards, asking questions like, "And how does that make you *feel*?"

Psychologists aren't altogether to blame for this sour relationship. Financial professionals have been trained to pay so much attention to numbers that they have become utterly mistrustful of fields that focus on words: Can't graph it? Can't express it in an equation? Then it's touchy-feely voodoo.

Fortunately, rigorous scientific disciplines have emerged in the study of decision-making. The goal of applied psychology today, particularly for those in the counseling and consulting fields, is to help clients develop better *habits* for going about their business—that is, to make people more effective at what they do—and that includes investing. As such, applied psychology and decision science are uniquely situated to help the individual investor.

Think of investing as a journey. There is a path you walk down and a destination you are trying to reach. The first steps ought to be the most carefully considered. The earlier you misstep, the farther and more quickly you wander off the path. Yet these first steps are the ones that are most likely to be taken in haste and carelessness. All too often investors plunge ahead to find they have not only wandered off their path, but perhaps chosen the wrong path entirely, or maybe even targeted a destination they will never reach. These initial missteps are most often caused by fundamental flaws in the investors' psychological framework. Beginning with the proper mental approach is essential. Psychologists can help.

Beginning the Journey

Let's turn to Edward Johnson again:

> What is it the good managers have? It's a kind of locked in concentration, an intuition, a feel, nothing that can be schooled. The first thing you have to know is yourself.

His words were referring to professional money managers, but his wisdom is universal; one has to understand oneself in order to be successful as an investor.

However, Johnson was not entirely correct about one thing. The lack of self-knowledge among most investment managers is not due to the fact that it cannot be learned (e.g., in business classes, training, etc.). The problem is that such characteristics have never been properly taught. With all due respect to Mr. Johnson, although self-knowledge can't be memorized from a book, *skills* for developing self-knowledge can be acquired.

The most cohesive attempt to integrate psychology and investing is a field called *behavioral finance*. This field made its name by demonstrating that traditional economics is based on a false assumption—that human decision making is typically rational, profit-maximizing, and self-interested. Dr. Daniel Kahneman, a psychologist who shared the Nobel Prize for Economics in 2002, won the prize for his research with Amos Tversky demonstrating that financial decisions are systematically biased in non-rational ways.

For all the great research done in behavioral finance identifying irrational investing behavior, the field has had trouble progressing beyond the realm of "investing parlor tricks," pointing out strange and quirky mistakes investors are prone to make. The findings are interesting, but *what do you do with them?*

While researchers in behavioral finance have identified systematic investor mistakes, they tend to offer these findings as solutions unto themselves, as if to say: "We've determined that investors fail to make rational and self-interested decisions. So, now that we established this fact . . . go forth and make rational, self-interested decisions!" [There are some notable exceptions, and one that comes to mind is the Save More for Tomorrow Plan (SMaRT Plan) devised by Shlomo Benartzi and Richard Thaler.]

Stopping at identifying mistakes would be enough, of course, if knowledge equaled change. ("You say this is bad for me? Great. I'll stop doing it, then.") But knowledge does not equal change. If it did, the world would be a different place. For starters, kids would eat their vegetables. Teenagers wouldn't smoke cigarettes. And stock market investors would average roughly 10 percent returns annually.

Knowing what to do is only a first step toward success—a necessary but insufficient condition for change. You do not lose money with your mind. You lose money with your actions—namely, buy, sell, and hold decisions that work out poorly.

If the problem isn't a lack of knowing (and it isn't), neither is the problem a lack of caring. Most people *don't want* to make decisions that are bad for them (Freudian notions of self-sabotage be damned!). And yet most investors not only make irrational decisions, they *persistently and reliably* make such decisions. Investors, generally speaking, know what to do and want to do it. The problem is . . . *they can't bring themselves to do it when they need to.*

It may be useful to think of investing mistakes in terms of an epidemic currently afflicting the United States. Americans have a higher percentage of citizens who are overweight than any other country. We are, simply put, the fattest nation on the planet.

Barring the rare cases of metabolic disorders, the best way to avoid weight problems is to eat a healthy diet and exercise regularly. Everyone knows this—children as well as adults. Every school district in the country drills this message into its students starting in grade school. And it doesn't take long for most people to recognize that the extent to which a food is bad for you is directly correlated with how good it tastes. So a lack of knowledge is not the problem.

The problem isn't even that people don't *care* about being overweight. The United States has an astounding number of joggers and gym-goers relative to its peers. Moreover, we are constantly being inundated with idealized body images in the media (thin for women, buff for men). We do care. We may even care too much. These unrealistic body images are widely blamed for the relatively high rate of eating disorders and steroid abuse in the country.

Nor is there any shortage of advice on ways to help remedy the problem of obesity. If you wanted to lose weight, you could go to the health and nutrition section of any major bookstore and find shelves upon shelves of books with detailed dieting programs. Moreover, most of those programs would work. But that utterly misses the point.

The question remains: What is the right plan *for you?* The right plan for you isn't the one that "would work if you follow it." (All those plans work if you follow them!) The right plan for you is the one *you can best follow.* In other words, the plan for you is one that is most suited to your preferences, values, beliefs, and emotional strengths and weaknesses. This book does not recommend a specific method of investing. There are many right ways for people to invest their money. Choosing one is primarily a matter of fit.

It's important to remember that both financial fitness and physical fitness are long-term goals. Sure, a lot of people like to drop some winter weight, slim down for a wedding, or get into "beach shape." But those are all short-term goals. We don't think you'd be reading this book if you were merely interested in growing your portfolio for the summer. We're talking about lifestyle choices that you can follow forever because they are consistent with who you are.

Again we see that the psychological obstacles that impede getting into better shape physically are the same ones that hamper getting into better shape financially. People attribute the inability to get into better financial shape to ignorance and apathy. This is a common misconception. In fact, a study of 1,115 investors by the Guardian Life Insurance Company demonstrated conclusively that people know they should be saving more money and investing it for the future in vehicles that have shown long-term returns. The survey also found that saving money and investing for the future were consistently rated as top priorities.[1] Yet the same study found that most respondents were woefully underfunding their retirements and risked hardship later in life.

We know what to do. We care. It doesn't matter, because our investing problems lie deeper, in what we call human nature. You cannot change human nature. But it is possible to plan around it. When it comes to your finances, you have to.

Risky Business

One of the most basic tools used in the investment community is the risk tolerance questionnaire. If you've ever worked with a financial firm or professional, you know one of the first things he or she will do is have you fill out a short survey designed to measure your preferences for investment risk taking. The results are then used to generate an asset allocation model (i.e., a plan made up of different investment vehicles) that matches your inferred investing style.

Matching people's investments to their personalities is a good idea. There is just one small problem with risk tolerance questionnaires. They don't work. They explain only about 20 percent of the variance in the average person's risk tolerance.[2] That's not to say there is no value in taking such a survey. It may lead to insights into one's investing proclivities. It certainly makes a good conversation starter for expectations. But that's about it.

The fact is human beings are lousy at predicting how they will react in future circumstances, especially those they have never encountered. The ability to comfortably handle financial risk is primarily what psychologists call *state dependent* (i.e., how you're feeling at the time), rather than *trait dependent* (i.e., a consistent characteristic that doesn't change).

In addition, there is no way to factor in all the ways in which one's life might change in the future or what the future positive and negative circumstances might be. By the time we encounter the predicted scenarios, we might be very different people in entirely different circumstances.

Additionally, many risk tolerance questionnaires start from false or skewed assumptions. It is sometimes called the Dentist Analogy. Imagine you've gone to see your dentist and the following conversation ensues.

Dentist:	I got your x-rays back and it looks like you're going to need a root canal.
You:	Oh wow . . . that's too bad.
Dentist:	Tell me about it. I have a three o'clock tee time, but there's *no way* I'm going to make that now!
You:	So, is this a painful procedure?
Dentist:	No! Of course not! Usually. So tell me . . . what do you think is the most amount of pain you can stand during the procedure?
You:	What?
Dentist:	My model is to use as little Novocain as possible, so I need a sense of your pain threshold. What is the absolute most pain you can stand during the procedure?
You:	Look, I don't think I want to—
Dentist:	Ah, don't worry about it. How about you just tell me when it hurts, and I'll add more Novocain along the way? Now sit back and relax. Open wide . . .

Of course, it deserves to be said at this point that no dentist would operate this way. But neither should an investment professional! And if you look at the assumptions behind using risk tolerance questionnaires you'll see that the analogy is not far off. Many such measures essentially ask you to rate your various pain thresholds, and then seek to base a plan around the maximum pain you can supposedly tolerate. Most people are asked to rate their pain tolerance while sitting comfortably in their advisor's office. Interestingly, because of a mental trap called the *projection bias*, it's extremely difficult to accurately estimate how we'll respond to pain in the future if we are not in pain in the present. To plan ahead for pain we've got to stay grounded despite changing circumstances.

Resisting Your "Idiot Friend"

An investing identity is important because it is so easy to get side-tracked along the road to wealth. Here's a brief anecdote that you may find familiar: I was 16 years old and had just done something stupid but entirely typical for 16-year-olds. It led to the following exchange:

Mother: Why did you do that? Are you crazy?
Me: But everybody was doing it!
Mother: And if everybody were jumping off a bridge, would you do that too?

The preceding conversation has been happening between every generation of mothers and sons in the history of time and, presumably, bridges.

The last question is meant to be rhetorical, but is nonetheless worth answering, because the honest response in most cases is, "Yeah, probably." What we see others doing around us has a profound impact on the decisions we make.

This exchange can happen between anyone, but it is most typical of teenagers and mothers. Why? Because the primary social developmental task of teenagers is to achieve a sense of "who they are." This search for an identity leads teenagers to test boundaries, engage in risk-seeking behaviors, and, yes, be more susceptible to peer pressure.

As we begin to grow more secure in our identities, we are better at resisting thoughts and behaviors that seem at odds with our self-image. We say, "I know it seems like everybody is doing X . . . but I don't like X. I'm not sure I ever did." And this deeper knowledge and acceptance of who we are allows us to resist the crowd.

Short-term market moves are your "idiot friend." Don't know what I mean? Sure you do. You remember your friend back in high school who was always getting you to do dumb stuff. He (or she) used to say things like, "Let's race that guy!" "Let's dye our hair green!" and, "They won't mind if we use their pool!"

These escapades usually started out great, but had a way of ending badly. How did your friend get you to engage in such foolish behaviors? Well, one reason is that the foolish behaviors are often fun—and we like fun. If we didn't, we wouldn't have the lottery, office pools, and the city of Las Vegas. But the second reason is that an underlying insecurity made you susceptible to pressure—usually in the form of such time-tested tactics as "You're not scared, are you?" "It'll only take a second," and the aforementioned, "Everybody's doing it."

To a teen these are remarkably effective manipulators. The average adult, however, is more likely to respond, "Of course I'm scared!" "Nothing takes a second," and "Everybody is NOT doing it and even if they were, I still don't want to." Such is the virtue of maturity.

The majority of investors are chronologically adults, but their investor identities are in an earlier developmental stage. They have some knowledge about the financial markets, but sometimes "just enough to be dangerous." They have some insights into themselves, but lack the realizations born of experience. They are still in the process of learning their investing strengths, weaknesses, values, and pain thresholds. This leaves their decisions vulnerable to the influences of other people in their lives, talking heads on TV, or the greatest pressure group of all, "The Market" itself. Most investors are—and in no way is this meant to be pejorative—the developmental equivalent of adolescents.

There is a consistency of approach that forms with self-insight and allows us to resist such peer pressure. The investing industry is not the fashion industry, but it all too often markets its products that way. Many financial pundits encourage the investing-as-fashion outlook by touting the "hot" investing options of the season as if they are strutting down a runway.

Spring is here! The leaves are turning green and so is Cyndi's portfolio! She looks positively verdant in this smart ensemble of solar, green-tech, and renewable energy stocks. Saving the planet never looked so good!

Come with Paulina this autumn to the exotic Far East. With the Red Star on the rise, you can't help but "fall" for these hot infrastructure plays. And with an annual GDP growth of 8 percent and the world's largest population, you won't have to be Shanghai'ed into this spicy number!

The thermometer is dropping this winter, but Giselle is heating things up with these red-hot selections from the oil sector. An OPEC production freeze will send crude prices—and your temperature—headed to 100 in these oil and gas plays!

A new fashion is always alluring. But fashion is also capricious. It changes on a whim and without warning.

Most people playing along are behind the curve. They join the trend after it has become the "cool" thing to do, and when they get out, it is usually after the new trend has reversed itself. The result is a wardrobe stuffed with outfits they have no intention of wearing again. Take a look at a picture of you and your friends from 20 years ago. Would you wear the same style of clothes today? Maybe, if you were going to a theme party.

And this would be fine if we were really talking about clothes. But the investing equivalents of leg-warmers, bell-bottoms, and scrunchies not only don't get sold off in a timely manner, they tend to collect in our closets (read "portfolios"), eroding our net worth in the process. (In later chapters we will discuss why the bad holdings tend to accumulate while the good ones tend to disappear.)

Some of us look back on those pictures of us with our friends 20 years ago and think, "Wow. I can't believe I wore that. I look like a goofball." It's usually good for a laugh. But a trip down memory lane through the wasteland of our investing errors, and the thousands of dollars we squandered in futile and transient pursuits, seldom elicits a chuckle.

When it comes to finding good places to invest our money, the vast majority of us are better off sticking to the classics. The little black dress. The blue blazer. Are they exciting? Well, no. But the goal of investing *shouldn't be excitement.* That's an emotional goal in direct competition with our financial ones, and a huge red flag. Nor should the desire to "stay current" be a motivator. The true motivators should always be rooted in our consciously developed goals—how we want our lives to look and what we want our legacies to be.

Finding Your Investor Identity

Now, the world don't move to the beat of just one drum. What might be right for you, may not be right for some.
—Theme song to *Diff'rent Strokes*

Have you noticed that it's uncannily common to invest at the wrong time—buy at the tops and sell at the bottoms? (We call it "Whack-a-Mole" syndrome). For most investors, real estate in 2005 and Internet stocks in 1999 appeared to be good buys. For most people it was only in painful hindsight that the tremendous overvaluations were apparent.

If we were to tell you that you can expect to earn an average of 1.87 percent a year in the mutual funds you invest in, would you still invest in mutual funds? Of course not. You'd buy a Treasury bond or something safer (and higher yielding). Yet 1.87 percent is what Americans have annually earned on average in their mutual fund investments over the past 20 years through the end of 2008.[3]

Those numbers are bad enough. But they look even worse when translated into real-life returns. As mentioned in the Preface, Dalbar Inc. found that $100,000 invested in the S&P 500 index on January 1, 1989, would have grown to a total of $292,329 by 2009, after accounting for inflation. However, Dalbar Inc. found that the average equities investor who invested that same $100,000, again accounting for inflation, would now have $82,288 over the same 20-year period. That is a difference of over $200,000, not to mention a net loss in actual purchasing power.

How could the average investor underperform so poorly that they can't even match the rate of inflation? Good question. Most of us don't want to arrive at a party before it's hopping or leave while we're having a great time. The same goes for timing our investments. But the inability to do just that is a prescription for underperformance. Thinking counterintuitively about investments is crucial. But it requires tremendous fortitude, confidence, and self-awareness.

Unfortunately, many amateur investors scoff at the idea that psychology matters to their performance. Yet the best investors in history—including Warren Buffett, Peter Lynch, Steve Cohen, Baron Nathan von Rothschild, Bernard Baruch, David Dreman (and the list goes on)—have mentioned the importance of understanding the psychological factors that drive both markets and individuals.

Managing yourself—your moments of greed, panic, and insecurity—can only be achieved once you've obtained the requisite self-understanding. And self-understanding comes from looking within.

In this book we're not endorsing any particular style of investing such as buy-and-hold or market timing. Nor are we endorsing any particular strategies (such as value or momentum) or assets (such as bonds, stocks, or commodities). Your optimal investing style and strategy depend on *who* you are.

If you're going to be investing, you've got to back up and take a good look at yourself. *Why* do I want to invest? *Who* am I trying to be when I invest? *What* are my long-term (and short-term) objectives? *How* am I likely to deceive myself along the way? Although it's important to answer these questions, they are incredibly challenging to answer honestly.

You may be wondering, "Why is knowing myself more important than knowing the markets?" It's true that you've got to have an elementary understanding of markets, assets, analysis styles, and potential strategies in order to invest well. Yet many investors go further, spending weeks or months learning specific trading strategies, or watching price quotes day after day, and yet never seeming to get ahead (and usually falling further behind). And they wonder, "Why am I trading the best stocks/real estate/commodities, and I'm still not making as much money as I should?"

You might have heard the advice from finance academics who say you can't beat the markets. They recommend you buy and hold low-fee stock index funds and forget the rest. When academics tell you to do this, they make it sound so easy. The more imperious ones seem to suggest you'd be silly not to do it. You may be surprised (if not amused) to know that most finance professors don't follow their own advice. And that raises the question, "If it's so easy to buy-and-hold low-cost stock index funds, why do the majority of mutual fund investors underperform?"

Let's get real about something: You're not designed to be a good investor.

No, we didn't say "destined." We said "designed"—as in anatomy. Investing is not like most other pursuits in life where the advantages can be readily seen. Great long-distance runners tend to be long and lean. Great pianists have long fingers. Great cyclists like to wear form-fitting spandex. And great investors, what are they like? Before looking into the secrets of great investing, let's first look at the causes of bad investing, since in order to be the next Warren Buffett, you've got to avoid being the next Nick Leeson.

On the surface, mutual fund investor underperformance can be attributed to buying at the peaks of the top-performing funds and selling when those funds are at their lows. On a deeper level, such behavior is driven by emotion. Greed and fear are the usual culprits, but there is also a lineup of supporting characters—shame, regret, and excitement to name a few.

Unfortunately financial experts erroneously leave rare events— and the emotions and stress surrounding them—out of their market models. This is insane. It is unexpected, rare events that cause the emotional reactions, which compel investors to jettison their long-term plans.

Ironically, "rare events" appear to happen on a regular basis in the financial markets. Before the financial paralysis of late 2008, Goldman Sachs' CFO David Viniar stated of early August 2007, "We were seeing things that were 25 standard deviation moves, several days in a row."[4] Twenty-five standard deviations implies odds of 1 in 1.3×10^{135} on any given day. That's one hundred thousand times more than the number of particles in the universe, and it is comparable to winning the UK lottery 21 or 22 times in a row.[5] Clearly, such financial models are based on faulty assumptions about human nature and human-driven markets. Leaving out emotion, uncertainty, and rare events is like forgetting to put flour, milk, and eggs in the cake you're baking. Is there anything left?

In the end, unexpected events and investors' accompanying emotional reactions will always be with us. But we have the ability to learn the skills to manage our emotions. It behooves us to do so to the best of our abilities. We're writing this book because for too long the psychological mistakes of investors have been diagnosed and subsequently ignored, and it's time for a prescription that goes to the core of the malady and provides a road to recovery. That road starts with a stronger sense of *who you are* as an investor, in other words, by forging an investor identity.

2

Investor Identity Fundamentals: Frames, Motivations, and Goals

This chapter addresses several of the core concepts that underlie an investor identity. This chapter is all about the first steps: the issues to be resolved *before* investing money, and to be periodically revisited along the way. We explain the frames of reference (frames) most investors carry and discuss techniques for "re-framing" damaging assumptions. We will dig into investing motivations, the often hidden reasons why we invest our money. The chapter goes on to cover the importance of setting goals for investing and understanding our intended destination. (Few people would recommend beginning a journey with no destination, after all.) Unfortunately these investor identity fundamentals are often overlooked by investors, perhaps in their eagerness to "get on with it" and pursue immediate profits. The chapter concludes with several questions to help you clarify that your frames, motivations, and goals are in alignment at the moment of making investment buy and sell decisions.

The Detail-Orientation Test: A Case Study in Frames

A human resources consulting company was looking to hire an administrative assistant for its New York office. The job would require preparing documents, proofreading, billing, and other responsibilities that demand attention to detail. In an effort to ensure hiring a qualified person, the company—whose job it was to help other companies make better hires—created a specially designed test that would assess applicants' meticulousness.

The test consisted of a mockup of a typical three-page report company consultants would produce for clients. The report contained 20 errors of grammar, syntax, and spelling, as well as mistyped figures and chart information. It was the test-takers' challenge to identify and circle all 20 errors.

Prospective hires needed to score at least 17 out of 20 to be considered. Out of the 15 applicants for the position, only 3 met the standard. The consultants in the office were surprised. Was the test that hard? They decided to take it themselves as a means of comparison.

All 8 consultants in the New York office scored 18 or better. Most scored 20 out of 20, including the office's managing director (MD), who appeared to revel in his perfection.

A visiting consultant from Philadelphia was in town and the New York branch decided to give him the test. They playfully challenged him to see if the Philadelphia office could "measure up" to the high scores of the New York branch. He accepted.

When he was done, the New York managing director wanted to know how he fared. "How many did you catch?" he asked.

"I found 21," the visitor replied.

The MD laughed. "Twenty-one? There are only 20 errors on the test! You must have made a mistake."

"Maybe," he answered. "But I found 21."

"Let me see that," the MD said, taking the test from the visitor. He pulled out his own perfect test out, laid it on the desk, and used it as a checklist.

After cross-checking the reports and matching mistake to mistake, he smiled. "Your test matches up with mine. You got a 20 after all."

The visitor paused, confused. "Yeah, I found all those. But the year at the top of the first page is wrong . . . are you saying that's not part of the test?"

"Huh?" the MD replied. "Let me see that again."

The MD picked the test off the desk and held it up for a moment, studying it. Then he frowned. Sure enough, at the top of the page, before the instruction paragraph and ostensibly before the test was meant to begin was a heading: "XYZ Company Administrative Assistant Test Version 1: New York Office, December 12, 200"—it should have read 2009.

The consultants' failure on the test was not due to a lack of detail-orientation. Where they focused on errors, the test-takers and the test designers indeed demonstrated impressive attention to detail.

No. Their failure was assured before the exercise even started. They didn't begin at the beginning.

Frames: Your Tinted Glasses

Investors frequently make the same mistake. Like the consultants who skipped ahead in the story that opened this chapter, investors often fail to ask the first questions first. All too often the starting point is "what to buy," "how much to invest," "is the timing right?" These are all important steps, but they are not first steps.

We must begin at the beginning. The first step to being a successful investor is to understand the assumptions and presuppositions that form the basis of our perspectives. We call them Investing Frames. What follows is a comparison of the three most influential Investing Frames in which investors operate.

Frame 1: Money-Focused vs. Life-Focused (a.k.a. Quantity vs. Quality or "Your Money or Your Life")

Why do you invest your money?

It's an obvious question, but an essential one for understanding an important frame through which you view the markets. A surprisingly common reason that people invest money is this: to get rich. It sounds tacky, we know. But although our investing motivation is rarely thought of as "to get really rich," when investors start from the assumption that they invest to "make money" and hopefully to "make a lot of money," that is unwittingly the frame from which they operate.

Of course making money is a desired investing outcome, but focusing on and worrying about making money leads to trouble (and less money in the long term). When your focus is on how much money you'll make versus the *actual* life you hope to live, you are in the money-focused frame.

It is not hard to see how investors get caught up in this approach. To make lots of money (without having to work) is as popular a daydream as it ever was (ranking just behind finding the "Fountain of Youth"). And there is no more alluring place to pursue this dream than in the equities markets. You may remember the popular trend at the end of the 20th century of quitting your job to become a full-time "day trader." Thousands of otherwise sensible people took their savings, pulled up to a trading terminal, and tried to cash in. When the tech-bubble burst it was like the song stopping in a giant game of musical chairs. The day traders suddenly found themselves out of the game and reeling from gut-wrenching declines in their net worth.

Operating from a money-focused frame has a subtle and insidious way of corrupting our outlook. Investing begins to take on the feel of gambling. The market becomes a slot machine, a roulette wheel, or a keno game; we pull the lever, spin the wheel, pick the numbers, and hope to hit it big. Vegas without Wayne Newton and strip clubs is how many investors unconsciously view Wall Street.

During good times the market is constantly roping investors in with the lure of easy money. There is no shortage of compelling anecdotes nudging us into this frame of mind. Apple, Microsoft, Intel—the investing world is full of mighty blue-chip oaks that started as nondescript little acorns, any of which "would have made you rich" had you gotten in early enough.

We have all heard variations of the "If you had bought $1,000 worth of Apple back in 1984, you would now have $4 gazillion" story line. It's part of the Wall Street mythos. When investing is described in these terms it practically *is* the functional equivalent of winning the lottery.

Making lots of money is a good thing. So what's wrong with this framework?

Plenty, it turns out. For starters, most gamblers lose. And a "hit the jackpot" framework opens the door for covetousness, laziness, greed, and many other base instincts to seep into the process. Investing successfully is a get-rich-slow scheme. Trying to speed up the process corrupts it. But beyond that, it sets investors up for binary (e.g., "all or nothing") thinking. With a lottery ticket, this approach is fine—you will likely lose your original investment, but to many, it's worth a shot at a jackpot. Our investing goals are anything but binary. No one says, "It's $10 million by the time I'm 65 or bust!" There are infinite shades of gray and investing success takes many forms.

But perhaps the biggest problem with the money-focused frame is that "getting rich" or even "making money" isn't a helpful goal. It's amorphous and idiosyncratic. How much money does it take to actually "be rich"? It's hard to say and most people can't. They describe "being rich" in the way Supreme Court Justice Potter

Stewart famously described the concept of pornography: "I can't define it . . . but I know it when I see it."

All other things being equal, having more money is better than having less. But the question still remains, why do you want to have money? Money is a means, not an end.

Rather than thinking in terms of making a lot of money, a much more productive frame is to focus specifically on what we'd like to achieve in life: the experiences we'd like to have and the misfortunes we would like to avoid, the nature of how we would provide for the people we love, the legacy we'd like to leave behind.

These are the true reasons we put our money away. Working from a life-focused frame roots our investing choices in tangible outcomes. It gives us a more grounded idea of what to shoot for and what to expect. It also helps us avoid the traps that lure investors into the false choices and gambling mentality that torpedo so many portfolios. When we have clear life goals, we can design an investing approach that aligns with them—one that can be measured and adjusted accordingly.

When you find yourself tempted to think diffusely about "making money" with your investments, try picturing how you'll use that money to live a more fulfilling life. Think in terms of the safety net it provides, the standard of living it affords, and specific accomplishments you'd like to ensure.

When you find yourself thinking of a potential investment as if it were a lottery ticket . . . throw cold water on yourself.

Questions: Are you operating from a money-focused or a life-focused Investment Frame?

- Do you have specific visions of how you would like your quality of life to be?
- Do you know what it will take to achieve them?
- Do you know how on track your current investments are to achieving these goals?
- Do you consider it important to find the "Next (Fill in Huge Successful Company Name Here)"?
- Do you think in terms of a specific wealth level (e.g., $5 million) as equaling success?

If you answered no to any of the first three questions, or yes to the last two, than you have a tendency to drift into a money-focused frame.

Strategies for Reframing

- We can all be seduced by the "get rich quick" potential of investing. Write down the sage words of trader Jon Polesuk: "Losers focus on returns. Winners focus on risk." In this case, risk refers to the risk to your long-term quality-of-life goals.
- Avoid all or nothing thinking. Define your successes in a range and not by specific dollar figures that represent failure or success.
- Tie your investing choices to specific, vivid goals for your future. Use the Slide Show Method (detailed later in this book) as a guide.

Frame 2: Market-Orientation vs. Self-Orientation (Outcome vs. Process)

Perhaps the greatest misconception—and hence the most common misframe—about investing is that successful investing is about what the market does. It isn't. Successful investing is about what you do.

Consider the statistics in Table 2.1.

Every year since 1932, if you were to invest broadly in the market, 10 years later you would have made money. (The exception being a 10-year period ending in 2008—a period that has seen the two biggest drops in the Index since the Great Depression.) In 86 percent of those years you would have had an average annual return of more than 5 percent. So investing broadly in equities ought to be a safe, reliable, long-term wealth generator for investors.

But how do investors actually fare?

The indispensable Dalbar Inc. (see Chapter 1) has provided irrefutable data that investors underperform the market. Much of the failure is due to an attempt to "beat the market" rather than be content with the historic long-term returns it has provided. This failure

Table 2.1   Average Returns over Rolling 10-Year Periods (1927–2009)

Negative Returns	4.6%
Between 0 and 5%	6.8%
Between 5 and 10%	23.33%
Between 10 and 15%	18.26%
Greater than 15%	19.27%

Source: Thomson Financial.

manifests itself in reactive, chasing behavior that inevitably leads to a "buy high, sell low" dynamic we call "Whack-a-Mole" syndrome.

Yet even when we devise measures to take merely what the market offers, the same human failings undercut our efforts. Exchange-traded funds (ETFs) were supposed to be the answer to matching market performance. Their sole purpose was to give investors the ability to buy stocks that match the components of a particular index. Don't paddle. Just float down the river. No more would investors be doomed to underperformance.

It turns out that the most recent data (2004 through 2008) indicate that ETFs have returned negative 1.9 percent as an asset class. (Not the result investors are looking for, but this period includes one of most severe declines in the history of investing.) But what did the *average investor* get for a return in the "market-matching" vehicle? The average investor received negative 8.2 percent. As this dismal underperformace in ETFs indicates, "Whack-a-Mole" syndrome is apparently not limited to those seeking to beat the indexes in high-fee mutual funds.

So if you accept that equity markets tend to go up over time (and they do), and that people consistently underperform the securities they hold (and they do), you may rightfully conclude that *how people manage their holdings* is almost always a bigger factor than *what the holdings actually are.* This is why it is so important to force ourselves into a self-oriented approach to our finances. In addition to drawing our attention away from the most important factor (our own behavior), the market-oriented frame has the added disadvantage of focusing our attention on precisely the things we can't control. Why is this bad? Because a sense of control is the best fear-fighting weapon we have in our arsenal. Operating in a market-oriented rather than self-oriented framework is inherently disempowering and anxiety-provoking. It stacks the emotional deck for failure. The relationship between fear and control is so nearly perfectly converse that if fear were a virus, the vaccine would be an injection of control.

We have—except perhaps in the rarest of circumstances—zero input on what the S&P 500 does, or how any of its components perform. What we can control is our emotions, our impulses, and the decisions we make, which, as we can see, are much bigger determinants of success, anyway.

When we operate from a market-oriented frame, we put an onus on ourselves to choose the elusive "right path" amid the tangled map of potential routes. But the fact of the matter is, there is no one right path to accumulating wealth in the markets. There are a multitude of them. The most common investing problem is not that people choose to walk down the wrong paths. It's that they choose the right ones and fail to stay on them.

To paraphrase Shakespeare: "The fault, dear investor, is not in our stars but in ourselves."

We do well to operate in a frame that reflects this reality.

Questions: Are you operating in a market-oriented or self-oriented Investment Frame?

- Do you believe that success means finding investments with the highest historical performance?
- Are you without a clearly defined and well-thought-out strategy for long-term success?
- Do you find yourself deviating from a deliberate strategy in pursuit of less well-thought-out options?
- Do you believe that you can predict whether it is a "good" time vs. a "bad" time to invest in stocks (i.e., market-timing)?

If you answered yes to any of these questions, then you are at risk of falling into a market-centered frame. Following are some steps to reset/maintain a self-oriented frame.

Strategies for Reframing

- Consciously forge an approach born of your investment philosophy (this will become easier as you continue to read this book). When you have formed complete thoughts, discuss them with an advisor—professional or otherwise—and *commit them to paper*. Writing down ideas and formalizing them on a piece of paper does wonders to increase both their sticking power and your commitment to them. Take the time. Do it.
- Make a simple postcard that says P>O, or if you prefer, I>M, to signify that investing process is more important than short-term outcomes or that you are more important than the market. Place the postcard in a place where you will be forced to read it when you look at your portfolio (e.g., in your file, taped to your computer).

- No idea that is relevant to your long-term future needs to be decided on in a day. To avoid impulsiveness, institute a one-week waiting period before buying into any position that deviates from your long-term plan. In the meantime, make sure you talk over that position with an advisor or trusted partner. The initial shine of a position is often a reflection of our mood. When we give ourselves a chance to think, that shine often goes away.
- Take the step of translating the data into what they would mean for you. Make a list of all the things you could pay for with the $200,000 mentioned in the Dalbar example in Chapter 1 (e.g., college educations, a second home, a new business). This is what you stand to lose from falling into a market-oriented frame.

Frame 3: Sporadic vs. Consistent Investing Frames (Fair Weather vs. All Weather)

During the 1986 Major League Baseball season, something remarkable occurred—the New York Mets shed their public image as inept but lovable losers and won the division championships. The long-suffering and long-dormant Mets fan base was brought to life. And not just their long-suffering fan base, but a legion of new converts. Whereas Mets paraphernalia used to stand out like remote, exotic islands in a dark blue Yankees sea, now everywhere you looked were the Mets' orange and royal blue adorning caps, shirts, and bumper stickers.

And when the Mets cemented their legacy by defeating the Boston Red Sox to win the World Series, the celebration was like few others. The fans loved this team. Mets pride was back.

But pride is tied to performance. Five years later, the ravages of age, free agency, and some tragically self-destructive behavior of the players reduced the core of the championship team to a shell of its former self. Mets gear was once again scarce on the streets, playgrounds, and bumpers of New York.

This sort of bandwagon-jumping is common in the world of sports. The ranks of a team's supporters always swell in the good times and recede in the bad.

There is a term for these supporters: fair-weather fans.

With sports there is no harm in this approach. Unfortunately, many people behave in much the same way with equities markets. They only become "fans" of investing after the markets have achieved an appreciable level of success (i.e., during fair weather), and their attention to the process is fleeting. What they need is a more consistent approach that captures the market throughout all of its peaks and valleys (i.e., all weather).

A "sporadic frame" is a dangerous one from which to operate for a number of reasons. One is that a sporadic frame leads to sporadic investing—a prime driver of "Whack-a-Mole" syndrome. If you tend to pay attention to or reengage the market only after it has had a nice run up, you inherently violate one of the greatest maxim of investing, "buy low."

This inconsistent approach hurts us when we're investing in blue-chip companies, funds, or indexes, and the problem is geometrically worse when we're in more speculative areas of the market. The same instinct that moves sporadic investors to get into markets that are "hot" is the same instinct that leads them to gravitate toward individual investments that are "hot." These may be smaller, much more speculative holdings. Often the reason these companies are in vogue is because of highly short-term and volatile circumstances (energy stocks during an oil squeeze, metal stocks during a construction boom, biotechnology stocks after an innovation).

The sporadic investor is at risk of taking a long-term approach to a short-term play. Think of it this way: The sporadic frame is the investing equivalent of driving down a highway and only looking at the road once every five seconds between reading e-mails on your BlackBerry. Sure, the road looks straight (for now), cars in front of you are moving, and there are no obstacles. But you've covered an awful lot of ground in the time you've looked away. If you look away long enough, you guarantee that you will crash.

We would never do this driving a car. But sporadic investors do this with their investments all the time.

The experience of opening up the statement from a long-ignored account can provoke the same reaction countless investors have had before: "Oh my gosh, I still own *that*?"

But the sporadic frame does not only mean "looking away" from investments for extended periods of time. Another symptom is looking too often.

Constantly checking the performance of your portfolio during a bull run in an effort to be "rewarded" with good news calls to mind the Skinner box made famous in behavioral psychology lab experiments. These experiments typically involve a rat compulsively pressing a button in its cage in hopes of being rewarded with an occasional food pellet. So if you keep hitting the "check prices" button on your keyboard every five minutes in an effort to give yourself a treat, then—and we say this with absolutely no disrespect intended—you're the rat.

Checking for micro-movements in investments that are *not* doing well is essentially a psychological coping device to manage your anxiety.

In the case of hyperfocus in a bull market, the behavior will simply extinguish itself when the action no longer sufficiently generates a reward or instead consistently generates punishment (i.e., bad news).

In the case of hyperfocus in a bear market, the anxiety will become too overwhelming and you will eventually be forced to sell out (usually at the worst possible time, judging by "Whack-a-Mole" syndrome). In either case it is unsustainable and unhealthy.

You can see why healthy investing is so difficult within a sporadic frame. Long-term, healthy investing requires a consistent frame that yields a steady approach in which you never get too close, nor too far, from your investments. Think of yourself as the investing equivalent of a satellite and the Earth as your portfolio. Too little attention, and you will drift off into space. Too much attention, and you will reenter the atmosphere, crash, and burn. The key is to maintain an equilibrium of involvement that keeps you in a safe, geosynchronous orbit.

All markets ebb and flow. But the great virtue of investing has always been that the long-term trend of the market is up. A consistent, "all-weather" frame ensures you will be part of that long-term trend.

Questions: Are you operating from a sporadic or consistent Investing Frame?

- Do you find yourself tuning in to investing media (TV, radio, print articles) after the stock market has had a 25 percent run up or better?
- Do you find yourself tempted to invest in companies you were totally unfamiliar with because of stock tips from friends or media outlets?

- Do you like to go online and check the up-to-the-minute performance of your holdings?
- Do you let statements go unopened and unchecked for extended periods of time during down markets?
- Do you know what you own in all of your investing accounts?
- Can you say—in less than five seconds—how many accounts you have?

If you answered yes to any of the first four questions or no to either of the last two, you are at risk of lapsing into a sporadic frame for your investing.

Strategies for Reframing.   In order to maintain a consistent frame, we have to impose structure on ourselves. In other words, we need rules. Some potential rules include:

- You will only own X amount of positions in your profile, so they may be properly kept track of (more than a dozen and you're starting to push the limits of what you can follow).
- You will open your statements and read them at the same defined interval both in good times and in bad.
- You will not be a rat in a cage searching for food pellets nor will you give in to your obsessive-compulsive tendencies. Once a day is more than enough to check your portfolio.
- You will have regularly scheduled reevaluations of your positions, either on your own or with an advisor.
- You will invest a set amount of money each month/quarter/ paycheck that you are not allowed to withdraw for any circumstances other than a legitimate emergency.

Where possible, automate the process. It is natural for all of us to lapse into a sporadic Investing Frame, but we can ensure that we are being consistent if we set up our accounts for direct deposit, regularly scheduled investments, and DRIP (Dividend Reinvestment Plans). Talk to your bank or your brokerage. These processes can often be set up with a quick phone call or by spending five minutes on the Internet.

Dollar cost averaging (the practice of investing the same amount of money into the same position on a regularly scheduled basis) is ideally suited to keeping investors in a consistent frame.

It ensures regular investing, time diversification, and prevents "chasing" hot markets.

Frames Summary

The first step in a journey will be followed by countless more, making the distance covered in the initial stride practically irrelevant. It is tempting to use this logic to discount the importance of how you start your journey. But that first step will determine, more than all the subsequent steps, whether you are heading in the right direction.

Like the consultants who started the test after the instruction paragraph or the investor who jumped into the market without a clear sense of purpose, establishing the proper Investing Frames is vital to success.

Because no matter how clearly you think you see the picture (i.e., the facts, the data), if that picture is viewed within an inappropriate frame (i.e., starting assumptions, presuppositions), you are seeing a distortion of reality—an illusion.

Consider whether you have been approaching the market from a money- or life-focus (quantity versus quality), a market- or self-orientation (short-term outcomes versus long-term process), or a sporadic versus consistent frame (fair- versus all-weather). In periods when you find yourself pulled into one of the more destructive frames, consider using a visualization exercise such as the Slide Show technique we describe later in this chapter. Such visualizations can reduce the short-term stress that pushes one's focus away from the long term and into the short term, where the most damaging frames reside.

Motivations: The Iceberg Theory

Why is it that so many smart and motivated investors who know what it takes to accumulate wealth fail to do so? This question lies at the heart of this book, and its answer is very simple:

Most investors operate from the assumption that making money is the only goal of investing.

In the earlier stages of investing identity development, people tend to consider "making money" to be their chief, if not their only motivation. But money is the tip of an emotional iceberg, the most visible and readily comprehensible portion of a much deeper mass of needs, desires, and motivations that lie below the surface. Money is pieces of paper, numbers on an account statement. Its value lies in what it buys us—what it represents. Safety, freedom, fulfillment, contentment, self-esteem (pride), even power—these are the vast majority of motivations that lie below the surface. They are the ultimate emotional payoffs for our investments.

Nonetheless, it is only natural for us to concentrate on dollar figures. We all do it. The stock price, the net profit/loss, the number on the bottom of the financial statement; the language of numbers makes communication and comprehension easy. It's shorthand. The problem is, if the conception of investing is constrained to the language of numbers, so is the understanding of investing. And therefore one's ability to improve decision making is severely handicapped as well.

A common refrain in this book is the question, "why?" Why are you investing your money, generally speaking, and why are you doing it in the specific ways you have chosen? At the most fundamental level, this chapter is dedicated to answering these questions by exploring the hidden motivations that lie below the conscious surface. A big part of developing an investor identity is gaining true insights into what is driving our money decisions. When we understand those unique, often idiosyncratic drivers of behavior, we are no longer at their mercy.

Maslow's Hierarchy of Needs

So what are the real reasons we seek to make money? In 1943, psychologist Abraham Maslow wrote an influential paper titled "A Theory of Human Motivation."[1] Unlike the Freudian school of motivation that saw human behavior patterns as dictated by early childhood psychosexual needs, or the behavioral school, which saw behavior as determined purely by "conditioning" (i.e., rewards and punishment), Maslow took a decidedly more optimistic view of human nature.

He posited that human beings were innately motivated toward something called *self-actualization*, a sort of enlightenment that we attain when we reach our human potential. But before we can reach this higher plane, we must first satisfy more basic human needs.

To illustrate this concept he created his Hierarchy of Needs (shown in Figure 2.1) in the form of a pyramid of what motivates human behavior. It was shaped as a pyramid to accentuate how

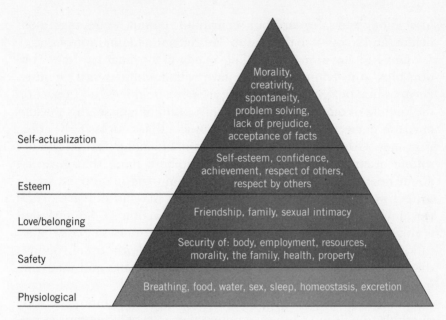

Figure 2.1   Maslow's Hierarchy of Needs

attaining the next level was predicated on forming a solid foundation at the level below it.

You will notice that "money" as a goal does not appear at any
stage in the hierarchy. It does, however, play a role in achieving success at various levels.

Where do investor motivations fall in this hierarchy?

The purpose of investing is not to meet the **physiological needs
at Level 1** of Maslow's pyramid. That may be the purpose for working (ask people why they work and "putting food on the table" is
one of the most common answers you will find). But investing is taking a surplus of money and putting it aside so that it can increase in
value over time. Burying your money in mason jars in the backyard
or in a mattress is not investing. It's saving. Investing is saving with
the intent to grow the value.

Level 2: Safety needs are the most basic motivations for investing.
These needs are less about upside than they are about protecting
against downside. People invest to guard against future scenarios in
which they could lose their security. As mentioned above, it is not
enough merely to make money—we want to have money in order
to protect ourselves and our family from future harm. But once we

have enough to safeguard our security—keep our house, insure our health, and so on—we don't stop. We continue to put money away.

Level 3: Love and belonging needs are primarily about relationships—the connections we have with family, friends, spouses. Perhaps in a perfect world, having money would have no impact on the success of our human relationships. But, of course, this world is far from perfect. The number one subject that couples fight about is money. Other than health (see Level 2), money is the greatest source of stress on families. Level 3 is about more than love, it's about needs for association and affiliation—the basic need for us to feel we belong. Money, and the role it plays in our lives, most certainly influences how and with whom we connect. So if Maslow is correct that once we have achieved a modicum of safety, we most fundamentally seek rewarding relationships with other people, then investing becomes a major factor in achieving and maintaining strong, healthy bonds.

Level 4: Esteem needs, as Maslow called this penultimate level of motivation, is most purely emotional in nature. Whereas the previous two levels involved feeling secure and feeling love, Level 4 pertains to how we feel about ourselves. And human beings have a tremendous drive to feel good about ourselves.

"It may be called the Master Passion," Mark Twain once wrote, "the hunger for self-approval." It is perhaps the most underappreciated motivation for investing. Feeling that we're doing the right thing, feeling respected, feeling adequate and worthwhile—these impulses are among the most powerful drivers of human behavior.

Level 5: Self-actualization may be the only level that transcends money's ability to impact it. But according to Maslow, the vast majority of people never satisfy needs above Level 4. (He considered truly self-actualized individuals to be rare and often historic figures on par with Eleanor Roosevelt, Mahatma Gandhi, and Martin Luther King, Jr.)

With an eye toward the hidden emotional reasons for investing, let's take a look at a case study.

Gary Gets Professional Help: A Case Study in Motivation

Gary was fed up. And today he decided to do something about it. Yes, there were ups and downs in the business, everyone knows that, but for six years in a row now he had lost money while watching less talented people slowly accumulate wealth. But that was going to change. No more impulsive decisions. No more overextending himself. No more chasing lost money.

Gary left his office at 5:30 P.M. to meet with his psychotherapist, as he had every Tuesday for three years. Today he felt different. As he pulled into Dr. Farmer's parking lot, he felt a wave of relief, and he broke into a broad smile. "Yes," he thought, "I finally feel like I have control over this situation." He couldn't wait to share the news with Dr. Farmer.

"Hi, Dr. Farmer," he said, as he plopped down on the big leather chair.

Dr. Farmer smiled. "Hello, Gary. You seem to be in good spirits today."

"I really am! As you know, I've been playing the game and losing money for years now. And that's where a lot of my stress comes from. It makes everything else in my life harder."

Dr. Farmer nodded.

"So I've decided to work with a professional—someone to help me make better decisions."

Dr. Farmer furrowed his brow, but didn't respond.

"I know what you're thinking. I never thought I would hire a poker coach, either. But this guy is really good, Dr. Farmer, he helped a newbie friend of mine make $30,000 last year. We've got an appointment set for tomorrow."

"Actually, after our last conversation, I thought you were going to quit. You said yourself, 'I'm not having any fun.'"

"Fun?" Gary interjected. "Doc, I don't play for fun! I play to make money. Do you know how much a good part-time online poker player can net? $50,000 a year, easy!"

Dr. Farmer shifted in his chair and opened his mouth to speak.

Gary quickly raised his hand. "Look," he continued, "It's a very misunderstood game. I mean, there's luck involved. But you know it's a game of skill. It's all about controlling your impulses and making better choices. There's no reason I can't build the skills and start making money. I would have thought you'd support me in that."

"Well," Dr. Farmer paused, searching for the right words to say. He looked at Gary and knew immediately that he was steadfast in his decision. "Good luck," he said.

Gary met with his poker coach the next day, and then weekly after that. His progress was immediate. He exhibited a newfound patience and discipline at the tables. His losses were capped to manageable levels and he began to have more winning games. For the first month in over two years he saw an increase in his bankroll.

And then, out of the blue, he fired his coach and went back to his old style of play.

Dr. Farmer was surprised to learn the news. "I thought you said you were doing better, Gary. You told me last week that you were making money."

Gary frowned. "I know, I know. I just . . . couldn't play that way. It was so . . . *boring*."

Hidden Agenda: The Emotional Returns on Investment (EROI)

Gary's (true) story contains a lesson for all investors. The reason he lost money wasn't a lack of ability or even bad luck. The reason was Gary's fundamental inability to understand his motivations. He thought his primary motivator for playing the game was to make money. He was wrong.

Sure, he had what it took to make money. He could be patient and disciplined and do all the things that make poker players successful. But where's the fun in that? Making big "all-in" bets, bluffing, overplaying weak hands to drive out stronger hands—that was why he played the game.

Investors often speak in terms of getting a financial return on their investments—an "ROI"; you make an initial investment in order to get more in return. For Gary the gambler, the financial return of the game was easy to recognize—it was literally right under his nose in stacks of clay chips. But Gary's more powerful incentives, those that formed the base of his investing iceberg, went unrecognized. We call them the Emotional Returns on Investment (EROI), and they make up the hidden motivations behind our actions. Gary's greatest EROI was excitement, "the rush," and it was a far more powerful force than the prospect of accumulating money.

For Gary, financial success required patience and discipline, but his emotional need was for excitement and risk. It is extremely difficult to serve two masters, but downright impossible when they demand contradictory things. When these two factors are in alignment, the investing plan is well suited to the individual and is likely to be successful. When they are not, it is a recipe for failure. See Figure 2.2.

Emotional Needs   Financial Needs

Figure 2.2   Emotions and Investing: Healthy Investing Requires Emotional Needs and Financial Needs to Be in Alignment

When given a choice between meeting a financial need or meeting an emotional need, we are naturally compelled to meet the emotional need—and the loudest, most immediate one gets served first. In this way, the EROI often precedes, exceeds, and supersedes the desire to make money.

So the question becomes: What can we do about it? Perhaps the best way to resolve this issue is to bring our hidden emotional returns to the surface, making them visible. We argue that the reason most investors underperform is because they pay too much attention to financial returns to the exclusion of nonfinancial rewards. Ask yourself what you gain besides money when your investments perform well—and what you lose besides money when they fail.

Following is a list of common EROI that serve as hidden motivations:

Safety

Excitement

Pride

Freedom

Fulfillment

Accomplishment

Social desirability

Tranquility

Influence

Power

Attention

Happiness

Imagine an enormous iceberg with just the tip breaking the surface of the water. All these words we've just listed fill the space underwater. And that tip? That's the part we see—our actual financial results—which depends entirely on what lies below the surface to keep it afloat.

Yet it's not just forward-looking emotional needs such as those above that motivate investors. Investors also have emotional needs to protect and preserve their wealth. For example, they may fear poverty, loss, or regret. Too often they are afraid they will continue to commit mistakes, fearful that the markets will never reward their efforts, or worried and insecure about the quality of their investments.

For most investors, it's quite a stretch to think that emotional needs could come before financial needs in motivating investing behavior. We occasionally have passionate discussions about this very topic.

What Is Your Motivation?

The following exchange is a composite of numerous conversations we've had over the years at MarketPsych seminars:

Market Psychologist (MP):	If there's one thing I hope you will all take away from my talk today, it's a new realization: Making money is not the goal of investing.
Investor:	What did you say?
MP:	I said, "If there's one thing I hope—"
Investor:	No, I mean the last part.
MP:	That making money is not the goal of investing.
Investor:	That's nuts.
MP:	Yeah. I get that a lot. Are you saying the goal of investing is to make money?
Investor:	Yeah, of course.
MP:	Great. So let me ask you, after you've accumulated a whole bunch of money and you feel like you've accomplished this goal . . . can you sign it over to me? I've always wanted a Ferrari and my wife would kill me if I cashed out our savings.
Investor:	What? No, of course not. It's my money.

MP:	Darn. You plan on keeping it, too. So maybe the goal of investing isn't really to make money, it's to have money.
Investor:	Well, yeah. But that's obvious.
MP:	It should be obvious. But it leads to very different kinds of thinking. If the focus is on making money, you're focused on how your investments are doing. But if the focus is on having money, you're focused on how you are doing. A much more important perspective, wouldn't you say?
Investor:	I suppose.
MP:	Okay, so why do you want to "have money"?
Investor:	So I can do things.
MP:	Things like what? Give me an example.
Investor:	Like, take care of my family. Hello?
MP:	Why do you want to take care of your family?
Investor:	Are you insane?
MP:	Possibly. But there is a reason—many reasons, actually—why a person would want to take care of his family. What are yours?
Investor:	What kind of husband—what kind of parent would I be if I didn't take care of my family?
MP:	You tell me.
Investor:	A terrible one. You think I want to be a complete failure? A deadbeat?
MP:	And what are some of your other reasons?
Investor:	So that we can live in a nice home, so my kids can go to a good school . . . to give my family a good life . . .
MP:	Why do you want to give your family a good life?
Investor:	You really are nuts, aren't you?
MP:	I wonder about that sometimes. But then the voices in my head assure me I'm not. Go with me on this. Aside from feeling okay about yourself, why do you want to give your family a good life?
Investor:	Because I love them! I want them to be safe. I want them to be happy! Geez, what the . . .
MP:	Exactly. So you don't invest your money to make money or even just to "have money." You do it because you believe having more money will achieve certain things—emotional goals you have for yourself. For

one thing, you want to feel good about who you are. You want to be able to look yourself in the eye. But if we asked more questions you'd probably also agree that you want the feeling of security that comes from knowing you can meet your needs. If you felt like being candid, you might even admit that you have an ego want to keep up with the Joneses who live in your neighborhood.

Investor: Hey—

MP: But it's not just about you. It's about the people you love. You're investing for emotional goals you have for them. To use your words, you want them to feel "safe," "happy." The ultimate driver of our money decisions is so that we—and those we care about—can feel a certain way. All investing decisions are means to emotional ends. They are never ends themselves. See what I mean?

Investor: Not really.

MP: So what's a more powerful motivator for a financial decision, a financial driver like "making money" or an emotional driver like "feeling good about yourself"?

Investor: Ah, but they're the same thing! If you make more money, you feel good about yourself.

MP: A lot of people don't, actually. You'd be surprised. But often our emotional goals and our financial goals are not the same thing, in fact, sometimes they're in direct conflict with each other.

Investor: What do you mean?

MP: Glad you asked. I'll give you an example. Let's say earlier this year you bought a stock and are still holding this position in your portfolio. Unfortunately, you bought right at the top and the stock is now worth half what you paid for it. And this was a stock in a company you really believed in, too. You even suggested to your in-laws that they should buy it . . . and they did. And now they're in the same boat you are. How would you feel?

Investor: I'd feel awful.

MP: Right. Who wouldn't? It's a sickening feeling. But think for a moment of the potential for intrapsychic conflict.

Investor: Huh?

MP: The cognitive dissonance.

Investor: English, please.

MP: Think of the pickle you're in. You said before that your financial goals and emotional goals are really the same thing, because when you make money you feel good about yourself. But sometimes it's like you have two brains and they're at war to see who controls your actions.

On one side is your Financial Brain. Its goal is to make money. This side knows you were wrong about the stock. It's telling you to get out of this position. It's saying, "Look, you've already held it too long. It's down 50 percent and its management is defecting and insiders are selling. All objective analyses say that there are better places for your money. Get out now. Cut your losses." It's very rational. That's the Financial Brain and it's telling you to sell.

Fighting on the other side of the conflict is your Emotional Brain. Its goal is for you to feel good. The only way that can happen is if you were not wrong. This side is hoping desperately that the stock comes back and will frantically grasp at any piece of information that tells you that you were right. In fact, that's the reason you've held it so long already. But even more than wanting us to feel good, the emotional driver wants us to avoid pain. If you sell now, it will be terribly painful. Not only will you have to admit you're wrong and lose a chunk of money, but you will have to tell your in-laws that you blew it and the best thing they can do is cut their losses.

Investor: Ugh.

MP: I know. Been there. So your rational Financial Brain is saying, "Get out of this stock, it's a total dog." But your Emotional Brain is saying, "Don't sell! If it still comes back, and you can avoid all that pain, you can face your family again, you can redeem yourself."

This battle is going on, but only one side can get its way. And if you consider that all financial decisions are motivated by an emotional payoff, which side do you think is more likely to win, the Emotional Brain or the Financial Brain?

Investor: I see your point. Even when we may know the right thing to do, it can be tough to do it.

MP: Exactly. You could argue in this case that the Emotional Brain already torpedoed your Financial Brain. Otherwise, you would not have allowed yourself to lose half your money. Our financial interests and our emotional interests are often in synch and usually match up well when it comes to the destination. But we haven't reached the destination. We're still on the journey.

In fact, to say that "making money is the goal of investing" is like saying "flying in an airplane is the goal of traveling."

On this journey, our Emotional Brain and our Financial Brain are often in flat-out war, and in that war our Emotional Brain has the superior firepower and holds the high ground.

Because in the end, investing is not primarily about making money. It's about creating the ability to feel the way we want.

Goals: Create a Slide Show® to Guide Your Investing

During a period of investment anxiety, when you're considering selling out of your investments until the latest market storm clears, what would happen if you could mentally transport yourself into your idealized future? What if you could see yourself in the vacation home in the Caribbean that you hope to own one day, with a refreshing breeze blowing through the house, sitting on the porch, drinking orange juice from one of your trees? If you could clearly envision such a scenario and recall that short-term fear is the greatest destroyer of long-term wealth, you're likely to make much less impulsive investment decisions,

One of the best ways to maintain a healthy outlook and positive motivation in your investing is to focus on specific goals and visions for your future. The Slide Show is a visualization/goal-setting technique that you develop to help you stay focused on the long term, even during stressful periods in the markets. The Slide Show technique involves first conjuring and then regularly imagining a vivid goal that represents the ultimate purpose of one's investing. Without a lucid and tangible goal, many investors find it difficult to stay in a healthy frame of mind, especially during market stress.

Visualization is a technique used by mental health professionals to relax clients and reduce anxiety. Mentally walking yourself through peaceful or pleasant scenarios decreases physiological symptoms of stress (e.g., rapid heart rate, muscle tenseness, shallow breathing). When the body relaxes, the mind follows—and for that matter, vice versa.

Using this approach creates an automatic shift from short-term to long-term thinking, which immediately puts the investor in a better frame of mind for good decisions.

The Slide Show also creates valuable anchors. Failure in investing decisions often comes down to losing sight of why you are putting your money away, which leads in turn to losing sight of how you should be investing. The Slide Show Method creates highly specific goals that recenter your focus. When you have a clear and accessible visualization—whatever it may be, a house you always dreamed of, the college graduation for a grandchild, the opening of a charitable foundation—it gives you a vital focal point. We have all heard the expression, "keep your eyes on the prize." It's good advice. But first you have to know what the prize looks like.

The Slide Show can become an emotional counterweight. There is so much focus on the fear of market loss that sometimes we fail to realize that in our attempt to avoid those losses (e.g., "playing it too safe") we lose something else—the ability to achieve our long-term goals. Fear of loss is the preeminent driver of investing decisions. The Slide Show Method is effective because it taps into this basic, primal motivator. It becomes a ballast that helps us reset our emotional scales.

It's helpful to create a Slide Show with a financial advisor—or at least someone with a comparable skills set. Such a guide is ideal because the purpose of the exercise is not merely to create vivid pictures of future goals, but to recognize what it would take to achieve them. This involves, among other things, portfolio allocation skills, knowledge of tax liabilities, and an appreciation of the historical returns of various investments.

Step 1: Identifying Slide Show Topics

The first step in designing a personal Slide Show is for the investor to identify important aspects of his or her future life that will be affected by the investment decisions made today. To phrase it differently, the investor should create/reveal a "goal" in this topic area. Create the future focus by mentally imagining yourself in an ideal scenario. Some sample questions to get the process started include:

- Imagine a time 20 years from today. Where would I like to be living?
- If I had an "extra" $100,000, what are some things I might want to do with that money?
- What are some dreams I have for my children and grandchildren?
- What are some of the places I've never been to, but would one day love to visit if I could have the chance?

Some Suggested Slide Show Topics

- Your home
- Education: sending children/grandchildren to a great school
- A foundation/cause you would like to support/start
- A vacation home
- Recreational goals
- World travel
- Luxury purchases
- Gifts for a loved one
- Visualization of holidays/wedding
- Whatever else you come up with

So we don't get ahead of ourselves, it is useful to classify Slide Show goals into three categories: On Track, Attainable, and Aspirational.

On Track Goals, as the name suggests, are those that that the investor can be expected to reach with his or her current investable assets and investing behavior, without major changes in circumstances or major deviations from historical market movements.

Attainable Goals are those that are within reach with an increase in the investor's investable assets and reasonable changes in investing behavior (e.g., a different asset allocation, saving more money, reducing spending).

Aspirational Goals are perhaps classified more as dreams than as goals. They are a chance to "think big" and to consider what would be possible with prudent saving, great performance, and good fortune along the way. They should be fun and exciting to think about. What the aspirational goals in the Slide Show should not be are self-indulgences that come at the expense of other, more important needs. (After all, one may very well be able to afford a private island, if one were to forsake all sorts of essentials such as health care, housing, and family needs.)

Remember, the focus of the Slide Show exercise is for an investor to get in touch with *what is most important* to him or her, to firmly establish *the why* behind the decisions he or she makes. The nature of that "why" will vary widely from person to person. By establishing the reasons for their investments and creating tangible visions in the Slide Show, investors arm themselves with a purpose, a plan, and a clearer vision of who they are and what they want for their future. One reason most investors fail to reach their goals is that they lack these essentials.

One's Slide Show should be enjoyable, not stressful, and most people we've worked with enjoy the process. But we recognize that some will find it a bit of a challenge. When asked a question about the future, many people's first reaction is "I don't know" or even "I never thought about it." That's fine. You don't have to know. But *you should think* about it. Having goals is imperative. All this "putting money away," all the effort, all the sacrifices . . . it's essential to *know why*. It keeps us focused and gives us motivation—much more so than having some vague sense of future well-being. So if it feels a little strange at first, that's okay. Give yourself some time. You will be glad you did.

Step 2: Make It Vivid

A key component to the method is to envision the goals more and more specifically. Vivid images are more easily recalled and more intensely experienced. The deeper into detail the image creation goes, the more powerful the technique. It pays to ask numerous follow-up questions and collaboratively arrive at the most detailed image possible. It may be useful to think of it as literally creating a photographic slide of the image, or as painting a picture together on a canvas.

- "Great. So you can see yourself living in a house near the ocean . . . "
- "What would you like your house to look like? What color would you paint it? Would there be a favorite room, a place where you could read a good book or listen to music?"
- "Would there be a garden? What would you grow there?"
- "It's a Saturday morning, and you've just woken up in this house. It's sunny outside . . . how would you like to spend your day?"

Step 3: Capture the Feeling

After you have created the image, the next step is to picture yourself actually being in the future and realizing that goal. A good question to ask is, "What would it feel like?" or even better, "How does it feel?" The ability not merely to picture the goal but to vicariously experience the feelings that come with achieving it completes the transition from an intellectual exercise to an emotional one. Some typical words/feelings would be "happy," "cozy," "proud," "satisfied," "fulfilled," "peaceful," "content," and "excited."

Speaking the words and verbalizing the feelings indicates that you have "done the work" of fully forming the thoughts and putting yourself in those situations. Let those moments linger a little bit. Reflect on them.

Our goals and dreams play like movies in our heads, viewed countless times and with an unconscious emotional reaction every time. Though they have not been achieved in reality, they have been realized in our imaginations over and over again. The ability to picture and experience these events (and the subsequent emotions they induce) forms an attachment to the future vision and gives you both an exciting and motivating goal as well as something to lose by veering off plan. Tagging the goal with an emotion is what gives it emotional sticking power. Feeling yourself in the sensory experience of the vision makes it real.

Critics of the Slide Show might say you can't miss something you've never had. That's nonsense. Those people have never recorded a Notre Dame football game, avoided all media for 24 hours so as not to spoil the ending, ordered a pizza, and sat down in front of their TV to stare at—Women's Figure Skating?!—because they had set their DVR on the wrong channel. We absolutely miss things we never had if we truly look forward to them.

Step 4: Recording

This process should be interactive and fluid. But it is vital that a response should be taken down and saved. It's what creates the common language and "anchors" that give the process its power. I recommend jotting down key words and descriptions on the worksheet in Figure 2.3. Here is a real-life example of a Slide Show description (in this case a retirement house) by a financial advisor who worked with a middle-aged couple:

> CLIENT would really like to have a part-time residence in Florida, somewhere near Palm Beach. It would be an apartment with an ocean view. They love the idea of hearing the ocean each night as they go to bed. They would love to get the newspapers delivered there and have coffee each morning on the balcony. They describe the feeling they have as "cozy" and "peaceful."

See Figure 2.3 for examples.

Step 5: A Matching Plan

It is important for investors to match their real-life finances to their visions. Some investors may be vastly underestimating what they can realistically achieve. Some may have visions that are unfortunately out of their reach. It behooves us to have a clear sense of the attainability of the Slide Show images. It may be useful to classify the goals as either "On Track," "Attainable," or "Aspirational." Likewise, if an advisor or investor chooses to use the Slide Show Method in a more regimented and structured format, an importance score (e.g., 1 to 10) can be a useful way of filtering and prioritizing goals.

Slide Show Topic: _____

Date Today: _____   Estimated Date of Goal: _____

Detailed Description: _____

_____

_____

Associated Feelings: _____

Total Investable Assets: _____

Estimated Cost of Goal: _____

What Will It Take To Get There: _____

_____

_____

Attainability: On Track ____   Attainable ____   Aspirational ____

Importance: 1 2 3 4 5 6 7 8 9 10

Other Notes: _____

_____

_____

Figure 2.3 Slide Show® Worksheet

The Five Questions to Ask Before Investing

While we've shared with you the emotional origins of investment mistakes and a tool for reducing the short-term pull of strong feelings, it's essential to mention that sometimes investment fear is justified. If you haven't asked yourself some tough questions before investing in the first place, then you won't have the confidence to remain a consistent investor. If you don't know what bad news or information should cause you to sell, then you're susceptible to the vicissitudes of the market's many moods.

Even with a solid plan and well-grounded investment philosophy, most investors will at some point consider deviating from their discipline. At such times, it's important to consider the answers to five questions.

If you are using technical analysis or momentum-based strategies, in which you buy and sell assets based on price movement, then your buy and sell criteria should be clear-cut. If you're using fundamental or hybrid (both technical and fundamental) information to dictate buying and selling, then it's important to ensure that you have a reliable and consistent source of that information and you've identified what type of information would drive you to sell.

Consider asking yourself the following five questions before each investment and a different four questions when contemplating selling (see Tables 2.2 and 2.3). Keep your answers in a journal and revisit them when needed.

These questions require reflection—which can be uncomfortable. Most investors, in the heat of the moment, will not stop to answer them. This reluctance of investors to do what they "know" they should do is why we wrote this book and why this chapter is primarily about understanding and aligning your motivations and frames with a healthy long-term outlook.

Table 2.2   Five Questions to Ask before Investing

Primary Buy Questions	Clarifiers
What is my advantage?	What do you know that others don't?
	How does your information about the investment provide an advantage for you?
What could change my opinion of this investment?	What new information is on the horizon?
	What would change your assessment of this investment?
What is the worst possible outcome?	What is the worst-case scenario for your losses?
Under what conditions will I sell?	Considering the information that drove you to buy, under what circumstances would that no longer be valid?
	What news or information will indicate that it's time to sell?
	How can you stay abreast of such information?
	Is there an alert that you can establish for the long term?
	What is your schedule for checking up on new information?
How can I prevent myself from making my most common mistakes?	What mistakes are common for you when you invest in a security like this?
	What do you need to do to prevent these mistakes?
	How often is the minimum that you need to monitor prices (preferably, not at all)?

Table 2.3 Four Questions to Ask When Considering Selling an Investment

Primary Sell Questions	Clarifiers
Were my criteria for selling met?	If yes, then sell. If not, then also consider if you didn't select adequate criteria.
Are the reasons I bought it still in place?	Recall why you bought this investment. Are those reasons still intact? If not, you should consider whether a change in those reasons should have been part of your sell criteria.
Do I need to sell it for cash, risk reduction, or diversification reasons?	Sometimes we simply need to sell for a functional reason. However, it's all too common to focus on the winners rather than the losers when it comes time to rebalance. Be sure to decide with an objective weighing process if you need to sell to free up a specific amount of cash.
Would I buy this today?	If you could do it all over again, would you own this investment today? If not, why not? If your reasons for not owning this investment don't meet your criteria for selling, do you need to reformulate those criteria? Did you neglect something important in those criteria?

Conclusion

A big part of developing a healthy investing identity is recognizing the first steps in the investing process—the ones we usually take before we've even realized it. These steps involve both our motivations (the reasons why we're investing—often related to satisfying our emotional needs) and our frames (predetermined mind-sets about investing). Investing success depends considerably on these first steps being appropriate, well suited to our needs, and well understood. Working within bad frames is tantamount to losing the battle before it has even begun.

Establishing healthy frames is perhaps the most challenging task. Most of us are unaware of the deep-seated beliefs and presuppositions that underlie our respective investing approaches. As was the case with the consultants in this chapter's opening vignette, it is vital that we take the proverbial step back to make sure that we are starting the task from the beginning, with the proper perspective.

We are best served by operating from a life-focused frame that views our investing decisions within the context of what we specifically want to achieve, rather than from a money-focused frame, which uses dollar figures as the primary scorecard.

Likewise, operating from a process-oriented frame that puts the focus on ourselves and the process by which we make decisions is preferable to operating from a market-centered frame that places the focus on external outcomes that are beyond our control in the short-term and are often less important to long-term success.

Third, we do well to adopt a consistent frame that keeps us on an even keel by approaching our investments as a steady, ongoing process, rather than to adopt a sporadic frame in which investing decisions are made in fits and starts as circumstances (or our whims) dictate.

If appreciating our investment frames is the most challenging task, understanding our motivations cannot be far behind. It starts with a realization that making money is not the only goal of investing. Our motivations for investing are an iceberg in which the obvious financial gains form only the visible portion. Below lie emotional motivations that, though less conspicuous, can be more influencial.

It is important to make these hidden EROI conscious, via reflection, journaling, or good conversations with a trusted partner in order to assure that they are aligned with our financial goals (i.e., our FROI). When our EROI is misaligned it can lead to emotions such as fear, anger and pride hijacking the process and leading us into poor investing choices—and all without our awareness. Getting away from sound financial motivations because of unsound emotional motivations may be considered the primary reason that investors underperform the markets and fail to reach their goals.

Knowing who you are as an investor is a process of learning, discovery, and hard work. As with any process, you ought to start by mastering the fundamentals. These first steps—recognizing the lens through which you view the investing process and understanding why you make the choices you do—lay the foundations for building the healthy investor identity that is key to achieving long-term investing success.

3

Your Investor Personality: Your Character and Style

*Success in investing doesn't correlate with I.Q. once you're above
the level of 25. Once you have ordinary intelligence, what you need
is the temperament to control the urges that get other people into
trouble in investing.[1]*

—Warren Buffett

In the first season of the television series *Seinfeld* there is an episode called "The Stock Tip." It opens with George Costanza excited about a stock. He received a tip from an insider that the stock was about to rocket, and he made a proposition to Jerry.

George enthusiastically explained that his friend "Wilkinson" had inside information about a small company that was about to go through a "big merger." George's friend "wasn't even supposed to say anything." If George bought shares on this tip, Wilkinson would tell him the exact time to sell.

"What does the company do?" Jerry asks.

"It's called Centrax . . . . they've got some new type of technique for televising opera . . . some sort of electronic thingy," George explains.

They invest, but the stock doesn't go up as expected. In fact, the stock declines, day after day. Finally, after losing almost half his investment in a few days, Jerry can't tolerate the pain any more, declaring, "I don't want to think about this. I'm selling!"

George gamely replies, "I'm keeping it. I'm going down with the ship!"

A week after selling, Jerry looks up Centrax's stock quote in the newspaper. The stock is up considerably from where he had bought it. His girlfriend unhelpfully remarks, "I told you not to sell it. . . . I said the stock market fluctuates." To which Jerry responds with dismay, "I just got fluctuated out of four thousand dollars!"

George ultimately cleared $8,000 on his investment in Centrax ("a Hyundai!"), and to celebrate his windfall he takes Jerry and Elaine to lunch. After lunch George leans across the table, and whispers conspiratorially, "Wilkinson's got a bite on a new one. The TramCo Corporation out of . . . uh . . . Springfield, I think. They're about to introduce some sort of robot butcher. If you want to get in, there's very little time."

Most investors have at some time made decisions like Jerry and George—investing large amounts of cash on limited information. Sometimes they buy on impulse, sometimes they sell in fear. George and Jerry had different perspectives on buying shares of Centrax. Jerry was cautious at first, while George was impulsive and enthusiastic. They also responded differently to the pain of the loss: Jerry sold out while George stayed invested. These different responses are, in part, functions of their unique personalities.

In the *Seinfeld* series George was portrayed as a brazen risk-taker, tormented by a conflict between his innate greed and opportunism and his lowly position in the social pecking order. Yet George's impulsivity often hamstrung his grand business and romantic plans, and it lent a tragicomic element to his character.

Jerry's character is successful in his career as a comedian, but he struggles with neuroses. He can't tolerate taking big risks. Nonetheless he is often coaxed into taking risks by his less responsible friends (Kramer, Elaine, and George), and many of the show's laughs come from his neurotic back-and-forth about the vicissitudes of daily life.

George's impulsivity and Jerry's chronic caution are key aspects of their personalities—traits that change little over time and reflect how they see and interact with the world. In the parlance of personality psychology, George is low in "conscientiousness"—he makes spontaneous and unplanned decisions—while Jerry is high in emotional sensitivity—he is chronically cautious and hyperalert to potential dangers.

Researchers have identified five major personality traits that describe much of how we see and interact with the world. Two of those traits are conscientiousness and emotional sensitivity, while the other three are openness to new experiences, extraversion, and agreeableness. Not only do your specific personality traits affect how you perceive and get along in the world generally, but more specifically, they influence how you invest.

Although many people assume that there is one correct "personality" for success in investing, research doesn't uphold that belief. In our work, we have found that it is true that individual personality traits are associated with investment success in different economic climates, but no one trait or combination of traits is consistently correlated with investment profits over time.

It turns out that both *knowing* your personality propensities and *understanding* the conditions in which they predispose you to thrive are greater predictors of success than the traits themselves. In part, knowing your personality allows you to understand the conditions in which your vulnerabilities will be exposed. At the same time, it's important to press your advantage. Understanding and leveraging your strongest traits when an optimal environment arises is key to successful investing. Pressing your personality advantages facilitates capital growth, while withdrawing when vulnerable is the best way to preserve capital when you're not in an optimal environment.

In this case, we're suggesting that market timing can be helpful for long-term investors. While you may feel pulled into sporadic versus consistent Investing Frames, depending on the latest market fad or news release, we're suggesting a more deliberate approach. By understanding your personality and your optimal investing style, you can be more strategic about when it is a good time for you to begin searching for investments. For example, an emotionally stable person may be better prepared to "bottom-fish" during a bear market, since he or she is less likely to panic if conditions worsen before the recovery (as they often do). An extravert is likely to do better at identifying fast-growing companies when volatility is low and the economy is growing.

What Makes a Great Investor?

Some characteristics of great investors are popularly known. For example, Warren Buffett has a keen intuitive sense of probabilities.[2]

George Soros enjoys examining his investment thinking process for flaws, taking pleasure when he finds one. Most great investors are extremely confident in their ability to succeed.[3] Yet these characteristics are not common to all great investors, and for the most part they are anecdotal. In this chapter we'll demonstrate that recent personality research is moving the understanding of great investors beyond the anecdotal.

Over the past decade there have been exciting developments in the scientific study of personality and emotional intelligence. Personality refers to a collective pattern of character, behavioral, temperamental, emotional, and mental traits.[4] Recent academic research has shown that personality can be broken down into five general characteristics.[5] These five traits (the "Big Five") are related to how people describe themselves using language. Remarkably, personality traits remain generally stable over the adult life span (exceptions are noted where applicable).[6]

Emotional intelligence (EI) describes the ability to identify, assess, and manage the emotions of oneself and others.[7] There is evidence suggesting that higher scores on some emotional intelligence traits are correlated with superior investment performance.[8] Because there is a confluence between several personality and key emotional intelligence traits, we will focus primarily on personality in this chapter.

Using emotional insights, whether about one's own personality or the tendencies of others, can lead to greater understanding of and success in the markets. In some investment situations having an emotional "feel" for the market may pay off; in others, it is more profitable to be quantitative and analytical. The investor who understands the value of emotional cues will be able to decide which "type" of market he is in and which style of analysis is likely to be more productive. Understanding your investor identity leads to more productive investment decisions because you will have more mental flexibility—the ability to select the most productive style of investing—an essential virtue in a constantly evolving market.

Important Note: Before you read on, *please* take one of the free personality tests—for Businesspeople, Traders, or Investors—on the MarketPsych.com website (www.marketpsych.com/personality_test.php). If you read on and choose to take a test afterward, your results will be biased by what you learned in this chapter.

The "Big Five"

*Most great men and women are not perfectly rounded in
their personalities, but are instead people whose one driving
enthusiasm is so great it makes their faults seem insignificant.*
—Charles A. Cerami

In 1936, two American psychologists, Gordon Allport and H. S. Odbert, hypothesized: "Those individual differences that are most salient and socially relevant in people's lives will eventually become encoded into their language; the more important such a difference, the more likely is it to become expressed as a single word."[9]

In the 1970s, Lewis Goldberg, a professor of psychology at the University of Oregon, compiled a list of 1,250 phrases describing personality characteristics. He and his students went door to door, asking 750 homeowners in Eugene and Springfield, Oregon, to rate how well each of the 1,250 phrases described them. The phrases were statements such as "Like parties," "Follow rules," or "Fear the worst." Subjects rated how well that phrase described them on a 1-to-5 scale. They then circled an answer: "Strongly disagree," "Disagree," "Neither agree nor disagree," "Agree," or "Strongly agree."

Responses from 300 of the original 1,250 phrases statistically grouped into five different clusters. For example, people who agreed with "Like parties" also tended to agree with the statement "Radiate joy," implying that social and optimistic people have a common personality trait (subsequently called "extraversion"). The five clusters were named the "Big Five" personality traits:[10]

1. Emotional sensitivity
2. Extraversion
3. Openness
4. Agreeableness
5. Conscientiousness

Many of the following trait descriptions and item examples are adapted from Professor John Johnson's free online NEO personality inventory, available at http://ipip.ori.org/,[11] which grew out of his work with Goldberg. See Table 3.1 for a description of the "Big Five" personality traits.

Table 3.1   The "Big Five" Personality Traits

Personality Trait	High Scores	Low Scores
Emotional stability	Emotionally stable. Relaxed and mellow.	Emotionally sensitive, scattered, indecisive, pessimistic, nervous.
Extraversion	Gregarious, optimistic, and social. Derives energy from others.	Introverted. Often enjoys and derives inspiration from solitude.
Openness	Open to experimenting with new ideas and experiences.	Traditional and conventional. Prefers continuity over change.
Agreeableness	Values cooperation and getting along with others, generous and altruistic.	Self-interested. Often mildly suspicious of others' intentions.
Conscientiousness	Self-disciplined, delays gratification, organized, follows rules, punctual. Uptight.	Impulsive and disorganized. Difficulty following set methods or rules. Spontaneous and relaxed.

Statistically, test-takers' responses distribute in a normal curve, with 40 percent of people scoring in the "average" range. Each test-taker scores on a range from "very low" to "very high" on each trait. One who scores low on the extraversion scale is called an introvert, and one who scores high is called an extravert. "High" and "low" scores are more than one standard deviation from the average. Each personality trait has a primary pole and an opposite pole. Thus, a low scorer on extraversion is, by definition, high on introversion.

Taken together, all five personality traits comprise one's personality *style*. Some people have multiple strong personality traits, and it is generally the strongest scores, whether on one or five of the traits, that are what we think of as our unique personalities. People who score highly on both conscientiousness and emotional sensitivity are commonly seen as "perfectionists." An example of a celebrity high in multiple traits is Jerry Seinfeld, described in the opening vignette.

Seinfeld often makes light of his strong tendency to emotional sensitivity. He is also extraverted and open, as apparent in his public persona. Being both extraverted and open, he enjoys putting his nervousness on display, to humorous effect, in his comedy routines. Having some traits but not others does not make a better or worse person. Each trait represents a way of seeing the world that is useful in some, but not all, situations. As we'll see later in the chapter, some traits do correlate with financial success, but the usefulness of traits depends on context. The same traits that facilitate success for a venture capitalist may impede the performance of a short-term trader.

Personality traits are somewhat heritable, which indicates that they have a genetic basis (although it is multifactored and complex).

Emotional Stability vs. Emotional Sensitivity

High emotional stability scorers tend to be calm and free from persistent negative feelings. They are more "thick-skinned," mellow, and unflappable. They are more likely to find the phrase "Remain calm under pressure" descriptive of themselves. Freedom from negative feelings does not necessarily mean they experience more positive feelings. In general, they are secure, hardy, and relaxed even under stressful conditions. The super-relaxed attitude of the emotionally stable can be a problem when real dangers loom. Emotionally sensitive people may sound the false alarm more often, but they also are attentive to potential risks.

Emotional sensitivity is on the opposite pole from emotional stability. Those who score high on emotional sensitivity tend to be more "thin-skinned" and to experience more negative feelings such as anxiety, anger, or depression and are more emotionally reactive than others. They are more likely to identify with the phrase "Panic easily." Their difficulty in emotion regulation when under stress can impair their ability to think clearly, make decisions, and cope.

In one brain imaging (fMRI) experiment, the degree of activation in one of the brain's pain centers—the anterior insula—when threatened was correlated with study participants' personality level of emotional sensitivity.[12] This finding implies that high scorers are more sensitive and reactive to signs of danger than emotionally stable people. This hypervigilance to threat can be exhausting and can lead to many false alarms, but it also ensures that they are prepared to take quick action when real calamity strikes.

One consistent finding in our research is that high scores on emotional stability are correlated with both short-term trading—and investing—success.

Extraversion vs. Introversion

On the extraversion scale, high scorers are called *extraverts* and low scorers are called *introverts*. Extraverts enjoy being with people, are full of energy, and often experience positive emotions. Extraversion is characterized by a desire to socialize and a tendency toward optimism. Extraverts are more likely to strongly agree with phrases such as "Love life." They tend to be enthusiastic and action-oriented and engage in opportunities for excitement. In groups they often like to talk, be assertive, and draw attention to themselves. Interestingly, brain imaging (fMRI) studies show that extraverts have more reward-system activation to financial gains than do introverts.[13] That is, extraverts are more excited and motivated by opportunities for financial gain.

Introverts are typically quiet, low-key, deliberate, and less engaged with the social world. Introverts are comfortable without much social involvement, and this is neither due to shyness nor depression; they simply need less stimulation than extraverts and are more likely to prefer being alone. Introverts agree with statements such as "Avoid crowds." Introverts are motivated from an internal drive rather than from outside stimulation. That is, they generate motivation and excitement internally rather than seeking external sources.

Openness to New Experiences vs. Traditionalism

Openness to new experiences describes a willingness to experiment, to seek out new experiences, and to think broadly and abstractly. Open people are intellectually curious, appreciative of art, sensitive to beauty, and they are more likely to identify with the phrase "Like to solve complex problems." Open people often think and act in individualistic and nonconforming ways. Compared to traditionalists, open people are often more aware of their feelings.

Traditionalists prefer the plain, straightforward, and obvious over the complex, ambiguous, and subtle. Traditionalists agree with the statement "Am attached to conventional ways." Open and traditional styles of thinking are useful in different environments. An open intellectual style may serve one well as a psychologist or professor, but research has shown that traditional thinking is related to superior job performance in police work, sales, and a number of service occupations.

Jim Rogers is probably the most famous open investor. He actively seeks new experiences and is in the *Guinness Book of World Records* for his long motorcycle and automobile journeys crisscrossing the continents. He has written several books: *A Bull in China*, (Random House, 2008) *Adventure Capitalist* (Random House, 2004), and *Investment Biker* (Random House, 2003). He created a commodity index in the late 1990s, when few investors were paying attention to that sector, and he has recommended investing in markets as diverse as Botswana, Nicaragua, and Bolivia. More recently, his family relocated from New York City to Singapore, so he could be closer to the business epicenters of the new millennium.

Agreeableness vs. Self-interest

Agreeable people believe others are basically honest, decent, and trustworthy. Agreeableness reflects concern with cooperation and social harmony. An agreeable person is more likely to agree with the statement "Sympathize with others' feelings." Agreeable people thrive in collaborative environments.

Self-interested people place their own concerns above getting along with others. They are generally less interested in others' well-being, and therefore are unlikely to extend themselves for other people. Self-interested people are more likely to endorse the statement "Am not interested in other people's problems." Competitive environments are comfortable for self-interested people. Most traders score highly on self-interest, which is important in their daily work, while competing for the best possible price.

Conscientiousness vs. Impulsiveness

Conscientiousness concerns the way in which people control, regulate, and direct their impulses. Conscientiousness describes a tendency to plan and organize toward achieving goals, to follow rules while pursuing those goals, and to control one's impulses along the way. Conscientious people typically agree with the statement "Know how to get things done." In occupational research, conscientiousness is correlated with career success and wealth accumulation. In general, pursuing immediate gratification and impulsiveness erodes prosperity.

Impulsiveness is on the other end of the conscientiousness pole. Impulsive people are likely to identify with the statement "Often make last-minute plans." In times of play rather than work, their spontaneity and impulsivity can be fun. A problem with impulsive acts is that they may produce immediate rewards but undesirable long-term consequences. Their accomplishments may sometimes appear small, scattered, and inconsistent.

Alan Greenspan, former chair of the Federal Reserve, is famous for his conscientiousness and attention to detail. The detailed analyses of important economic trends he developed for his consulting clients in the 1960s and 1970s were legendary for their thoroughness. His insight and detail-orientation led to his ascension at the Federal Reserve. Until the financial crisis of 2008, most businesspeople viewed him as a powerful sage. Subsequently, the dangers of his rigorous focus on detail, without adequate appreciation of the larger regulatory (and psychological) forces guiding the economy, were revealed. Conscientiousness and attention to detail are generally beneficial, but one must also maintain a willingness to periodically challenge conventional models and assumptions.

The Character of Performance

Do investors' scores on the "Big Five" correlate with performance? To investigate the performance/personality link, we set up a 75-item online personality test. The test uses 60 of the most significant NEO personality phrases, and it has 15 research questions at the end. In designing this test we looked for correlations between personality traits and financial decision making. The test measures the "Big Five" personality traits: emotional sensitivity, extraversion, openness, agreeableness, and conscientiousness.

Table 3.2 shows the linear correlations between personality trait scores and investor returns, and common investor mistakes (up arrows indicate a positive correlation and down arrows an inverse one). Up arrows on the table indicate that the personality trait in the header row is correlated with a self-reported item in the leftmost column. Down arrows describe an inverse correlation, and "0" represents no relationship.

Items in the leftmost column include investment returns, net worth, and lifetime largest loss. Below those three items is a list of several common investment traps or "biases" (more on those in Chapter 6). Common investor mistakes are abbreviated from the full list, which is below:

- Exit Plans in Place: "I have exit plans in place before I enter my positions."

- Hold Losers Too Long: "I hold my losing positions too long." (Like the "Down with the Ship" trap described in Chapter 6.)
- Let Winners Ride: "When I make more money than expected, do you sell some of the position or buy more?"

The data set includes 3,000 self-described investors, traders, and businesspeople from developed economies who took our personality test from 2003 to 2009. The test data were rigorously edited for quality.

Factors such as net worth and average annual returns showed few significant correlations. However, net worth was directly correlated with the personality trait of openness. Additionally, average annual investment returns were inversely correlated with "holding losers too long" and open investors reported the highest average annual investment returns.

Certain personality traits appear to predispose investors to some common mistakes in their investing, such as doubling-down on losing positions and cutting winners short (not letting winners ride) for emotionally sensitive individuals; however, emotional sensitivity was negatively correlated with net worth. The common investor traps noted in the table are discussed in more detail in Chapter 6.

Test-takers also were asked to report their largest lifetime loss from a single position and whether they have "exit plans in place" when they enter an investment position (i.e., what information will lead them to sell the position). Several personality traits predictably

Table 3.2   Correlations of the "Big Five" Personality Traits with Mistakes, Planning, and Investment Performance (2003 to 2009)

Reported for Investors	Extraversion	Emotional Stability	Conscientious	Open	Agreeable
Investment Returns	↓	↑	0	↑	0
Net Worth	↓	0	0	↑	↑
Large Lifetime Loss	0	0	↓	0	0
Exit Plans in Place	↑	↑	↑	↓	↓
Holding Losers Too Long	0	↓	↓	0	0
Let Winners Ride (Momentum)	0	↑	0	↑	↑

correlated with these two behaviors. As expected, conscientiousness, emotional stability, and extraversion correlated with having exit plans in place in advance. Interestingly, openness and agreeableness were associated with a lower likelihood of having exit plans in place when a position is entered. We have been collecting personality data since 2003, and we see that the personality traits correlated with high performance shift dramatically when the bull and bear market periods are analyzed separately. Additionally, the results for traders and investors are significantly different. For investors, extraversion was positively correlated with investment returns during the bull market period, but negatively correlated during a bear market. Emotional sensitivity showed the opposite correlations—apparently nervousness protected investors during the bear market but led to less risk-taking (and lower overall returns) during the bull market. On average during the volatile market of the past six years, openness and emotional stability correlated with investment returns.

The long-term correlations we've identified between personality traits and investing success and mistakes demonstrate the need to understand our personality traits and their influence on us. It's thus prudent to develop a workable plan to take advantage of your optimal investing environment or style when it comes into favor.

Working with Your Traits

Now consider how your personality affects your investment decisions. Do you have a propensity to feel unbearable nervousness during market declines (emotional sensitivity)? Or are declines exciting for you—do you see them as buying opportunities?

Although personality traits tend to stay fixed over time, how we adapt to them does not. You have the opportunity to change your investing environment in order to better accommodate your personality-based strengths and vulnerabilities. If needed, take a moment to consider how that might be done.

For example, we've worked with short-term traders who had high scores in emotional sensitivity. They couldn't handle the stress of trading—especially the daily P&L feedback—and they ultimately transitioned into longer term investing styles. They found the most success in investing styles where they could not access (or chose not to access) daily performance results, such as in real estate or dividend–paying investments. Another strategy they used was to monitor a company's asset value or return on equity (reported quarterly) rather than its market share price. Additionally, many emotionally sensitive investors spend their time looking at details on a company's balance sheets, and they invest with the intention of "holding forever" (as Warren Buffett has famously described his favorite holding period).

Emotionally sensitive investors may also enjoy bottom-fishing for "cheap" companies when sentiment is negative. For example, periods when consumer sentiment is in the lower quarter of its historical range have been good times to invest in small-cap value stocks in the U.S. stock markets, and emotionally sensitive investors may find this easier to do.

Open investors tend to do better with "exotic" research into new investment classes, businesses, or regions. On the other hand, traditional investors thrive in predictable and established markets, such as in developed-world mutual funds.

Conscientious investors are able to follow rules and stay organized during turbulent periods in markets. Conscientious investors often thrive in rule-based fundamental analysis that relies on the discipline to scour SEC filings and accounting data. On the other hand, since impulsive investors have a less deliberate analytic process, they should be especially careful to avoid external information sources (e.g., the financial media) that might prompt them to make spontaneous, and often regrettable, decisions.

Extraverted investors are often good salespeople (especially if they are high in conscientiousness), and they tend to thrive in bull markets. However, extraverts should keep a tool handy to remind them when to reduce their risk exposure. A straightforward "switch" to tell extraverts when to pull back on risk occurs when prices cross below their 200-day moving average. Historically such a crossover has signaled a "regime change" from bull to bear markets. Extraverts may enjoy looking for momentum investments again when prices again rise above the 200-day average, indicating a shift back into a bull market.

Please write your personality test results into the worksheet shown in Table 3.3, and consider how your unique personality traits guide your investing. Write down the strengths and vulnerabilities of your personality. How can you lean on your strengths in your

Table 3.3   Personality Worksheet

Personality Trait	My Score	How It Affects My Investing (adapt from your test results)	My Plans to Accommodate
Conscientiousness vs. impulsiveness			
Emotional stability vs. sensitivity			
Extraversion vs. introversion			
Agreeableness vs. self-interest			
Openness vs. traditionalism			

chosen style of investing? Or do you need to change course and find a more appropriate sector, market, or style of investing that better fits your personality traits?

A financial advisor we know worked with a married couple who were frequently bickering about each others' budgeting and spending habits. The couple had argued over money issues since before they were married, and their advisor wanted to help them smooth their communication. Usually their arguments went along these lines:

Husband: My wife won't stop spending. She has no idea how wasteful she is being, and it makes me sick to think of all the money she is squandering. She just doesn't get it.

Wife: He pesters me constantly about money, and it seems like his main focus is controlling me. We have plenty of money, I stay within our agreed budget, and I'd really like him to back off.

Their advisor wanted to see if he could gain any insight into their personalities. He asked them to take MarketPsych's investment personality tests and report back to him with their results. Perhaps, he mused, he could smooth their communication about financial issues if there were some glaring discrepancies.

It turned out that both partners had high conscientiousness scores on their personality tests. In itself this is unremarkable. But what the advisor noticed of interest was that the husband's score was "extremely high" while his wife's was "high." As they discussed their scores and the husband once again implied that his wife was wasteful and irresponsible, their advisor pointed out to the husband, "You know, your wife has a high score on conscientiousness. She follows the agreed budget, and she takes care of her financial duties. Maybe you're being too hard on her because you're *extremely* high in conscientiousness. No one will ever match up to your high standards. In fact, is there anyone you know who handles money to your satisfaction"

The man paused and contemplated. "Well, I guess you're right," he said. From that day forward he was more accepting of his wife's financial behavior, and while he had trouble agreeing to *all* her spending, he was able to stop "monitoring" her account statements. And most importantly, the couple no longer bickers about money.

Sometimes simply gaining insight into your strongest personality traits, and understanding how they color your views of the world around you, is enough to make lasting change.

The Genetics of Successful Investing

> *The information encoded in your DNA determines your unique biological characteristics, such as sex, eye color, age and Social Security number.*
>
> —Dave Barry (comedian)

All of us are endowed with inborn psychological differences rooted in our genetics. The environment we grow up in, even as far back as our mother's womb, affects which genes are "expressed" and ultimately influence our physical growth and development. Such ingrained biological differences are the basis of personality, and they are expressed as early as infancy. Fortunately, recent research shows that over our lifetime, we can change the developmental biases we acquire through life experience when we're young. Unfortunately, biases rooted in our genes tend to persist.[14]

In the past four years, DNA analysis has revealed two personality findings related to genetics and investing. The serotonin transporter (5-HTT) gene can have a polymorphism (producing a short version of the 5-HTT protein) that is present in a significant proportion of the population. Emotional sensitivity scores are correlated with the presence of the short serotonin transporter gene in individuals[15] (however, with high variance). Additionally, people with this gene polymorphism have been shown to be susceptible to anxiety and depression in some (but not all) studies.

Another gene–personality link involves the dopamine 4 (D4) receptor. The D4 receptor regulates sensation-seeking (an aspect of personality similar to "novelty seeking"). Sensation-seeking is a facet of extraversion. People who have the D4 polymorphism (7-allele repeat) have more difficulty staying in monogamous relationships, are more likely to move, and in one study, they reported significantly more extramarital affairs.

A high score on the personality trait of sensation-seeking (a facet of extraversion) is indicative of risk-taking propensities in many domains (financial, recreational, social, and health). Sensation-seeking is a highly consistent predictor of various kinds of risk taking, including compulsive gambling and participation in high-risk activities.[16] In fact, a Finnish study found that the sensation-seeking personality trait is correlated with overtrading stocks.[17]

Researchers have identified several genes that contribute to investment risk-taking. Professor Camelia Kuhnen at Northwestern University near Chicago found that the presence of the serotonin and dopamine genes mentioned above appear to alter investment decision-making: "The 5-HTTLPR s/s allele carriers take 28 percent less risk than those carrying the s/l or l/l alleles of the gene. DRD4 7-repeat allele carriers take 25 percent more risk than individuals without the 7-repeat allele." The presence or absence of these specific genes has a strong and significant influence over individual financial risk taking.[18] The genes associated with investment risk taking are:

Genes	Abnormal Variant
Serotonin transporter 5-HTTLPR (s/s allele)	Anxiety and depression sensitivity, and take 28% less investment risk.
Dopamine D4 receptor (7-repeat allele carriers)	Novelty and sensation seeking, and take 25% more investment risk.

You can't alter your genes, but you may be able to influence your "epigenetics." Epigenetics refers to the genes you possess that are actually expressed. Only about 20 percent of our genes are "turned on" at any one time. Your environment with its continuous challenges and variability in resources determines which genes are likely to be activated. There is a feedback loop in which your genetic expression is influenced by your environment and even indirectly by your behaviors. In fact, the premise of this book is that by modifying your physical activity, practicing psychological and emotional training, and setting up behavioral modification systems to guide optimal choice, then new patterns of thinking and behavior can be learned and can perhaps influence your biology as deeply as the expression of your genes.

At MarketPsych we've begun offering genotyping tests for investors to understand the genetic factors that may be influencing their investment decision making. Please contact us via our website for more details.

Using What You've Learned

As we've emphasized repeatedly in this book, knowledge does not equal action. Even though you may now understand how to improve the synergy between your personality and your investing, for most people it's challenging to get started. To begin we need an emotional impetus and the *discipline* to follow through. Discipline is a facet of "conscientiousness." Low scorers on conscientiousness are likely to be lacking in discipline.

You don't actually have to be conscientious to set up and follow a disciplined investment plan. A very successful hedge fund manager we know scored "extremely low" on the conscientiousness personality trait (he is very spontaneous and impulsive). When we discussed his personality results with him, he remarked, "The key is that I know I'm undisciplined and I don't follow through on things." He went on, "I hired an extremely conscientious and obsessive assistant to keep my life together." This strategy allowed him to remain spontaneous and creative in his problem solving, while at the same time his assistant scheduled his meetings, travel, and research, and she set up a fail-safe system of alarms and reminders to keep him on track and on time.

The essence of self-discipline is emotion management, which is different from emotional control. Management focuses on awareness and redirection rather than confrontation and repression of emotion. The internal tension resulting from the confrontation with and repression of undesired feelings strains cognitive resources. At the turn of the nineteenth century, Sigmund Freud even theorized that the repression of emotions was the root cause of mental illness. Redirecting strong emotions toward productive outlets is important for maintaining personal happiness and harmonious relations with others.

Self-discipline does not refer to a rigid adherence to an investment strategy, but rather to a focused and organized mind-set about examining investments. Unfortunately, many investors have inadequate experience and education with the markets to understand the roles of rigid rules and the times when flexibility is required.

Traders such as Mark D. Cook, featured in Jack Schwager's book *Stock Market Wizard* (Marketplace Books, 2008), have learned to use emotional awareness and self-discipline to their advantage. Cook is considered one of the most successful short-term traders in history. Cook remarks, "Whenever I am most fearful of the market, that emotion helps me decide to go long and buy. Whenever my fears become overwhelming, my discipline tells me to buy and discipline must win out or you are doomed to failure."[19] It is not only important to identify emotional impulses, but Cook actually uses those impulses as contradictory trading signals. He summons enough courage to do the opposite of his strong emotional drives.

Because you'll need a good deal of discipline to go through this book and its exercises, much less to spend time reflecting on what they indicate about your investor identity, we recommend that you take a moment to consider how to increase your self-discipline. Techniques for enhancing your level of investing self-discipline are outlined in Table 3.4.

Table 3.4   Identifying the Emotional Precipitants of Lapses in Self-Discipline

Self-Discipline	Questions to Diagnose Lapses
Self-Awareness	What feelings compel you to break your personal rules? Is this a pattern for you? What are your reasons or rationalizations?
Perspective	What do you stand to lose by exercising self-discipline?
Courage	What has prevented you from creating a strategy or disciplined mind-set? What are the tough issues you'd prefer not to address?
Structure	Can you design a program of analysis that fits well into your strengths but does not overlook other key factors? Can you set up a behavioral system to keep you on track? Do you need to hire a conscientious assistant?

With a balance of self-discipline and cognitive flexibility, rules can be applied to enhance performance without inducing excessive rigidity. Short-term investors and traders will especially benefit from the following ideas, but analysts and portfolio managers can use them as well.

1. **Start every day fresh.** Former options specialist Richard Friesen (currently MarketPsych Director of Trader Training), no matter what his recent performance had been, reminded himself daily that risks were lurking in the markets by thinking: "There's a bullet coming toward my head today, and I've got to figure out where it's coming from and how to stop it." This mantra brought down overconfidence, instilled humility, and encouraged preparedness.

2. **Invest an amount of money that's comfortable.** If you are fearful or excited about the money you have on the line or what you stand to gain from a trade, then your judgment will be useless, and you're not going to think clearly. Don't invest more than you can tolerate losing. When emotions become overwhelming, "throw a maiden in the volcano." (Sell a small portion to take the pressure off so you can think clearly).

3. **Plan and anticipate, don't react.** Plan what you are going to do *before* the market opens. Start with the worst-case scenario and work from there. Once you are in a trade, emotions take over, so the plan must be in place in advance.

Conclusion

In this chapter you learned about the effect of your predominant personality traits and genes on your investing. Regardless of your unique personality traits or genes, you can always take actions to change your situation. The first step is beginning a process of self-understanding, getting in tune with your motivation, and cultivating the self-discipline to organize your plan of attack and carry it through.

Using the knowledge you gained in this chapter, we hope that you filled out Table 3.3 and generated ideas for avoiding personality weaknesses and increasing your reliance on strengths. For example, if you lack self-discipline, consider hiring someone (or even using a software program) to help keep you organized and on task. If you are emotionally sensitive, consider investments that are longer term and reduce the frequency of checking prices—or even better, schedule your updates at regular intervals (and don't check during the interim!). If you are an open person, consider looking internationally or at new products for exotic investments, since you are likely to enjoy such variation of the routine. Such insights are key to discovering the foundations of your investor identity.

Alongside our personalities, which are ingrained habits and emotional tendencies, we have learned beliefs. Such beliefs about money, investing, and the markets often influence our behavior unconsciously. We adopt these beliefs at a young age from role models and peers, parents, religious organizations, and our communities. Such long-standing beliefs are also called values, and they can both serve us and undermine our efforts in the markets. The next chapter will help you begin an exploration of your financial values.

4

Your Investor Emotions: The Hidden Drivers of Behavior

"But I don't want to go among mad people," said Alice. "Oh, you can't help that," said the cat. "We're all mad here."
—Lewis Carroll, *Alice in Wonderland*

F ew subjects are more emotional than that of money. We feel anger, fear, and sadness when we lose it, security, satisfaction, and joy when we acquire it. Money is a great source of pride for some and shame for others. This vast ocean of emotions churns below the surface of consciousness driving us in different directions. Knowing why, how, and when money influences our emotions is a crucial step toward establishing a sense of who we are as investors, and ultimately becoming a better financial decision maker.

This chapter will explore the range of emotions investors feel, the effects they have on our investments, ways to manage those emotions, and ultimately techniques for making better choices when emotions run high.

Restless Ed, the Redemption-Seeking Channel Trader

Ed is a 61-year-old male who no longer works. He has close to $12 million in investable assets, but prior to the collapse of the stock market in 2008, he had $1.5 million. In March 2009 he met with his financial advisor and revealed that he wanted to make some changes in his investment strategy.

The following is part of a transcript from that meeting.

Ed: The Dow has been moving up and down constantly. I want to use my cash to buy the Dow when it hits 7,000. When it comes back to 7,500 I'll sell. When it goes back down to 7,000, I'll buy it again.

Financial Advisor (FA): You realize that the market generally isn't so predictable. There's no guarantee it won't keep going down.

Ed: Well, I want to be invested in the Dow anyway, so I don't mind buying and holding it if it goes down.

FA: I guess my main question is, why do you want to do this?

Ed: (Slightly annoyed) Because I want to make money.

FA: You can make money investing a lot of ways. What I mean is why this, why use this specific trading approach?

Ed: Because the market has been going up and down a lot.

FA: Right . . .

Ed: So, I'm not making any money on it.

FA: Well, okay, but that's not part of our plan. Our plan is designed to preserve and grow your wealth for the long-term, not to make money every month along the way.

Ed: Right. But just because I want to make money for the long run, does that mean I should miss opportunities to make money now?

FA: It sounds to me like you get frustrated watching the market trade in a zone and you feel like every time the market comes back down you've missed an opportunity to make money.

Ed: Exactly!

FA: Where did this idea come from?

Ed: I just noticed the market going up and down a lot the past six months, and I felt like I should be doing something about it. (Long pause) I had a friend back in Long Island who used to use this approach and he made a lot of money. He'd do it with a single

	stock. But I don't feel confident enough to do it with a single stock.
FA:	Your friend did well?
Ed:	He did very well. He made a fortune.
FA:	When was this?
Ed:	This was back in the 70s, I think.
FA:	You mean . . . 35 years ago?
Ed:	Yeah.

The preceding is a classic example of an emotional investor with a long-term plan who was pulled into a short-term focus (more on that in Chapter 6, "Your Investor Blind Spots: Identifying [and Avoiding] Investor Traps"). The question was why. What was driving Ed to make this decision?

Ed didn't realize he's emotional—which is part of the annoyance you sense in his words. He believed he was being 100 percent rational. The market had been trading in a zone. He saw an opportunity to make some easy money. (It is, of course, not as easy as it appeared to Ed, but that's not our focus here.) But what were the hidden motivations in this particular case? Why did Ed want to adopt this specific course of action?

When asked what his financial and emotional goals were, Ed identified the following.

Long-Term Financial Motivations

- To have enough money to support his current lifestyle, including yearly trips with his wife to various places around the globe
- To have money to know he can meet all health/long-term care costs (there is a family history of Alzheimer's disease on both sides of the family) for his wife and himself
- To help out his children with down payments on their houses
- To have enough money to invest/help out in a business his oldest son wants to start

Long-Term Emotional Motivations

- A sense of security for his family and himself
- Feeling free to do the things he wants to do
- To feel a sense of pride, knowing he fulfilled his duty as a provider

The stated financial goals were very much in synch with the articulated emotional goals. You can see that by meeting the financial goals he laid out for himself, Ed would get his desired emotional return on investment (EROI).

The problem is that Ed was no longer operating within a long-term, goal-based, rational framework. Instead he was lured into the dreaded short-term, market-based, emotional framework.

Short-Term Financial Motivations

- To capitalize on market volatility by channel trading for a series of 7 percent profits

Short-Term (and Hidden) Emotional Motivations

- Relief from his frustration
- To avoid (short-term) regret of missing out
- To redeem himself for missing a perceived opportunity long ago
- To "keep up with the Joneses" (in this case, an old friend who made a lot of money trading)

If the river Ed was riding had been flowing steadily toward his financial goals, he likely would have felt no urge to make changes. But the river was not moving briskly at that time; it had led him to a stagnant pool, the ideal breeding ground for investing disease. And sure enough, it had spawned some emotional bacteria that were now threatening the health of his financial plan.

Ed felt *restless* and *impatient* that his portfolio had been down the past year. And with his perception that he should have made money on the recent volatility, you can add *frustrated* to that list. He found himself thinking, "Time is running out. I need to make money now." Trying to play catch-up or to make money in a hurry is one of the most dangerous things an investor can do. It practically ensures reckless, emotionally driven decisions.

Ed had never truly made peace with the fact that years ago he had watched a friend "get rich" from trading while he had done nothing. Put aside for a second just how accurate Ed's interpretation of his friend's finances really are. (If there is one thing you can rely on, it's that people love to talk about their investing success stories. Their blunders tend to get nowhere near as much promotion.) He was haunted by the sense that his current (perceived) difficulties were the result of his missing out years ago.

"If I had taken action, if I had had some guts, who knows how much better I'd be doing today?" These are the thoughts that were running through his head, but he didn't connect these internal dialogues (brow-beatings?) with his then-current behavior. Like an archaeologist who finds hidden cities layered on top of one another, it is a safe bet that if you dug beyond the restlessness, you would find the emotion of *regret*, and if you dug deeper still you would find a sense of *shame*.

Financial Wounds and Emotional Wounds

In effect, Ed was suffering from an unhealed emotional wound from nearly 40 years ago. And (to stick with the metaphor), his recent frustrations had caused him to pick at the scab. Now this old wound had been reopened and was bleeding once again. Worse yet, it had become infected with negative emotions (e.g., regret, anger, envy).

Financial wounds are easy to see. They are cuts to our net worth measured in easily grasped numbers. Ed had $1.5 million. Then he had $500,000 less. But financial wounds are always accompanied by emotional wounds that are not so visible and less easily remedied.

Here is where the greatest threat lies. With prudence going forward and adequate time, most financial wounds heal. The money comes back. But emotional wounds offer no such promise. Emotional wounds that don't heal correctly (e.g., that aren't "processed," "dealt with," or otherwise accepted) can become emotionally infected. Anger, envy, confusion, hopelessness, and other destructive emotions can seep in and turn an isolated problem into one that is systemic, one that corrupts the decision-making process going forward. In Ed's case it was the equivalent of a nasty gash going untreated, turning gangrenous, and risking the life or limb of the victim.

Ed had reached a crossroads for his investing future. Compelled by his emotions, he sought to deviate from his plan and engage in a trading strategy that he clearly had not thought out thoroughly. The question became: What should he do?

Bearing in mind that emotions at the base of the motivational iceberg typically carry more weight than the rational, financial portion at the top, there are two general courses of action that Ed could take:

1. *A Course of Healing:* Resolve the emotions by working through them so that his feelings wouldn't drive his investment decisions.
2. *A Course of Managing:* Allow his emotions to dictate decisions but in a way that would do the least harm to the financial goal.

If Ed could have adopted a healing approach, he would have been well served. That would have required making his peace that he did not "make a fortune" going in with his friend. But his urge was strong and immediate. He was not be capable of doing that at this time, or possibly ever. What he was capable of was enough self-insight to recognize this and adopt a management strategy—indulge the emotional goal in the most appropriate/least harmful way.

The answer in this case was to adopt a Course 2 strategy in which Ed turned a small portion of his portfolio into "active money" designed to capture short-term moves in the market. Ed had advocated taking as much as 50 percent of his holdings, but his financial advisor convinced him to "start" with only 10 percent. This is one of the most underappreciated services a financial advisor provides, being an emotional buffer and behavioral break during emotional periods. This ensured that Ed could indulge his restlessness, but did not seriously jeopardize the long-term goals he had been working toward.

Understanding the Science behind Emotion

The science behind our understanding of emotion has advanced dramatically in the past decade. Because emotions underlie so much of thought, behavior, and perception, they, and the psychology and neuroscience underlying them, are discussed in detail in this chapter.

All decisions relating to risk and potential reward engage the emotional centers of the brain. Because it is a subtle but essential aspect of all decisions, we cannot set out to consciously "control" emotion. Rather, we must learn to understand and artfully manage the influences of emotion (particularly the positive influences and destructive aspects). For example, excellent intuitive decision making is often based on "gut feel." However, at moderate to high levels, emotions may overwhelm intuition rather than support it.

Emotions are subjective feelings that serve as easy shortcuts for the brain. In particular, emotions summarize our progress toward goals and away from dangers. On the one hand, the emotion of excitement indicates that one has identified an opportunity, and it helps the body and mind prepare for action. Excitement propels increased risk seeking and exploratory behavior. On the other hand, the emotion of fear notifies one of potential danger. Fear gives rise to behaviors of risk aversion and withdrawal. Simplistically speaking, emotions are like a traffic light for the brain.

Such emotions as fear and excitement are *anticipatory*. They help people prepare for threats or opportunities, and they are fundamental to the coordination of thought and action away from danger or toward opportunity.

When a threat becomes reality, resulting in immediate danger, then we are compelled to flee, freeze in terror, or become combative (fight), giving rise to the colloquial expression "the fight or flight response." This response is a *reaction* to danger. If one is anticipating danger, fear is experienced, but if one is reacting to danger, then the "fight or flight" response is provoked.

This distinction between anticipatory and reactive emotions is important. Amateur investors often buy stocks based on excitement about an expected price change in their favor. What they don't realize is that their excitement biologically diminishes their ability to detect potential dangers, preventing adequate due diligence. Excitement decreases fear through a neural feedback mechanism. Excited investors are *physically incapable* of thoroughly processing information about potential risks.

Investors often sell stocks in reaction to events, such as a bigger than expected profit or a piece of unexpected negative news. Such reactive selling is typically not in response to a rational plan or logical interpretation of facts (although because they think they are being rational, most panicky sellers will disagree with this assessment), but rather it is emotionally driven selling.

Affect is a word that broadly refers to emotional experience. Feelings, moods, and attitudes are all affects. Shortcuts in the thinking process facilitated by feelings are functions of "the affect heuristic." A *heuristic* is a type of mental shortcut. Rather than objectively reasoning through a decision, individuals choose based on a "hunch."

The term *affect heuristic* refers to the feeling "tags" that people place on complex judgments. For example, when asked about the prospects of the stock of Apple or IBM, an investor may feel (and subsequently think): "Apple is sexy and exciting" or "IBM is old and boring." Their thoughts arise from internal emotional tags that are attached to each company. These tags serve as simple and rapidly accessible judgments, which are especially utilized when deciding under time pressure or uncertainty.

Emotions can be short-term (lasting minutes to hours) or longer term, such as *moods* (lasting hours to weeks). When emotions are chronic, they are called *attitudes*, and when they represent permanent ways of thinking about and dealing with the world, they are *personality traits* (discussed in Chapter 3).

There are many ways in which emotions alter our decision making. Short-term emotions arouse an inclination to take action because "doing something" is how we discharge that emotion. When we fail to take action, that emotion will linger—even if we're no longer conscious of it—and subtly affect our judgment and decision-making. Think of a short-term emotion as a pebble in your shoe: You have to get it out, or it will irritate you and can eventually affect the way you walk.

Our friend Doug Lennick (of Lennick Aberman Group) related the following analogy about unconscious emotions: "Suppose you've had a bad day at work—maybe you lost money in the markets, or a major client expressed doubts about your talent. After such a bad day, when you arrive home everyone seems so *inappropriately upbeat*. On some level this aggravates you further. Somewhere in the back of your mind you might even think, 'Don't they know I had a bad day?' Maybe you slam a door, criticize someone, or start a petty argument—anything to bring them to your negative level. Usually they get on with their cheerful lives, and you're left alone to bring yourself out of your own emotional funk."

It is human nature to react emotionally when events do (or do not) go one's way. Furthermore, nothing has to *happen* for someone to experience emotional reactions. The simple act of imagining possible outcomes, such as great successes or terrible losses, stimulates emotion. Every investor has emotional reactions to market price action, although this diminishes with experience. Most investors have felt nervousness during sideways markets; elation, pride, and fear of missing out during bull markets; and intense doubt, anger, fear, or panic during sharp market downturns. Each emotion uniquely alters how investors think and what they subsequently do with their capital.

Using Your Emotions for Good: Damasio and the Iowa Gambling Task

The conventional wisdom is that emotions are "bad" because they interfere with our ability to use reason in decision making. It's easy to tar the concept of investing emotions with that brush, but it's actually not true. Emotions aren't inherently bad. They only become negatives when we take ill-advised actions based upon them. Being afraid or angry or utterly confused—those are feelings. They don't lose us money. Your subsequent buy, hold, and sell decisions are what could do you in. Some of the best investors in the world are highly emotional individuals.

In fact, there are times when our emotions can be a positive if we are able to recognize, understand, and use them in a constructive manner. (We are trying hard not to get through an investing psychology book without resorting to the expression, "get in touch with your feelings.") Nonetheless, the ability to tap into "gut feelings" or what we call intuition is not only a weapon in our arsenal, it's the hallmark of some of the world's greatest investors.

A study in the early 1990s by neurologist Antonio Damasio, then at the University of Iowa, demonstrates this point well. Damasio took an interest in several patients with unique lesions in his neurology clinics. His patient group had lesions of an area of the brain called the ventromedial prefrontal cortex. These lesion patients retained their basic intelligence, memory, and capabilities for analytical reasoning and for logical thought,[1] but they made poor decisions in risky situations.

Many of these patients reported that they knew when they *should* feel afraid, but they had difficulty both (1) experiencing emotions and (2) associating their feelings with anticipated consequences. Essentially, they had a deficit in their ability to integrate emotions and thinking.

It turns out that the part of the brain these patients were missing evaluates the relevance of emotional input to one's decision making.[2] Damasio's patients could not understand what emotional information was important. They knew when they should be afraid, but they could not use fear to help them avoid taking a dangerous financial risk.

Damasio wanted an instrument to detect his patients' problem with risk processing, but no formal tool was available. Being innovative, he designed a card-playing game called the Iowa Gambling Task to measure the responses to risk in these patients. The patients were connected to electrophysiological arousal monitoring devices (as in lie-detector tests) such as a skin conductance response (SCR) monitor. In Damasio's task, four decks of cards were laid out in front of brain-lesioned patients and normal individuals.[3] The subjects then selected cards from any of the four decks of cards provided with the overall goal of maximizing their financial gain. See Figure 4.1 for a depiction of the card decks, outcomes, and odds for each deck.

Subjects were not told the overall odds or payoffs of the card decks. They were simply told to play the game and to try to make as much money as possible. Each deck contained 40 cards. Returns varied in magnitude and frequency in decks A and C. In decks B and D one loss occurred in every series of 10 trials. Overall the average expected return after 10 card flips was –$250 for decks A and B and $250 for decks C and D.

Damasio found that the patient group was more likely to choose cards from decks A and B (the "bad" decks). The patients did not generate anticipatory SCRs to the risky decks (A and B), and they played deficiently overall. "Even after several of them realized which decks were bad, they still made the wrong choices."[4] The patients' risk-assessment of the "bad" decks was intellectually intact, but it did not alter their decision making, and they continued to choose cards from these losing decks.[5]

Unlike the brain-damaged patients, normal subjects learned to avoid the losing decks. After flipping the first 10 cards, normals began to show physiological "stress" reactions on the SCR measurements when hovering over decks A or B. Patients never showed

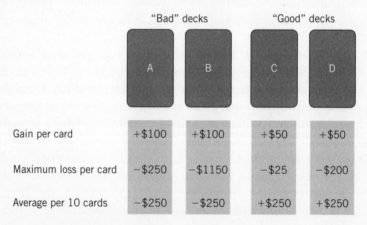

	"Bad" decks		"Good" decks	
	A	B	C	D
Gain per card	+$100	+$100	+$50	+$50
Maximum loss per card	–$250	–$1150	–$25	–$200
Average per 10 cards	–$250	–$250	+$250	+$250

Figure 4.1   The Iowa Gambling Task.
Note: Notice that the net return per deck is negative for decks A and B and positive for decks C and D. Additionally, the range of gains and losses is much smaller in decks C and D.
Source: Reprinted with permission of John Wiley & Sons, Inc.

such responses. Furthermore, even though the normal subjects experienced a physiological stress reaction after 10 card flips, they could not consciously identify that decks A and B were the money-losing decks until over 50 card flips later. Normals began to flip more cards from the "good" decks C and D before they were consciously aware that these decks were "good." That is, normal people had "gut" stress reactions to the losing decks after 10 flips and changed their behavior to prefer decks C and D. Yet they only articulated a "hunch" about which were the losing decks after 50 card flips. They could explain their hunch with certainty only after 80 flips.

Damasio's research implies that people *need* feelings to signal when to avoid losses in risky environments. When making risky decisions, there is a gap between what the emotional brain (the limbic system) knows about risk and one's conscious awareness of the actual danger. Intuitive decisions, where "gut feel" drives judgment, arise from such limbic knowledge. In the brain-damaged gamblers, a brain region that integrates risk-related feelings with reasoned decision making had been taken off-line.

Investors can tap into the wisdom and foresight that comes from our own instinctive emotional reactions. It starts with looking out for our own particular early warning signs; what happens to you mentally and physically when you begin to experience stress? Some people may notice they become irritable for little reason. Others may notice their bodies tensing up. George Soros is famous for sensing danger in his portfolio because he begins experiencing lower back pain. The ability to perceive our emotional distress signs early on, listen to them, and use them to reflect on our investments is the key to tapping into this early warning system. Read on to learn about the common investing emotions, their triggers, and how you can learn to harness them for your own good.

Stirring the Unconscious

In a study of subliminal emotion during financially risky decisions, subjects decided among risky options after viewing a photo of an emotional face.[6] The faces were expressing prominent emotions such as fear, anger, or happiness. Participants were asked to name the gender of the face before proceeding on to the gamble, to ensure that they had been paying attention, though they were not warned that the facial expression might affect their decision making.

The researchers ran three experiments in which subjects chose between different risky financial options. Interestingly, but unsurprisingly, participants were most likely to select the riskiest option after viewing happy faces. However, after seeing an angry or fearful face, participants were more likely to choose the safe option.

Importantly, the faces' emotional expressions influenced participants' decisions regardless of their performance feedback (how much money they made or lost). In conclusion, the researchers speculated that transient subconscious activations of the brain's fear, anger, and happiness processing centers biased the ability of the brain's cortex to correctly value risky gambles.

Perhaps most surprisingly, the study subjects reported feeling no different regardless of whether they had seen a positive or negative face. What's more, they did not believe that the face's expression affected their choice of the risky versus the safe bet. They were completely unaware that an unconscious emotion, introduced by simply looking at a picture of a smiling or frowning face, had strikingly altered their financial choices.

Of course, investors are unconsciously influenced by emotions besides those on faces. The workplace mood, the tone of business news broadcasts, the content of the morning newspaper, and one's home emotional environment may all be factors that unconsciously bias how one approaches risky decisions. Even if the influence of these factors is small, a 1 percent alteration in investment choices can lead to a large cumulative gain or loss over years.

The Difference between Positive and Negative Feelings

Positive emotions signal that life is going well, goals are being met, and resources are adequate. In these circumstances, people are ideally situated to "broaden and build."[7] Negative emotions, such as fear and sadness, are characteristic of a self-protective stance in which the primary aim is to guard existing resources and avoid harm. Each stance—optimism and pessimism—has characteristic effects on financial judgment.

Researchers have found that people in a positive emotional state tend to reduce the complexity of decisions by greater use of mental heuristics ("shortcuts") such as stereotypes.[8] Positive people more quickly disregard irrelevant information, consider fewer dimensions of problems, recheck less information, and take significantly less time to make a choice than people who are feeling negative.[9]

During financial gambles, positive people choose differently from negative people. When stakes are high, people in positive emotional states try to maintain their positive state and avoid substantial losses.[10] In contrast, if stakes are low, joyful decision makers become risk seeking in order to benefit from small potential gains (though without wagering so much as to risk their happiness). So while happy people make more optimistic judgments overall, in situations where they foresee a reasonable likelihood of large losses, they avoid taking a risk. The problem is, happiness often blunts one's ability to detect risk.

Whereas positive emotions broaden a person's focus, negative emotions narrow it. Negative moods are associated with a more ruminative and vigilant (hyperalert) thought process. Negative emotions predispose a person to excessive risk perception and overreaction to losses.

Table 4.1 provides a summary and comparison of positive and negative emotions on decision making, judgment, and behavior.

Table 4.1 Positive and Negative Emotions' Effects on Thought

People in a Positive Mood	People in a Negative Mood
Reduce the complexity of decisions.	Detail-oriented.
Adopt a simpler process of information retrieval.	Vigilant and broad analysis.
Disregard irrelevant information.	Often excessively focused on minutiae.
Consider fewer dimensions.	Broad observations.
Recheck less information.	Repeat and double-check.
Take significantly less time to make a choice.	Slow and thoughtful, occasional "analysis paralysis."
Take more risk in low-stakes gambles.	Avoid small risks when possible.
Take less risk in high-stakes gambles.	More likely to spend excessive amounts of money on large purchases or risky bets.
Less reflective after a failure; more resilient after losses.	Ruminate about setbacks and have more trouble getting back on their feet.

Regret

> *There's no shame in losing money on a stock. Everybody does it.*
> *What is shameful is to hold on to a stock, or, worse, to buy more*
> *of it, when the fundamentals are deteriorating.*
>
> —Peter Lynch

Regret is an uncomfortable but intrinsic part of investing. Inevitably, some decisions are bound to go wrong. Those who can't "take a loss" objectively—which is virtually everyone—will experience regret. It is regret's discomfort that drives two of the most common behavioral biases.

In behavioral finance research, one of the most prevalent biases is the tendency to hold losing stocks longer than winning stocks. Investors too frequently "let their losers run." Many academics believe that to avoid regret, investors hold on to losing stocks while hoping for a comeback that will vindicate their initial buy decision.

Experimenters asked subjects to participate in a game where they made their own investment decisions (buy, sell, or hold) over several periods of a simulated market. During the experiment, subjects were given the opportunity to follow the recommendation of a hypothetical stockbroker.[11] When the broker had given accurate advice, and the subjects had followed the good advice, they reported less overall satisfaction with the investment outcome than if they had made the buy decision independently. Making one's own profitable investment decisions is more emotionally gratifying than following a broker's advice. However, if they lost money on a stock, they felt more regret if the initial buy decision had been theirs alone. Following a broker's recommendation reduced the emotional impact of losses. Brokers' recommendations were *emotional shock absorbers* that attenuated reactions to both profits (happiness) and losses (regret).

The "emotional shock absorber" effect may explain why many investors pay a premium for actively managed funds and personal investment advisers. These professionals function as intermediaries between the individual and the emotional consequences of investment decisions, and they remove many of the emotional ups and downs (and the resulting bad decisions) from the process of investing.

Sadness and Disgust

> *The most common cause of low prices is pessimism—sometimes pervasive, sometimes specific to a company or industry. We want to do business in such an environment, not because we like pessimism but because we like the prices it produces. It's optimism that is the enemy of the rational buyer.*
> —Warren Buffett, 1990 Chairman's
> Letter to Shareholders

Professor Jennifer Lerner at Carnegie-Mellon University induced states of sadness and disgust in subjects using short movie clips. She wanted to know how sad and disgusted people differed in their "trading" behavior. After emotion induction the subjects placed bids and offers in a simulated market. For example, she asked participants to fill out a questionnaire in which they chose a price they would accept in exchange for an item they had been given (such as a pen highlighter set). In another condition, subjects without the item indicated how much they would pay for it.

Lerner found that participants in a disgusted emotional state were emotionally driven "to expel." That is, disgusted people want to "get rid" of items they own, and they do not want to accumulate new ones. As a result, they reduced both their bid and offer prices for the consumer items. They wanted to get rid of their holdings even at unfavorable prices, and they didn't want to accumulate any new ones.

In the case of sadness, Lerner noted that "sadness triggers the goal of changing one's circumstances, increasing buying prices [bids] but reducing selling prices [asks]." Compared to people in neutral emotional states, people who had viewed sad movie clips subsequently valued items they owned less and items they did not possess more.[12]

Lerner speculated that "retail therapy" (in which people go shopping to lift their depressed spirits) is a result of sadness-induced buying behavior. Lerner noted that compulsive shoppers tend to experience depression, that shopping tends to elevate the depressed moods of compulsive shoppers, and that antidepressant medication tends to reduce compulsive shopping.[13]

Did public disgust about the financial abuses that led to the 2008 financial crisis lead investors to undervalue stocks and "expel" (sell) their shares from their portfolios? The rally of 2009 and early

2010, which carried most shares well above their crisis lows, would seem to confirm that most investors who sold during the crisis got a bad price for their shares.

Fear and Anger

> *The key to making money in stocks is not to get scared out*
> *of them.*
>
> —Peter Lynch

In another series of experiments, Professor Lerner examined the roles of anger and fear in financial risk taking. In advance of the experiment, she measured participants' dispositional levels of fear, anger, and "optimism about the future" using standard surveys.[14]

According to Lerner, emotions characterized by a sense of certainty (such as happiness and anger) lead decision makers to rely on mental shortcuts, while emotions characterized by uncertainty (such as anxiety and sadness) lead decision makers to scrutinize information carefully.[15] Anger and fear, while negative, differ in the dimensions of control, certainty, and responsibility that accompany each feeling. Angry people feel more certain about the nature of an infraction, they feel that they have more control over outcomes, and they feel that others are responsible for the provocation. Fearful people are uncertain where the source of danger lies, lack a sense of control over stopping it, and are unclear who or what is responsible for the threat.[16] In order to identify the danger, they investigate their surroundings and new information more thoroughly.

Fearful people are averse to risk, while angry people are as comfortable with risk as happy people. The decisive factor in risk taking is perception of control. Fearful investors feel insecure and out of control. As a result, during market declines, the fearful are more likely to sell out. Angry investors have identified the enemy, sold the relevant stocks, and feel in control of the remainder of the situation. They hold on to declining stocks because they are more certain of their position.

Pride

> *Pride goeth before destruction, and a haughty spirit before a fall.*
> —Proverbs 16:18 King James Version

Nothing sedates rationality like large doses of effortless money.
—Berkshire Hathaway 2000 Annual
Report, February 28, 2001

As an investor you've certainly made some good and some bad investments. If you've ever been proud of a good call you made, then you've probably also noticed that publicizing your recent sagacity to friends, family, and colleagues immediately preceded a comeuppance. It must be a third law of thermodynamics: As the body burns with excitement and confidence, and the brain swells with appreciation of its own genius, a reversal of fortune takes place whose severity is inversely proportional to the height of one's pride.

Pride leads to hubris. Hubris is itself known among military historians as victory disease. *Victory disease* refers to the tendency for military commanders, after a series of triumphs in the field, to subsequently demonstrate poor judgment. The fortunes of victors reverse due to arrogance, complacency, reliance on stereotypes of enemies, and an ignorance of or inability to develop new tactics. Famous examples of victory disease include the failure of the imperial Japanese navy to set up a defensive perimeter following their initial string of victories in World War II and Napoleon's ill-fated invasion of Russia.

The business press has coined the term *CEO disease* to refer to the tendency of CEOs to underperform after achieving the top position in their organization.[17] Victory disease and CEO disease follow a similar psychological pattern, one commonly called "hubris."

The English word *hubris* is derived from the Greek word *hybris*. It refers to the excessive pride that usually precedes the downfall of the tragic hero in Greek drama. Hubris is found among successful individuals who see external goals as their primary metric of success and who have made a series of advances towards their goals. Investors operating from a money-focused or an outcome-oriented frame are susceptible to hubris. Anywhere acclaim is awarded according to some extrinsic metric, such as wealth, beauty, or athletic prowess, achievers are vulnerable. Hubris is one of the most dangerous emotional states that investors can experience, as it often precedes the greatest losses.

The first stage of hubris is to have a series of gains or acclaim. If those gains are attributed to one's unique talents, skills, or intelligence, then they can contribute to a persistent pattern of overconfidence. For overconfident investors, risks are ignored and their belief in themselves is hypertrophied.

When hedge fund consultant Steven Drobny asked hedge fund manager Christian Siva-Jothy what he learned from a large 1994 loss, he replied, "Confidence is a very, very dangerous thing. Simply because you've had a good run doesn't mean it will continue. In fact, once you've had a good run you're at your most dangerous. Overconfidence is an absolute killer. It doesn't matter how well things are going, you should always kind of pinch yourself, take a step back, and ask, 'what can go wrong?' In fact, the better things are going, the more you should look at where your risks are and what the downside is."[18]

Siva-Jothy reports, "I impose discipline on myself by keeping a trading diary. Every morning I go through the same process: If I have my positions on, I ask why do I have the positions? What has changed?"[19] Siva-Jothy's process reveals a truism of investment success: Great investors have an abiding humility that drives an honest appraisal of both successes and mistakes.

Greed

> *There are two times in a man's life when he shouldn't speculate:*
> *when he can afford to and when he can't.*
>
> —Mark Twain

Warren Buffett wrote to a hypothetical market timer in the 2004 Berkshire Hathaway annual newsletter: "And if they insist on trying to time their participation in equities, they should try to be fearful when others are greedy and greedy when others are fearful."

For millennia, greed has been identified as a source of financial folly. In the Bible, as one of the seven deadly sins, greed is called *avarice.* In some biblical accounts, it is the deadliest sin—the "root of all evils" according to St. Paul. The Buddha referred to greed as *desire* and called it the source of all human disappointment and suffering. Charity (the antithesis of greed) is one of the five pillars of Islam. In Victorian England, Charles Dickens parodied the greed of his character Ebenezer Scrooge, who today serves as a stark reminder of the loss of human connection that can accompany an excessive desire for financial gain.

Michael Douglas, playing the fictional corporate raider Gordon Gekko in the 1987 movie *Wall Street*, waxed philosophical about the true nature and necessity of greed before the shareholders of a corporation he intended to buy, Teldar Paper. One of the most memorable scenes in the movie is a speech by Gekko to a Teldar Paper shareholders' meeting:

> The point is, ladies and gentleman, greed is good. Greed works, greed is right. Greed clarifies, cuts through, and captures the essence of the evolutionary spirit. Greed in all its forms, greed for life, money, love, knowledge has marked the upward surge in mankind—and greed, mark my words—will save not only Teldar Paper but the other malfunctioning corporation called the U.S.A.

Gekko's self-serving desire to lay off Teldar workers and auction off its separate divisions for profit lay beneath his self-proclaimed altruistic motives.

Gekko's speech was reportedly based on Ivan Boesky's 1985 commencement address to the graduates of the University of California at Berkeley, in which Boesky declared: "Greed is all right, by the way. I want you to know that. I think greed is healthy. You can be greedy and still feel good about yourself." Boesky was a Wall Street arbitrageur who was later convicted of federal crimes. He paid a $100 million penalty to the SEC to settle insider-trading charges in 1986.

Economists from Adam Smith to Milton Friedman have seen greed as an inevitable and, in some ways, desirable feature of capitalism. In a well-regulated and well-balanced economy, greed helps to keep the system expanding. But it also ought to be kept in check, lest it undermine public faith in the entire enterprise.[20]

Among investors, greed leads to impulsive decisions that erode wealth through overtrading, chasing positions higher, and inadequate due diligence. Broadly speaking, greed is a result of a convergence of factors: the desire for gain, the strong motivation to pursue opportunities, the disregard of risks, and a penchant for excess. Greed following a series of profits is fuel for hubris.

On an individual level, greed has deleterious effects on performance, yet greed is a common facet of human behavior. Can learning about greed improve one's profits in the markets? For many investors, locating stocks with large profit potential and anticipating their high returns is one of the exciting (and occasionally addictive) aspects of investing. Managing the greed that accompanies a normal investment process is an enduring challenge—one that can be managed with disciplined self-reflection.

Summary

To summarize:

- Fear of regret prompts conservatism with existing assets (selling too soon) and increased risk taking with money-losing ones (holding onto losers too long).
- Anger gives rise to mild optimism, a sense of control, and certainty about one's financial choices. Overall, angry investors have less stock turnover.
- Sadness leads to increased investment risk taking and increased trading.
- When afraid, investors usually overestimate danger.
- When happy, investors underestimate risks and trust positive prognostications from similarly optimistic experts.

Table 4.2 describes the causes and consequences of common emotions on our financial decisions.

Table 4.2   Summary of Emotional Influences on Investing

Emotional State	What Causes It	How it Affects Investing
Positive: Happiness, Optimism	Recent gains. Liking an investment. Receiving an exciting stock tip.	When happy, investors underestimate risks and over-rely on positive prognostications from similarly optimistic experts.
Negative: Pessimism, sadness, grief, helplessness, hopelessness	Financial or other losses. Sad news.	Sadness leads to increased investment risk taking and increased trading.
Fear: Anxiety, nervousness, anticipation of danger, uncertainty	Learning of potential dangers or threats to your investment. News that projects negative events.	When afraid, investors usually overestimate danger and are more likely to believe threat-related information.

Emotional State	What Causes It	How it Affects Investing
Anger: Irritation, blaming, self-righteousness, certainty	Learning of unfairness (e.g., rich executive bonuses at AIG after its government takeover). Feeling betrayed or hurt by others.	Anger gives rise to mild optimism, a sense of control, and certainty about one's next action. Overall, angry investors have less stock turnover.
Regret: Memories of pain	Financial losses that you feel responsible for. Reflecting on avoidable losses.	Fear of regret prompts conservatism with existing assets (selling too soon) and increased risk taking with money-losing ones (holding on to losers too long).
Greed: Excessive desire for gain	Seeing an opportunity that appears to have few or easily manageable risks. Feeling a need to make a quick or very large profit.	No efforts to identify risks or think in a contrarian manner.
Pride: Hubris, overconfidence	A series of gains. Public recognition of excellence. Often overconfidence is innate (e.g., especially in young men).	Lack of due diligence. Investing without investigation of potential risks.

Being Triggered

When was the last time you stubbed your toe? Probably at night, you got up from bed, you were walking in the dark, and BONK . . . OUCH!

What was the first thing you did after stubbing your toe? Curse? Grimace? Grab your toe and jump around the room on the other foot?

In our mental lives there are events that are the psychological equivalent of stubbing your toe. Imagine checking an investment value and seeing that it plummeted due to a fraud allegation. "Ouch!" you mutter. This "ouchie" was an emotional trigger, and its influence on your investing won't just go away.

After we are triggered emotionally, we are in a new state of mind. Little events that usually would have been ignored (for example, a naïve comment by a colleague or a doubt expressed by a friend) add fuel to the emotional fire burning inside. Triggers can cause a chain reaction of emotion that climaxes in a counterproductive, emotion-driven decision. This climactic decision discharges the triggered feeling once and for all.

In general it is the negative triggers that we remember most vividly, but keep in mind that unexpected positive events can also trigger us. For example, after a week of high performance in their investments, some investors fail to readjust their risk management stops. The high performance triggered a state of optimism, which resulted in ignoring future potential risks and loss of discipline.

Emotionally triggering events are various and include:

- Seeing an investment value drop (rise) steeply
- Being insulted (complimented)
- Technology glitches (enhancements)
- Receiving an upset (congratulatory) phone call from a client

Please take a few moments to identify the "Ouch!" or "Eureka!" moments that create strong emotional reactions for you in the typical week. Ensure that you document the triggers that have real impact—that is, they change the tone of your day. Table 4.3 helps

Table 4.3   Identifying Your Emotional Triggers

Triggering Event	Feeling Reaction	Behavioral Response	Alternative Response
Example: Seeing a stock I own disparaged on CNBC.	*Example:* Angry and contemptuous	*Example:* Losing my composure and yelling at the TV. Talking up the stock to colleagues.	*Example:* Investigate the negative points identified by the TV analysts and update my model if appropriate (and e-mail the show with a rebuttal if incorrect).
1.			
2.			
3.			
4.			
5.			

you identify your emotional triggers, describe your usual reaction, and write out a healthy alternative reaction. That is, describe how you could discharge the emotion to prevent it from unconsciously affecting your future behavior.

Identifying and writing about your triggers isn't emotionally easy. Triggers provoke reactions that are habitual and comfortable for us at the time, even if they lead to trouble later. Identifying your triggers and your common reactions is one step toward improving coping responses. Increasing awareness of emotions—even unconscious ones—allows us to work through them.

Name That Emotion

As we've discussed so far in this chapter, your emotional state unconsciously biases your financial decisions. Fortunately there are simple techniques for neutralizing the effects of unwanted feelings.

A technique used with success in reducing emotional reactivity is called "affect labeling." Affect labeling is a mindfulness technique (see Appendix A for an explanation of mindfulness). Mentally identifying and labeling our emotions ("affects") appears to interrupt the neural circuits that underlie repetitive emotional reactions. As a result of practicing such interruption, we can rework thoughts and behaviors away from our habitual (and often destructive) responses. Such an emotional awareness practice interrupts our habitual and automatic responses to triggers.

Affect labeling involves noting the presence of an emotion, stepping back from it, and giving your experience a name. Then letting it go. The emotion will likely return, in which case you can label it and release it again, each time labeling ("ah, here is Fear again") and releasing it. Don't block, push away, or suppress the emotion. Trying not to have the feeling will increase your focus on it and thus its intensity.

Once you have identified and interrupted a habitual (and presumably destructive) emotional reaction, you are then prepared to challenge it. Labeling your own emotional states is similar to going against the prevailing mood of the market—you've got to step outside of yourself in order to observe events. Contrarian investors should be familiar with this concept. It is not easy to do, but once you begin to do it, your flexibility in the markets (and life) improves. By labeling emotions dispassionately as they occur, we are able to see reality more clearly.

Emotional Defenses

If you are distressed by anything external, the pain is not due to the thing itself but to your own estimate of it; and this you have the power to revoke at any moment.
—Marcus Aurelius (Roman emperor,
A.D. 121–180)

While we can change our experience of pain by changing how we think about it, we usually don't do this consciously. We do it unconsciously and automatically, using mental techniques learned over our lifetimes. The techniques we use for reducing our experience of pain are called *emotional defenses*. Emotional defenses offload the distress of uncomfortable emotions. Emotional defenses can be anything from telling jokes or altruistic acts (mature defenses) to denial of the problem or regression into a childlike state (immature defenses).

Emotional defenses were first described by the Viennese neurologist and father of psychoanalytic psychiatry, Sigmund Freud, who observed that people can adjust their thought processes to avoid negative feelings such as anxiety and guilt. Defense mechanisms can be viewed as a form of emotion regulation, in which the brain moves toward minimizing negative and maximizing positive emotional states.

Defense mechanisms operate unconsciously, yet they have a profound effect on our perceptions and behavior. Common defense mechanisms and their effects are listed in Table 4.4. Defense mechanisms are generally classified as primitive, neurotic, and mature (I'm excluding the "pathological defenses" here, which are characteristic of severe mental illness). All of us utilize different defense mechanisms at different times. Primitive defenses are immature, and they are prevalent in children and adolescents. Neurotic defenses are common in adolescents and adults, and they are maladaptive techniques for dealing with anxiety. Few people consistently use mature defense mechanisms, but in psychotherapy one goal is to help clients transition to greater use of mature defenses.

Emotional defenses are inevitable adaptations to negative feelings, but they manifest in a great variety of ways. Distorted logic (rationalization), avoidance of painful facts (denial), believing an internal feeling is also being felt by another (projection), or

Table 4.4   Upgrading Your Defenses

Defense Mechanism	What Is It?
Primitive Defenses	
Fantasy	Tendency to retreat into mental fantasies in order to work through inner conflicts. ("Star Trekkies," perhaps?)
Projection	Attributing one's own emotional experiences to others. For example, repeatedly asking a spouse, "what's wrong?" (when in fact the questioner is the one feeling discomfort).
Denial	Ignoring distressing facts. Many investors denied the financial crisis' damage to their investments by refusing to open account statements (in some cases this could be adaptive if one knows that the account statements will motivate bad short-term decisions and thus deliberately avoids them).
Externalization (blaming)	Blaming others or external causes rather than taking responsibility for working through a distressing situation. Supports a victim-stance and undermines adaptation to challenges.
Neurotic Defenses	
Rationalization	Using logic to find an acceptable explanation for unpleasant feelings or inappropriate behaviors in order to avoid confronting an actual, and more painful, explanation.
Intellectualization	Focusing in detail on the isolated, emotionally neutral aspects of a problem. This leaves the anxiety-provoking characteristics of the situation unaddressed. Financial engineers should beware of this defense. The possibility of outlier events was uncomfortable, and it was ignored in risk modeling prior to the 2008 financial crisis (oops!).
Hindsight bias	Rooted in memory, it involves excessively optimistic assessments of one's past accomplishments, often leading to future misguided endeavors. Learning from one's mistakes is prevented by this defense, making it particularly dangerous.
Repression	Repeatedly pushing negative emotions into the unconscious. It can lead to chronic problems as the negative emotions distort ways of thinking and interacting with others (rather than being discharged or addressed directly).

(*Continued*)

Table 4.4   (Continued)

Defense Mechanism	What Is It?
Mature Defenses	
Humor	Releases the tension of negative emotion by outlining the absurdity inherent in the situation.
Sublimation	The tension caused by negative feelings motivates one to improve the situation.
Altruism	Negative feelings are used to motivate helping behavior toward others (often so that they won't have the same negative experience that motivated the altruism in the first place).

attributing unpleasant circumstances to factors out of one's control (externalization) are all emotional defense mechanisms.

One clear example of the externalization defense is blame. Occasionally we hear from retail traders blaming their market losses on "manipulators" (e.g., computerized traders, government interventions, or a global cabal). They have difficulty taking responsibility for their losses, but if they did realize that they themselves are accountable, then they could begin working to adapt to market conditions. Blaming keeps them in a state of victim-hood rather than adaptation. Two common defenses, motivated reasoning and projection, are detailed in the subsequent pages.

Motivated reasoning is a neurotic defense mechanism related to rationalization. Motivated reasoning is thinking that is biased to produce preferred conclusions and support strongly held opinions.[21] Professor Peter Ditto at the University of California at Irvine set up an experiment to investigate motivated reasoning. He videotaped participants as they self-administered a bogus medical test. The subjects were coached that one test result was a favorable diagnosis, while the other was an unfavorable (but unnoticeable) diagnosis. Subjects who received the unfavorable diagnosis required more time to accept the validity of the test result, were more likely to spontaneously recheck it, and believed that the test had lower accuracy than those with the favorable results.[22] Not only do people underestimate the likelihood of negative feedback about themselves, but even after they are presented with it, they tend not to believe it.

Importantly for investors, people who engage in motivated reasoning perform more poorly on decision-making tasks than those who are less anxious about negative information. Researchers designed a card-sorting task where the fastest solutions were achieved by considering threatening information. "A skeptical mindset may help people avoid confirmation bias . . . in everyday reasoning."[23] Actively confronting uncomfortable information leads to superior decision making in investing and in life.

Emotional individuals often have trouble predicting how they will feel in the future. They incorrectly assume that their future emotional state will resemble their current one. Because they cannot accurately project themselves into the future and subsequently empathize with their condition, they have a bias of "projection" when planning for their future selves.

In one study of people working out at a campus gym, everyone entering and leaving the gym was asked to read a short vignette and answer a question in exchange for a bottle of water. The vignette described three hikers who had become lost in the dry Colorado mountains without food or water. One follow-up question asked whether hunger or thirst would be more unpleasant for the hikers. Another question asked whether, if the subject were in the hikers' position, they would find hunger or thirst more unpleasant. Of people entering the gym, 61 percent thought the hikers (and themselves) would find thirst more unpleasant. Of those leaving the gym after their workout, 92 percent thought the hikers would find thirst more unpleasant. Those leaving the gym were projecting their own feelings of thirst onto others.[24]

It is difficult to imagine a future outside one's window of recent experience, and the markets are no exception. If the markets are calm, investors tend to project such tranquility into the future. Similar projections hold true for established bull markets, bear markets, and long periods of price volatility. Fearful investors project that their anxiety and distress will continue indefinitely. They sell in order to escape the angst caused by declining investments—pain for which they can see no end.

Projection of current wealth continuing into the future is a common trap for investors, but nowhere has it been demonstrated more clearly than with professional athletes. Regardless of their high salaries during their careers, "by the time they have been retired for two years, 78% of former NFL players have gone bankrupt or are under financial stress because of joblessness or divorce." And it is little better for other sports: "Within five years of retirement, an estimated 60% of former NBA players are broke."[25]

One remedy for the projection bias lies in appreciating how one's current and future emotional states alter one's perceptions of financial risk. Take the time to think ahead about your feelings.

Courage is essential when facing uncomfortable negative emotions. During a bear market it is easy to think about the economy pessimistically—everyone is doing it. The goal in such a situation is to look for the positive aspects of the economy—the ones that are being overlooked. This requires balanced thinking, courage, and a willingness to look at all available information with equanimity. George Soros indicated that one of the keys to his investment acumen is the ability to nonjudgmentally think about why his investment reasoning process may be wrong (his theory of fallibility).

During calm markets most investors don't prepare adequately for volatility. They cannot accurately forecast how they will feel and what they might do in such conditions. They project their current sense of security onto their future self. Some naïve investors take on excessive credit risk because they see no threats on the horizon and they project an excellent borrowing climate into the foreseeable future. Investors caught with excessive risk exposure during a credit contraction are the origin of the Wall Street adage, "It's only when the tide goes out that you learn who's been swimming naked." When credit dries up, those who took excessive risk, whatever their justifications, are exposed.

Ed's Epitaph

Recall the story of Ed that opened this chapter. After the conversation with his financial advisor, Ed embarked on his new strategy with part of his assets. He put all his cash into equities when the DJIA crossed below 7000. Then the market stayed range-bound within Ed's parameters for about a month. He sold out in late March 2009 when the DJIA moved past 7,500, netting a 7 percent profit—as was his plan. As of the writing of this book (16 months later), the DJIA had climbed steadily to over 10,000. It has yet to return to the 7,500 mark, let alone the 7,000 plateau at which Ed's second buy signal would be activated. So the end result was that rather than making multiple trades as he had envisioned, he made one. That money went into cash and did not see the benefits of the subsequent market run up.

Did Ed make a mistake? Perhaps he was using an intellectual defense—finding a detailed investment strategy that he could control in the short term—to contain his overall market anxiety. If you consider that Ed's decision to take money from low-yielding cash and put it to work in a controllable strategy allowed him to turn a 7 percent profit in one month, you might consider this a "quick win." If you consider that, had he bought and held, he would be up an additional 33 percent, you might be inclined to think it was a mistake. We view our investments through an emotional lens. Your lens may be rose-colored glasses or a pair of Ray-Bans.

In fact, it is futile to declare victory or defeat at all. Who is to say what Ed would have done in those subsequent months had he not turned that portion of his account into active money? He may have felt more confident and decided to buy into the index as it climbed, or he might have found himself waiting for a big market drop, keeping his powder dry for a market "buying opportunity." Ed thought he was following a logical investing system. Of course, he wasn't. He took on huge risks for a tiny (and lucky) profit—all the while driven by his unconscious emotional needs.

In order for investors to move forward in a healthy manner, they need to have an emotional equilibrium. In other words, we have to feel okay about what we're doing. If we are too restless or too anxious or too complacent, we put ourselves at risk for making decisions based on those feelings (emotional drivers), rather than on sound reasoning (financial drivers).

Looking down the road, finances and emotions appear to be perfectly aligned for most people (e.g., "I'll make my money, have the life I want, and then I'll be happy.") But there's a problem. We aren't down the road. We're *never* down the road. We are eternally stuck in the present where our emotions constantly sidetrack our journey. The ability to understand these emotions, reconcile them, and when necessary, suitably indulge them are the keys to staying on the financial path to our goals. When we fail in that effort, we inevitably get detoured to some place we never intended to go.

Conclusion

We each experience emotion differently. Our emotional needs, the emotions we experience day-to-day, how we react to events (our triggers), and how we deal with anxiety and uncomfortable realities (our defenses) are largely unique to us as individuals. By learning about and reflecting on our common emotions, their triggers, and the defenses we use, we can better manage such emotions, both for financial good and to prevent investment harm.

This chapter has reviewed the influence of immediate and short-term emotions. In the next chapter we will visit the role of longer-term emotional tendencies—as manifest in our values—and the effects of our values on how we see the world and invest in the markets. By gaining insight into and learning the origins of your financial values, you are strengthening the foundation of your investor identity.

CHAPTER

5

Your Investor Values: What's Most Important to You?

Far better is it to dare mighty things, to win glorious triumphs, even though checkered by failure . . . than to rank with those poor spirits who neither enjoy nor suffer much, because they live in a gray twilight that knows not victory nor defeat.
— Theodore Roosevelt

All I need are some tasty waves, a cool buzz, and I'm fine.
— Jeff Spicoli, *Fast Times at Ridgemont High*

Bob was a coaching client of Dr. Peterson's in the mid-2000s. In August of 1987, Bob had predicted that a stock market crash was imminent and decided he needed to prepare for it by buying stock index puts (insurance in case of a market fall). But, being a frugal man, he didn't like to pay "fair value" for his investments. Throughout the months of September and October 1987 the prices of puts had been rising. Bob had placed his bids well below the asking price, and his buy orders hadn't been filled.

During a trading week in mid-October Bob had the gnawing sensation that the market was about to plummet, and by Friday was convinced he had to take action to protect himself. That morning he contravened his underlying reluctance to "pay up" for the put options and upped his bid to the "current bid," becoming the next investor to buy if a seller entered a market order. Other investors interested in purchasing insurance quickly outbid him, and the prices of puts drifted higher all morning. On Friday at noon he once again raised his price to that of the last trade, and once again other bidders entered higher buy prices. Near the end of market hours on Friday he called his broker with urgency to raise his bid one last time before the market closed, but he was unsuccessful and his order remained unfilled going into the weekend.

The next Monday, October 19, 1987—a day that would come to be known as Black Monday—the Dow Jones Industrial Average lost 22.6 percent, and wiped out 30 percent of Bob's net worth by lunchtime.

Bob told Dr. Peterson, "I absolutely knew the crash was about to happen. I had been an architect of portfolio insurance plans for two mutual funds . . . . later I realized that those schemes would lead to a positive feedback effect on selling once they became pervasive and the next correction started. There aren't many times in the markets when you know a price move is inevitable. I was just waiting for the trigger, which happened for sure the week before Black Monday." Why didn't Bob take the asking price for the puts if he was certain the crash was imminent?

As he spoke it became clear that this was not the first time Bob had stubbornly refused to pay the market price despite his certainty of an impending market move. And his refusal to pay "market" prices wasn't only related to investing. Bob despised paying full price for any item, whether a suit or a car or an airplane flight. He always waited for a great deal, and he wouldn't buy an item otherwise.

This thriftiness helped Bob accumulate wealth over his lifetime, and he had profitably invested it in undervalued companies. But at the same time, his thrifty nature had limited the growth of his wealth. Over his lifetime there were several instances when he was 100 percent certain about impending market moves, but he refused to enter market orders that would enable him to profit from them, and as a result he failed to capitalize on his insights. Ironically, because his orders were limit orders outside the market's current bid-ask spread, they were more likely to be filled when he was wrong than when he was right about the short-term price direction.

Although Bob was wealthy as a result of his long-term investing, he was nowhere near as wealthy as he could have been. Bob valued getting "the best price"—this was very satisfying to him. This is an important and admirable "financial value," and it usually leads to wealth accumulation, but in this case it became a liability. His problem arose because exercising this value in the small picture prevented him from acting on his insights into the big picture. Frugality is a virtue, but it has its place. If you're on the *Titanic*, you don't say, "I'm holding out for a better lifeboat."

In 2005, after approximately 10 sessions, Bob felt that he was finished with coaching. In part, he believed the price for coaching was too high. He again contacted Dr. Peterson in 2009 to reenter a coaching relationship.

As he explained, the 2008 financial crisis had exposed flaws in his investing process. He had successfully bought puts in July 2007, and he profited on those in 2007 as the financial crisis began, but by early 2008 he felt the prices were once again "too high" for puts, despite his conviction that a massive decline in the markets was imminent. He had bids to buy puts well under the market price for several months in 2008. His orders to buy puts were never filled because he wasn't willing to "pay up," and in 2008 he *again* lost about 30 percent of his net worth, despite his conviction that the ship he was on was about to go under. (Sometimes a virtue taken too far becomes a vice. It calls to mind the classic skit in which the notoriously frugal Jack Benny encounters a mugger. The mugger points a gun at him and demands, "Your money or your life!" and then waits while Benny stands there silently with his hands in the air. After several seconds he repeats his demand, "I said, your money or your life!" *"I'm thinking it over!"* responds Benny.)

Such financial values as Bob's are shaped by many forces. For example, culture, family upbringing, early experiences, and emotionally impactful events form how we think about spending, saving, borrowing, and investing money. This was very much the case with Bob. He grew up in a modest household where conserving money was important. His family didn't have the same luxuries other, more fortunate, families did. They had enough food to eat, but at the dinner table you ate everything you were served—there were no leftovers. On birthdays, you received "a simple homemade gift," not a room full of colorful presents. His parents had survived the Great Depression and imparted the survival strategies to their children at a young age. You were rewarded for taking on a paper route, for walking the extra blocks to save bus fare, for saving coins in a jar. And—for the most part—those values served him well in his quest for financial security.

Our financial values amount to a powerful, often hidden force, that drives our investment decisions, both small and large. And as the quotes that open this chapter illustrate, values aren't uniform from person to person. Roosevelt and Spicoli had slightly different visions of "the life well-lived." Sometimes a person's values can lead to advantages, and in other situations to disadvantages. As a result, it is important to review your financial values and to understand how and why they affect your money decisions—for good or ill.

Enjoying the Process

When our values are unaligned with our activities, an internal tension develops. That tension causes a buildup of stress, which often leads to impulsive (and ineffective) actions to alleviate it.

Simply knowing how your values affect your investing behavior is the start of relieving that tension and a major step toward establishing a firm investing identity. Too often values that serve us well in one area (e.g., finding a good deal on long-term investments) can create stress and hold us back from acting on our convictions in other contexts (e.g., taking the necessary actions for short-term market positioning).

A central theme of this book is that there are any number of "right ways" to invest. But the right way for *you* must possess a quality of singular importance; it must be a way that you can follow. One means of ensuring that a path is easy to follow is to enjoy traveling it. In this way our values are closely related to our interests, the things we find stimulating and fun.

Warren Buffett derives pleasure from understanding how businesses work and devising ways to make them more profitable. George Soros loves practical philosophy. His motivation for investing is driven in part by his desire to test his theories and ideas in the financial markets. Buffett and Soros are two of the world's greatest investors, and they got that way because each took pleasure in his particular investing process.

Do you have to love what you do as an investor to be successful at it? No. But it helps. And enjoying the investment process signals a compatibility between your investing identity and your investing approach.

Do you enjoy a particular aspect of investing or the markets? If so, it's important to identify and center on the aspects you find enjoyable—those you value—as you read through this book.

This chapter will help you explore several aspects of your financial values:

1. Identifying your financial values
2. Understanding how your values influence your investment decisions
3. Identifying existential values that motivate your life's work and provide a sense of meaning
4. Learning about how your family history and past experiences may have shaped your financial beliefs
5. Understanding your social values around money

We'll help you get started identifying your values and their origins. This process of self-inquiry should be light-hearted and enjoyable. If you find yourself taking the questions too seriously—which you'll know if you start to fret about the "right answer" or the implications of one of your answers—then take a breather. There's no hurry in this process.

The Financial Values Questionnaire

What are some of your unfulfilled dreams?

Can money buy greater happiness for you?

What aspects of business, investing, or the markets do you feel passionate about?

These questions get to the heart of why you invest—or fail to.

By thinking about such questions, you can deepen understanding and alignment of your values, passions, and actions. Since 2005 MarketPsych.com's Financial Values Questionnaire has been collecting data on investors' financial values. Feel free to read ahead without referring to the questionnaire, but before the chapter is over we hope that you will have answered the questions online (they're free at www.marketpsych.com/test_question.php?id=9) and thought about how your own values affect your life (financial and otherwise).

Test-takers' answers to our values questions run the gamut from hilarious to profound. For example, test-takers have described their unmet life goals and dreams in a range from the personal, "alleviating financial concerns," to the global, "making a huge difference in people's lives," to the transcendent, "developing a deep spiritual practice," to the self-centered, having less than 14 percent body fat" and "having sex with a supermodel." Such goals may be either extremely engaging or empty, depending on your perspective.

The most common traditions and values that test-takers cite, when asked which values they hope to pass on to future generations, include honesty, integrity, family involvement, hard work, faith, business acumen, philanthropy, loyalty, higher education, humility, ambition, investment knowledge, and community involvement.

It's important to ask yourself, when you emphasize one value or type of values, what might you be missing in another realm? Does the ambitious person trade off family involvement? Does the pursuer of investment knowledge miss out on the creative life? And if so, does it matter to you?

There aren't global answers to these questions, rather, they are personal, and everyone can take the time to look at his or her life and values, ensure that they are aligned, and make changes where compelled. Trying to value something you "should" care about, but don't feel compelled by, is a dead end.

Values Leakage

Values that serve us well in the workplace, in social life, or in health matters are often *unhelpful* when misplaced as financial values. Humans have a tremendous capacity to learn and adopt new ways of thinking and behaving more effectively. The problem is, investing well is too often counterintuitive.

Most often confusion about values arises because we "mis-attribute" values that apply to social relationships to financial transactions. Bob couldn't buy at market price not only because he was frugal, but because he didn't want to enrich human "cheaters." "Why should I cave in and pay an inflated price so that some other person can take advantage of the system?" he thought. It offended not only his wallet, but his sense of fairness. He indulged this sense of what's fair, but it came at a large financial cost to himself. Which values of yours might be costing you? More importantly, is that a trade-off you are willing to make?

A study of the traits of the best stock analysts in the late 1960s identified some surprising characteristics as being of value: higher levels of hostility, feeling apart from others, and taking an outsider's perspective. These are not traits that will make a person a role-model in the community. Nonetheless, these traits seem to aid investment analysis by contributing toward skepticism (of market trends, overconfident executives, and overhyped companies).

All of these characteristics share (1) a strong sense of self, and (2) a comfort level with being different. In other words, successful stock analysts have a well-developed investing identity, and with it a willingness to break from the herd when it is headed over a cliff. It is important to note that these traits can be applied situationally as long as we're aware of the different "hats" we need to wear in social relationships as opposed to when we're doing financial analysis.

Table 5.1 will help you understand where your global values might be leading you astray when they emerge during an investment decision–making process.

The gist of this table is that investing is not like daily life— just because we feel good or bad about something: we like it, it is performing well, it is cheap, or it is glamorous—does not mean

Table 5.1   Understanding the Common Financial Values

Value or Belief	Explanation	Potential Problems
Thrift	One should only buy items at a discount. Buying cheaply saves substantial expense.	A stubborn refusal to "pay up" can lead to missing some of the biggest opportunities. Cheap ≠ bargain.
Glamour	If something is expensive, then it's of higher quality.	Often buy "at the top." Overpaying for stocks. Mistaking hype for substance.
Loyalty	You should stand by people (or investments) who have served you well in the past. You owe your investments the benefit of the doubt.	The story of your investments change. Your opinions should too. The "Halo Effect"—an early return causes us to "fall in love" with a position.
Safety First	You feel strongly that risk is to be avoided at most any cost. To behave otherwise is to jeopardize your financial well-being.	Perceptions of risk are often skewed. Long-term returns of stocks are higher than for bonds precisely because they are viewed as more risky (academics call this the "equity risk premium").

(Continued)

Table 5.1   (*Continued*)

Value or Belief	Explanation	Potential Problems
Thrill-seeking	Investing should be exciting. If there isn't the potential for a big win, it isn't worth investing.	Excitement is an emotional goal, not a financial one. The gratification from investing well comes in the very long term.
Morality	You shouldn't invest in companies whose products, services, or management contravene your values.	Investing should not violate your conscience. But if you invest to improve your *life*, then that prospect should govern your decisions.
Altruism	Money should be used for the greater good.	A noble sentiment that should not be confused with self-denial or passivity. Markets are impersonal and competitive.
Hard work	Money should be earned through hard work and sacrifice.	Sometimes we work excessively to achieve returns that would be easily available with a slight shift in effort or perspective.

we should invest our money in it. The counterintuitive nature of investing well is one of the most difficult lessons to internalize and implement.

The Impact of Financial Traumas

If, like Bob, you've got relatives who lived through the Great Depression, you may have noticed some unusual habits of theirs. For example, despite having more than adequate assets, they spend time washing and drying Ziploc bags for re-use. Or you might have observed them picking up pennies off the street, clipping coupons, cleaning their plate of all food—even if they don't like it—or gorging themselves on free samples at grocery stores. In the markets, they are often scared of stocks, keeping their savings in low-yielding cash or savings accounts.

If you try to change their behavior, reminding them that they have more than enough money, your reasoning falls on deaf ears. If you demonstrate that many of their habits, on a cost-benefit basis, are costing them money, they respond with a shrug and continue as usual.

The financial changes experienced by many people during the Great Depression were so sudden and shocking that as survivors, they permanently changed how they see the world. Depression survivors adapted to the sudden changes by learning and sticking with habits of extreme thrift and resourcefulness. Such ingrained thrift is also seen in survivors of wars or severe poverty, refugees, and new immigrants.

Thrift of this nature often leads to the accumulation of wealth and is usually not maladaptive. Problems arise when such thrift becomes hardened into habits that prevent further growth and flexibility in response to changed circumstances. Coping strategies that safely carried us through those traumas can become automatic behaviors that are difficult to change even when they no longer serve their original purpose.

Researchers Ulrike Malmendier and Stefan Nagel found that "Depression Babies" were more reluctant to invest in stocks. In fact, among any generation, poor stock returns several decades previously altered their general willingness to take risk in the stock market.[1]

Studies of the brain's response to traumatic experiences show that memories of the experience and events surrounding it become burned into the brain's amygdala (an emotional learning region). Subsequent reminders of similar events trigger anxiety and defensive behaviors. The task for the investor is to identify (1) any experiences of severe financial loss or hardship you have faced, (2) the coping strategies you built up to protect yourself, and (3) the triggers that can elicit any anxiety-ridden or maladaptive responses:

1. What types of high-impact financial experiences have you or your family experienced (e.g., war, poverty, dislocation for work, market crashes, investment losses, health expenses, business failures, bankruptcies, debt, career changes)?
2. What were the coping strategies that helped you survive the trauma? How did they change you for the better?
3. What aspects of your coping strategies could be limiting you now?
4. What triggers remind you of the event and induce anxiety for you? Are there particular circumstances when you feel yourself falling into this pattern again (e.g., market plunges, losing investments, portfolio stagnancy, changes in your income,

unexpected costs/bills)? How do your coping strategies affect you when anxiety is triggered now?

All in the Family

Raj was raised as an only child by a poor single mother. Growing up, he moved frequently from city to city as his mother searched for better employment opportunities. Raj remembers feeling there wasn't enough money at home and that his clothes, grooming, and accent were never quite "right" for the kids at his latest school. He felt out of place and rootless, except when he was with one person—his father.

His father was a pilot who visited him as a surprise when he occasionally passed through town. During his visits he regaled Raj with tales of exotic locations, fast cars, and good times, and he gave Raj more gifts in one visit than he received from the rest of his family in a year. Inevitably he was accompanied by a pretty young flight attendant who was generous and kind with Raj, hoping to win his affection. Days with his father were like holidays from his difficult daily life.

After these too-brief visits, his father was gone again, not to be heard from until the next unexpected phone call. Raj's mother despised his father, both for his playboy lifestyle and for how little he contributed to raising his son. She was bitter and sometimes treated Raj badly after those visits, which only steeled Raj's resolve to live a life of ease and comfort like his father.

Shortly after he finished college, Raj's mother fell ill. He moved nearby to take care of her. His dreams of the playboy life had been put on hold, and his spirit was beginning to flag. Then Raj discovered online trading. He could be a "trader"—playing small stakes with dreams of getting rich and escaping from his humdrum lifestyle. Raj traded for a few years, but he never felt secure in either his developing career or his trading on the side. Unfortunately, he frequently "blew up" his trading account by taking excessively risky positions in his hurry to make a quick "million."

Through his work with Dr. Peterson, Raj came to realize that he was living two lives—one a stable, slow-paced life in which he sacrificed for his mother, and one a "fantasy life" he dreamed of. It was, in fact, the same childhood dynamic being played out in adulthood, only this time it wasn't surprise visits from his father that provided his chance for deliverance, it was the stock market.

In examining his values and where they came from with Dr. Peterson, the cause of his failure (and the means to change) became clear. This "I need to get rich" value that drove him to trade so recklessly—so *desperately*—was not the motivation of an adult trader at all; it was the motivation of a lonely 10-year-old boy who wanted to be like his dad. His trading behavior would not change until he came to a place of acceptance about his father and the pain and his childhood. When Raj realized this, he was able to change.

What outside observers may plainly see in us, we often don't see in ourselves without the use of a mirror. Such is the case with Raj's values. He thought he was just an aggressive trader who needed to tweak his "system." It came as a revelation to him that this value he placed on obtaining a thrilling lifestyle was rooted in his childhood experiences and inextricably bound to his relationship with his father. Through treatment Raj gradually stopped trading, redoubled his efforts on his career, and today is very successful in his profession (and he no longer trades).

Like Raj, we all have unconscious values that serve as drivers of our behavior. Making such motivations—and where they come from—conscious is a first step toward positive change, and, on occasion, the only step necessary.

These questions will help you begin an exploration of your values and the life events that may have shaped them. These questions, designed to facilitate self-exploration, were derived from the work of Dr. Robert Siroka, a New York City psychologist who, among other projects, offers workshops and psychotherapy related to money issues. As you go through these questions, consider how your answers might explain the origin of your career choice, investing habits (both successful and damaging), and opinions about money.

Think back to your early years:

- What would your parents say about social class?
- What was the financial status of your family?
- What were your family's values around spending, saving, and earning?

- What was the general tone around money in your family?
- Was money seen as good, evil, indifferent?
- Was money seen as easy to obtain?
- Who in your family controlled or was the authority on spending? Saving? Investing?
- Who was a positive role model?
- What is an early money memory?
- What are two messages you received from your family about money?
- Who are the money heroes in your family history?
- Where are the money ghosts hiding (that is, what are some financial embarrassments or shame in your family history)?

How have your parents' attitudes influenced you?

- Which attitudes have served you well?
- Which attitudes have been unhelpful?

What are your financial values?

- How do you speak to or educate children about money?
- What are your attitudes or beliefs about those without money?
- How wealthy do you want to be?
- How will you define being wealthy?
- What will it take (how much income or assets are enough) for you to feel financially secure?
- What scares you the most when you think about your financial future?
- Should you fail to reach your financial goals, what will be the reasons why?

This exercise is designed to help you start thinking about the role of your money history in guiding your present-day habits and beliefs. In some cases there are clear relationships between your answers and your life choices.

Once you understand how your values may have formed over time and through your early experiences, it is useful to turn toward another series of questions. How would your life and values change if you truly believed that money was no object? Thinking along these lines helps free up any underlying dreams or goals that may have been set aside in the pursuit of financial security.

George Kinder and the Three Questions

In middle age many people realize that their current work is incompatible with their personal values and goals. Yet because of their investments of time and education in their careers, they feel trapped—unable to change tracks. Such a conflict between one's innate values and career can lead to frustration and moodiness—often called a "mid-life crisis." Such emotionality may be due to chronic disappointment with the "rat race" or feelings of "selling out" at work.

Conflicts between a person's fundamental values and daily work often lie dormant in the unconscious, subtly influencing behavior. It is only when such conflicts are brought to the surface that they can be worked through and new, more harmonious pursuits initiated. The pioneer in unearthing conflicts between one's deepest values and current lifestyle is George Kinder, a certified financial planner and founder of the Kinder Institute of Life Planning.

Kinder established the Institute to help financial advisors understand and help clients with their entire lives (not just their finances). Kinder instructs his advisors to ask clients three questions about their current lifestyles and their deepest values. Their responses to these questions reflect their fundamental financial goals.

We've reprinted Kinder's questions here. As you go through these questions, think deeply about your answers. Take the time to consider if your responses to these questions are consistent with how you are currently living and working.

1. I want you to imagine that you are financially secure, that you have enough money to take care of your needs, now and in the future. The question is . . . how would you live your life? Would you change anything? Let yourself go. Don't hold back on your dreams. Describe a life that is complete, that is richly yours.
2. This time you visit your doctor who tells you that you have only 5 to 10 years left to live. The good part is that you won't ever feel sick. The bad news is that you will have no notice of the moment of your death. What will you do in the time you have remaining to live? Will you change your life and how will you do it?
3. This time your doctor shocks you with the news that you have only one day left to live. Notice what feelings arise as you confront your very real mortality. Ask yourself: What did I miss? Who did I not get to be? What did I not get to do?

According to Kinder, "When you understand what you want to do with your life, you can make financial choices that reflect your values."[2] Kinder's questions usually open up much soul-searching. Many clients wonder, "Should I make a change if my current trajectory isn't consistent with my dreams?" At MarketPsych we believe that such a self-analysis process should be done in partnership with a trained and trusted advisor in order to gain the most benefit, as can be found with a financial advisor trained through The Kinder Institute of Life Planning (www.KinderInstitute.com).

Digging into Money Taboos

Shafik Hirani is the top-producing financial advisor at Investors Group Financial Services Inc. in Calgary. While Hirani is good-natured, he asks incisive questions that get to the heart of a client's beliefs around money. Hirani excavates underneath clients' surface financial concerns with a series of intriguing and engaging dialogues. Some of his inquiries appear to have little to do with finances; nonetheless, they address the self-imposed limits that restrict thinking around money issues. We invite you to consider some of Hirani's favorite questions:

1. What about money is exciting for you?
2. What about money is stressful for you?
3. How do you deal with financial and other stress (how would your spouse know that you are "fretting")?
4. What are three things you lie to yourself about when it comes to your money?
5. What are three things you lie to others about when it comes to your money?
6. How much money would it take to compromise your values (e.g., how much would someone have to pay you to eat a live earthworm? Box with Mike Tyson? Rob a bank?)?

Of course, it's not easy to face what we lie to *ourselves* about. Nonetheless, it's a worthwhile exercise to think deeply about such issues. You might be surprised at what comes up.

Conclusion

We hope you learned about your investing values and how they affect your financial approach. Of course, there are no simple "answers" to the questions we've asked you to consider. Understanding your values will give you deep insights into who you are as an investor (i.e., your investing identity). Often meaningful change can come from simply becoming conscious of your money values and belief systems, particularly when you see that conflict with your desired way of life.

To complete the process we've begun in this chapter, please consider how what you learned about yourself may change how you want to live your life going forward:

1. How can you use an understanding of your own financial values to improve your investing (and your life)?
2. If you're a financial advisor, how can you use an understanding of your clients' financial values to improve your work with them (and their lives)?

The purpose of this chapter was to help you gain insights into your investing approach; however, we recognize that for many the process of addressing these questions can be emotional and could even end up opening old wounds. If this chapter has left a trail of "loose ends," we hope that you'll consider seeing a coach or psychotherapist in order to work through your thoughts. Psychotherapists can help you understand the narrative behind your values, your life, and how you're living. Additionally, they are specialists in helping you make long-term changes in life direction.

Although our financial values underlie the larger choices we make in life, there are subtle influences that affect specific types of decisions in predictable ways. The next chapter will introduce the concept of the systematic investing mistakes known as "biases." Unlike financial values, it is not unique life history or upbringing that create biased decisions. Most of the biases are biological in origin and "hardwired" from birth. Fortunately, investing biology is not investing destiny.

6

Your Investor Blind Spots: Identifying (and Avoiding) Mental Traps

Most investors who fail to reach their goals do so because they fall into identifiable and often predictable mental pitfalls along the way. If there were signs that said "Warning: Mental Pitfall Ahead!" there would be no problem. But such traps catch us off-guard precisely because they lurk in our blind spots. They already exist in our psyches, and they do their damage before we are aware of their presence.

Every investor has weaknesses and vulnerabilities. These make up the darker side of our investor identity. And though some are more at risk than others, these investor traps are universal human tendencies to which every investor is susceptible.

Forging a more effective investor identity involves not only recognizing these traps, but also realizing your personal susceptibilities to them and developing the ability to sidestep them along the way to your goals.

This chapter describes the most common and insidious investor traps. You will learn to identify and minimize the impact of these common mental mistakes.

Trap #1: Win/Lose Mentality

Most investors love to keep score, and there is no bigger, clearer scoreboard than that provided by stock markets. Our personal score cards are delivered in the form of monthly statements, but we no longer need to wait a week to get the final numbers. With Internet access, we can see how we're doing at any given moment of any given day. A gain on the day is translated as a win, while a loss gets classified as just that, a loss. Investors easily slip into such a win/lose, binary framework for evaluating their financial returns status.

Thinking in terms of numerical profits and losses leads to immediate emotional reactions whenever you get feedback about your gains and losses, which increases your overall stress level. Most people want to relieve short-term emotional pressure, especially the negative kind, even at the expense of long-term wealth accumulation. The win/lose mentality is a mental trap that increases stress and encourages a short-term, money-focused, and outcome-oriented frame of mind.

A win/lose mentality is appropriate in many settings. NFL football comes to mind. An NFL team plays 16 games during a season. Each game has a binary outcome: "win" or "lose" (I'm not counting ties here; they're fairly rare). It doesn't matter if you win a game by 30 points or on a last-second field goal. The resulting win has the same significance. The same reasoning applies to losses. If a team has enough wins at the end of the year, they qualify for the playoffs. At the playoffs, another series of binary outcomes will determine whether that team becomes the Super Bowl champion—the ultimate goal.

But what happens when you apply win/lose logic to investments? It is easy for investors to be drawn into a perspective that views individual holdings as games in the "investing football season." Holdings that yield a profit get mentally filed in the "W column," while those that take a loss go in the "L column." This is not only unsound, it's dangerous. For one thing, all wins and losses are not created equal. The first factor is how much money you have invested; the second is the percentage of the price movement. For example, a 10 percent loss in a $10,000 holding is clearly not evened out by a 10 percent gain in a $5,000 holding (you would need a 20 percent gain for that). Nonetheless it's a convenient mental shortcut to slap win/lose labels on our investments.

Even when you look at the total profit or loss of your portfolio, the win/loss framework remains a trap. You may have long-term financial goals, but it would be a mistake to approach them as win/lose (e.g., "$2,000,000 or bust!"). Another way investors keep score is by performance per time period. This week was a winning week. This month was a losing month. Last year was a losing year.

But introducing the notion of investing "quarters" creates the feeling of the ticking clock, and time pressure does awful things to our decision making.

You may hear a little voice in the back of your head whisper, "How are you going to make up for that loss? You have to make money now! Time is running out!" But the clock is not going to "run out," not the way it does in football. In an NFL game the need to take a big gamble may make perfect sense—it can be your only hope to win the game. But being baited into taking a big risk with your investments in order to make back lost money is never a good idea. In football these desperation heaves are called "Hail Marys." In investing they are called, well, "Hail Marys."

Another problem born of this win/lose framework is that in our effort to score a win (and consequently feel good about ourselves) we can be tempted into selling our winners in order to lock them in. The old saying, "No one ever went broke taking a profit," is true. Profit-taking is essential. But not giving yourself the opportunity to have meaningful, long-term appreciation with your investments is to guarantee an oppressively low ceiling on your portfolio's upside.

The win/lose mentality is similar to what is called "black and white" or "all-or-nothing" thinking. We see this not only with unsuccessful investors but also with unsuccessful dieters. Many chronic dieters approach their eating with no gray area, no room for moderation. They are either "on a diet" (very strict) or they are "off it" (no rules). When they veer off a plan, rather than stopping at one (okay, two) cookies with the reasoning that little harm has been done, they instead revert to the thought, "I've already gone off my diet. I may as well get my money's worth here," and proceed to finish the box of cookies (and possibly a pint or two of ice cream), consoling/justifying themselves with the refrain, "My diet starts on Monday. Again."

We need to see gray areas and moderation in our investing, too. It saves us from extreme decisions and destructive frameworks. Investing for the future is not a game to be won or lost; it's a process of accumulating enough wealth so that we can live and feel a certain way.

The financial media and casual conversations with friends will often draw us into thinking in terms of the win/lose mentality. Adopting and maintaining a life-focused, process-oriented frame is the key to beating this mental trap.

Avoiding Trap #1

- When you want to evaluate how your investments are doing, adopt a framework based on progress toward your life goals—they're the reason you're investing in the first place. Are you in line to achieve your retirement plans? Is the college fund on track? These are much better evaluations than whether you're beating the S&P 500 this year—much less competitive, too.
- Do not allow your actions to be dictated by arbitrary time-lines like a calendar or fiscal year. Tax implications aside, they are meaningless guideposts within the context of your long-term plan. The time to start investing is now, not January 1. Because you're "having a bad year" is no reason to take on big risks to make up for it.
- Fight the temptation to "break even" on individual positions. You have a choice to make with your portfolio. You can either try to win every battle, or try to win the war. You cannot do both.

Trap #2: Down with the Ship Syndrome

As the last section indicated, we love to win. But we hate to lose even more! In fact, seminal research in the field of behavioral finance indicates that the pain of losing is felt 2 to 2.5 times more strongly than the joy of winning.[1]

"Down with the ship" syndrome is rooted in this loss aversion. Intellectually, we know that not all of our investing choices in the stock market are going to work out. Some positions will lose money. But selling a position that is down means realizing the loss and experiencing pain, and not only the financial pinch, but the dull emotional ache that comes from feeling disappointed, foolish, or wrong. We possess, however, the means to evade these feelings—we just won't sell. Indeed, in some cases, we can delay this realization indefinitely.

In this way, down with the ship syndrome is quite similar to the snooze button on alarm clocks. We know we should wake up at the predetermined time. That's the entire point of setting an alarm clock. But some days the prospect of waking up for work is remarkably unpleasant (I call these days "weekdays"), and all we want to do is sleep in. The snooze button gives us the power to put off our fate for as long as we choose. Of course, the longer we postpone the inevitable, the worse our fate becomes.

Likewise, it sometimes becomes apparent that we should no longer be invested in a holding, but when that holding is in the red the temptation to press the "investing snooze button" can be surprisingly powerful. Of course, in the case of sleeping we accept that our fate (getting up) is sealed. But with our investments, we always hold out the hope that they can rally and that a painful future is not inescapable.

Consider for a moment the veritable ocean's worth of investments available to us. There are presently over 13,000 mutual funds in the United States alone. For the tiny bucketful of investments in which most people choose to invest their hard-earned money, they place an awful lot of faith and hope. That faith and hope, not lightly given, often creates a misguided sense of "loyalty." We may retain our hope in the face of negative circumstances, sometimes tinged with naïvete, sometimes with defiance. Unfortunately, it is this hope that keeps investors tethered to losing positions as they descend into the depths.

The investing ocean floor is littered with examples of stocks that went *Titanic* on their shareholders. (Bear Stearns and General Motors are recent high-profile examples.) Some of them sank like stones. Others drifted there over the course of years. But all of them sent warning signals and presented ample opportunity to avoid huge losses.

Most shareholders who ended up in Davy Jones's locker were aided on the journey by what is called the *sunk cost fallacy*, a bias which leads people to make such rationalizations as "It's down so far, I can't sell it now." Of course, near the very bottom, the position may be so low that selling it would only recoup a micro-fraction of the original investment. But something is always better than nothing. And in most cases, that something could have been considerable if the investor had the courage to voluntarily take a loss, rather than have a complete bust forced upon them.

What makes down with the ship syndrome doubly destructive is the opportunity cost it inflicts. Even in cases where our ill-chosen positions make their way higher and avoid total disaster, they are still prone to underperform many other options we considered during that span. Sometimes the best way to extricate ourselves out of down with the ship syndrome is to focus not on the loss of the position we're in, but our opportunity cost—the gains we're missing by not holding something else in its stead.

Avoiding Trap #2

- Set predetermined exit points (stop-losses) for riskier positions. Somewhere between 8 and 15 percent is typical, depending on its usual volatility. You don't need to completely liquidate the position. (In fact, moving completely in and out of positions is a great way to get stuck in a yo-yo style of investing.) Agree to take a preset percentage out of the market if specific fundamental changes occur.
- We avoid losses because they hurt. But learning to take manageable losses is what separates the great investors from the rest of the pack. Allow the good feeling of knowing you're building an invaluable skill to outweigh the bad feeling of losing a small amount of money. Congratulations—you just became a better investor.
- Process > Outcome. The ability to follow a plan is infinitely more important than what happens on an individual trade. Create a physical reminder of this all-important lesson that charts your progress. Every time you stick to a plan (e.g., doing due diligence, selling/buying, not buying) put a quarter in a jar. Every quarter that goes clink is a tangible representation of your becoming a stronger investor.

Trap #3: Anchoring

Anchoring is a subtle, if not completely unconscious, distortion in thinking. Anchoring refers to the use of a "reference point" to estimate our current level of success or failure. A common form of investor anchoring is to use the high-water mark for a portfolio—the day we had the most money ever—as our principal means of evaluating our status. For many investors this day was in October 2007 when the DJIA was over 14,000 and the S&P 500 index was over 1,500. Many investors look at their portfolios and think, "I'm still down 15 percent from my high," "I've lost $100,000 in the past year," and so on.

Is this an appropriate or healthy prism through which to view portfolios? Imagine for a moment that instead of talking about the best day ever for your portfolio, we're talking about the best day ever for your *entire life*. Maybe it was your wedding day, or perhaps the birth of a child, or maybe it was just a Saturday on which you broke your personal record by three strokes in the morning, hosted an afternoon BBQ with your closest friends, and then watched your team win the World Series that evening. Think about how satisfied you were, how fulfilled, how unbelievably *happy*.

Now think about comparing your happiness every day since then to *that day*. Can you think of a better recipe for misery and dissatisfaction? A better way to ensure your investing glass is eternally half empty? Yet this is essentially what we do when we adopt a "I used to have X, but now I have Y" framework for viewing our net worth.

We also use anchoring to form inappropriate baselines for individual stock positions. Some of the most common "anchors" include the purchase price, an all-time high, or an analysts' "price target." There is nothing wrong with using important numbers as a means of evaluating a position. The problem comes when we choose inappropriate benchmarks and fail to deviate from them.

How persistent can this bias be? I can still hear an investor I know well referring to Bear Stearns as a "$100 stock" after it had dropped below $20 per share.

It calls to mind a scene from the movie *The Return of the Pink Panther* in which the hapless Inspector Clouseau has just smashed a piano with a medieval weapon in an ill-conceived attempt to swat a fly.

Looking at the shattered instrument the owner wails, "But that's a priceless Steinway!"

Clouseau responds matter-of-factly with all the dignity he can muster, "Not anymore."

Anchoring is a trap because it causes us to evaluate our portfolios with the wrong tools. And the faulty measurements those tools yield lead to faulty decisions on how to proceed.

Avoiding Trap #3

- Separate the concept of what a stock's price has been and what it was actually worth. For example, during the "dot-com bubble" there were a multitude of stocks that soared to Olympian heights. Their underlying businesses weren't "worth" those prices then, and they aren't now. Factoring yesterday's numbers into today's evaluations distorts the reality and tempts us into buying on false expectations.

- Acknowledge that our portfolios will not stay at their "all-time highs." It would be nice if the market moved by climbing stairs, steadily rising with every step. It doesn't. It moves in fits and starts, rising and dropping without warning, sometimes for extended periods of time. Take a moment and accept this reality. Comparing your current net worth to your portfolio's "best day" will create an itch, one that you will seek to scratch at great cost to your mental health and net worth.

- Turn your position upside down. Ask yourself, how far is your investment above its all-time low? How much more could you have lost? While we don't want you to get attached to an inverse anchor, they can be helpful to break free of one that's been persistent.

Trap #4: Mean Reversion Bias

The mean reversion bias (MRB) is an example of an "overreach bias," one that carries an appreciation of a valid concept too far. Its primary hazard is that it leads investors to make unsound predictions that knock them out of an otherwise sound approach, often drawing them into an escalating game of "market timing"—a game they are destined to lose.

Mean reversion is another way of saying "the law of averages," that things will "even out" over time. It is an important concept, but one that is widely misinterpreted as it pertains to investing.

Market prices do indeed tend to even out. When stocks become overpriced they tend to correct back to a more reasonable value. When they drop to underpriced levels, the same mechanisms ensure that they will gravitate back to "fair value." The problem is that the market is under no obligation to conform to our often rigid timelines for "averaging out." And, to paraphrase economist John Maynard Keynes, "Markets can remain irrational longer than you can remain solvent."

In the case of any series of events based (in part) on randomness, there are always longer streaks than we anticipate. Professor Thomas Gilovich of Cornell University—a noted behavioral finance expert—has an exercise that he uses with his classes to illustrate the

MRB. Each semester he would ask his statistics class to write two sets of results on the blackboard while he left the room. The first was a progression of 20 actual coin tosses (e.g., HTTHT, etc.). The second was a set of 20 fictitious coin tosses. He would guarantee that upon his return, he could tell which was real and which was made up. The professor was always correct. How did he choose? Whichever series had the longest streak of heads or tails in a row was the real data set. The professor knew what many stock market investors do not, that in any set of unfolding results, you can rely on some runs lasting longer than they supposedly "ought to."

The MRB is a major component of what is often referred to as the *gambler's fallacy*. The gambler's fallacy is a common cognitive distortion in which a person uses a series of independent events to make a prediction of a future independent event. In the coin-flipping example, the students commit the gambler's fallacy when they base their reversals on the notion that if the coin has come up "tails" several times in a row, it is "due to come up heads."

It is perhaps fitting that the bias is called the gambler's fallacy because the gambling industry actively encourages it. They do so in a variety of ways, but perhaps none is more illustrative than the scoreboard at a roulette table. Roulette is a game of chance in which a wheel yields a random result between 00 and 36, with each number corresponding with the color black or red (and in the case of zeroes, green). The scoreboard is an electronic device that keeps track of and displays the previous 20 results the wheel has generated. There is no more irrelevant information in the world than what a roulette wheel has already done. The scoreboard might as well display a random list of Centigrade temperatures of Mongolia or point totals generated by the 1977 Pittsburgh Steelers. But what casinos know is that when something that looks like a pattern emerges (five "red numbers" in a row, "even numbers" for the last seven spins, a string of bets all in the "bottom third"), the gambler's fallacy creeps in, gamblers "see the pattern," and they become more likely to bet—and bet aggressively. In this version of the fallacy, they mistakenly think an existing "trend" (of independent events) is bound to keep on going.

While amateur investors often project a "trend continuation," the MRB manifests itself in professional investors acting on such beliefs as, "The market has been up 10 straight months. It's due for a correction. Let's move out of equities and wait for the pull back." In both cases patterns are seen in independent events.

The MRB is one of the few biases that is more prevalent among professionals than it is among average investors. A recent example involves the volatility that overtook the markets in the early part of the 21st century. We know that on average the DJIA returned approximately 9 percent per year over its history. But in 2000 the index performed poorly and returned negative 9.1 percent. Market strategists surveyed by *Barron's* predicted (on average) an 18.7 percent rise in 2001—one that, not coincidentally, would have the index reverting back to its prior strong uptrend. But instead of rising, the DJIA actually fell another 13 percent in 2001. So what did market strategists do? For the year 2002, market strategists played the regression to mean card even harder; they predicted a 21 percent increase for 2002. The actual return for 2002 was an abysmal negative 23.4 percent. There were three straight years of negative returns, each worse than the last. For 2003, market strategists appear to have caved in to the trend by lowering their expectations; they predicted (on average) a most modest 1 percent rise (meaning that many of the consensus predicted a fourth straight year of negative returns). The DJIA responded with a stellar 28.6 percent return for 2003. In 2004, market strategists finally decided not to outsmart themselves and predicted the most logical guess as to what the return would be—a 7 percent return for 2004. They were close. The DJIA returned 9 percent that year, very much in keeping with its long-term historic average.

There is nothing wrong with inaccurate predictions per se. They only become a liability when we act on those predictions. In the case of the early 2000s, we see that investors who followed the lead of leading Wall Street forecasters would have escalated their investing into the teeth of the storm, but would have begun to capitulate precisely as the skies cleared—textbook "Whack-a-Mole" syndrome.

These examples are not shared to make fun of market strategists. Market strategists are, as a whole, a highly intelligent bunch with more insight into equities markets than any other group in the world. It just goes to show that even the best and brightest are not immune to mental traps.

Avoiding Trap #4

- Fair value is a legitimate concept. (Over time, stocks get valued at what their underlying businesses are "worth.") But their journey to that place is notoriously capricious. Build a buffer around your buying and selling activities. If you buy a stock at $40/share, and you believe it's worth $50/share, do not be in a hurry to jump in again if it drifts to $39/share—and then again at $38/share. Allow for some variance. The gains from buying at the marginally lower price come at the cost of flexibility and in "bogging you down" in the position. You want to give yourself a chance to buy it at $30/share without owning too much.

- Remember Keynes's observation (learned through painful experience), "Markets can remain irrational longer than you can remain solvent." It is a lesson learned by everyone who has watched an irrational market stubbornly refuse to conform to their expectations.
- Sweeping market predictions are particularly susceptible to the MRB. Yet, you could assemble the top minds in the financial world in a room, ask them to make market predictions, and find their answers all over the map. The markets do what they will do on their own schedule. Make a vow that you will simply refuse to get baited into playing the prediction game. Just don't do it.

Trap #5: Endowment Effect

The endowment effect is the tendency we have to overvalue that which we own, while undervaluing that which we do not. Nowhere is the endowment effect more plainly seen than in residential real estate sales. There is on average a 12 percent gap between what the owner asks and what the average buyer is willing to pay (in a bad market the gap opens to 33 percent!). Certainly any pragmatic owner understands that selling a house may involve some give and take. The seller wants to set a nice high price from which to bargain (see the section on anchoring). But there is much more going on here than simply the desire to take in some extra bucks. The owner of the house truly believes the house is worth more.

How does the endowment effect impact stock market investing? In a word, *attachment.* Consider all the things we invest besides money.

We invest time and effort. Even if our time and effort are cursory, these two factors inherently increase our emotional attachment. (Do you treat $50 found in an old coat pocket the same way you'd treat $50 you worked for?) We know we invest our hope—we want it to go up, after all. But think for a moment how a rise in the position reveals other hidden investments: (1) our reputation (if it goes up, we will look good to others), (2) our judgment (if it goes up, we get to be proven right), and (3) our self-esteem/ pride (if it goes up we feel smart, wise, responsible—in other words, better about ourselves). When we invest in the stock market—or anything else for that matter—we invest a small part of our *selves*— that's the attachment.

(Of course, if the position goes down, these same hidden investments suffer, causing us pain.)

There is nothing illogical in an owner and a nonowner placing two different values on the same holding. It is worth more to the owner because it *contains more* to the owner. For that matter, there's nothing intrinsically wrong with this discrepancy, either. The endowment effect only becomes an investing trap when it impedes our ability to make good decisions.

Those poor decisions come when we invest so much of ourselves in a holding that we have trouble letting go. We can't give up that hope or that desire to be proven right. We can't face the blow to our self-esteem or pride that eating a loss would cause . . . we can't face our father-in-law.

Healthy investing means having a healthy level of attachment to one's investments. You should never love a stock—at least, not unconditionally. Unconditional love should be reserved for relationships with family, very good friends, and possibly college sports teams. Applying it to a relationship with your investments ensures what pop-psychology types call "co-dependency"—you're miserable, but stuck with each other.

The endowment effect is closely related to the status quo bias. It is always easier to do nothing than to do something. That's because doing something requires energy. Inertia plays a role in investing, just the way it does in physics; a body at rest tends to stay at rest. When the status quo bias teams up with the endowment effect, you have physical forces and emotional forces exerting pressure to stay put. This can harden the mold on a portfolio in desperate need of reshaping and keep us stuck in positions that have long outlived their usefulness.

Avoiding Trap #5

- Write down the objective characteristics of your beloved stock—its last three quarters' earnings, total debt level, cash flow characteristics, market share. Listing objective criteria reduces the endowment effect. (At the same time, DO NOT list the goodies: The hot new products that are so much fun to use, the phenomenal management team, and the cool logo should be ignored while you list those dry facts and figures).

- Mentally clear any attachment to the investment by imagining that you do not own it and someone is presenting it to you for the first time, saying, "I found this new stock/mutual fund." Ask yourself if you would buy this investment today at this price in this environment. If the answer is not a strong "yes," it is a sign that you're holding it for the wrong reasons.

- The endowment effect creates an irrational attachment making it difficult to consciously challenge our assumptions. Clearly articulate—or if you are unable, find someone else to clearly articulate—the best arguments *against* holding your investment.

- Often our head (reason) knows the right thing to do but our heart (emotions) won't let us. It is easier to agree to take a difficult action in the future than it is to actually do it in the moment. So take yourself out of the moment. Agree to liquidate a small, manageable portion of the position and set up an autopilot function to carry it out.

Trap #6: Media Hype Effect

There was a time, not too long ago, when access to financial information was highly restricted. If you wanted to know your stocks' latest prices, you would have to wait until the next morning, buy the *Wall Street Journal,* and check the ticker symbol—possibly with the aid of a magnifying glass—on the quotes page.

But now, thanks to the increased prevalence of 24-hour financial news networks—my cable package currently has five of them—and, of course, the Internet, investors have a nonstop news stream and instant information at their fingertips.

This should be a good thing. But is it?

The media hype effect is all about the misuse of information. We tune in to hear the latest "news" as it pertains to our holdings. We like getting information. The more we get, the more we feel on top of things; information increases our sense of control.

But this desire to feel in control often comes at the cost of our better judgment. The fact is, too much information is a dangerous thing. A famous example—with a lesson for investors—is detailed in the book *Freakonomics* (Harper Perennial, 2009) by Stephen Dubner and Steven Levitt. The authors detail the case of Cook County Hospital in Chicago. The emergency room was overburdened and therefore needed to improve efficiency. The administrator decided to refine the diagnostic procedure for patients presenting with chest pain so as not to waste precious resources. Instead of relying on the clinical judgment of the doctors to determine admissions to the CCU, all triaging would be performed based on a strict decision tree developed by a cardiologist, Lee Goldman. The tree had only four branches: (1) ECG evidence of acute mypcardial infarction, (2) low blood pressure, (3) fluid in the lungs (shortness of breath), and (4) unstable angina (chest pain).

That's it. Not weight. Not age. No other physical evidence. Not even a doctor's medical intuition. No other information that doctors usually factor into their diagnostic process. How did the new protocol fare? Goldman's method led to 70 percent more accurate recognition of patients who were not having heart attacks. Of course, many doctors resisted this new method. It didn't feel right to their clinical judgment. But that is part of the lesson for the investor.

It often feels as if we need more information to make a good decision about investing. But when we factor in extraneous variables, far from helping us, it actually hurts our ability to make good choices.

A study by Paul Andreassen at Harvard University[2] examined the effect of media reports on managing a portfolio. He had two sets of subjects manage an identical portfolio of stocks. One group was told to watch certain financial programs, read stock market articles, and stay on top of information regarding their holdings. The other group was explicitly told to avoid all information about their holdings, a financial sequestering, if you will.

When the gains and losses of the portfolios were later compared, the people who read articles and watched television programs on investing did significantly worse compared to those who avoided the media. In fact, in more volatile times the gains of the "nonwatchers" were twice as good. What makes the information even more compelling is that whether the (supposedly) relevant news was positive or negative made no difference. It wasn't the nature of the news that mattered; it was the consistently inappropriate response to information that proved to be the problem.

The media hype effect is amplified in volatile markets. Markets have rarely been more volatile than in the two years leading up to the writing of this book (2008–2009). The DJIA rose 30 percent in 2009. From its lows in March, the rise was more than 45 percent. It was by all objective accounts a good year for investors, provided they did not pull out during the market lows. Nonetheless, 2009 saw considerable volatility and a number of days in which the index dropped over 100 points in a session.

Dr. Murtha noticed that on those days, usually around 10:30 or 11:00 AM (EST), he would often receive a call from a concerned investor who wanted a second opinion. (Okay, it's his mom, a very bright and sensible woman by the way.) The nature of her concerns and her considered remedy were always the same. "Things are looking bad," she would say. "Maybe we should move to cash for a little while until things calm down a little."

He would ask her what brought on the sudden urge to sell. In every case her response started with, "Well, I was watching a financial news network." But that was never identified as the reason for the call. It was always "something I've been thinking about for a while." (That's the nature of the media hype effect. It doesn't typically cause a new thought; it tends to activate an existing thought, prey upon an existing fear.)

Dr. Murtha's response was always the same. "Fair enough. But let's not do anything rash. Call me back on a day when the market is up over 100 points and we'll consider taking action."

That call has yet to come.

Avoiding Trap #6

- Provocative media reports create a sense of financial urgency that leads to impulsiveness. In reality, it is rare that any long term plan would be meaningfully affected by waiting a bit before acting. Agree to a waiting period—don't trade for one to seven days after encountering "media hype." You will often find that when the waiting period expires, you no longer wish to make the trade at all.

- If the above seems difficult, agree to act on only a small fraction of the position initially, say, selling 10 to 20 percent (called "throwing a maiden in the volcano" by Jim Cramer). This relieves pressure and anxiety by allowing you to take some action while you wait for that calmer, clearer state of mind at the end of your self-imposed moratorium.

- The media can overload our data processing centers. Limit your information flow by identifying three or four relevant data points for a position. The chances are, anything more than that is actually getting in the way of making a good decision.

Trap #7: Short-Termism

Of all the investor traps, short-termism may be the most pervasive and the most dangerous.

The forces of investing—both internal psychological factors and external events—are perpetually drawing us into a short-term market focus in which our emotions rule. Yet healthy investing requires precisely the opposite approach, a long-term goal focus where rationality holds sway.

Short-termism is perpetual, unconscious, and virtually immune to data. It is like a relentless tractor beam constantly drawing us into this mind-set. To get an understanding of how much so, we need look no further than Ian Fleming's iconic superspy, James Bond. We all know what to expect when we watch Agent 007 in a movie. We know he's going to foil the villain, save the world, get the girl, and so on. But in any James Bond movie there are periods in which our hero is in great and seemingly inescapable peril (inordinately involving buzz saws, laser beams, and sharks). Provided the movie is done well, we audience members experience an unavoidable emotional reaction—we feel anxious. (The film industry calls it "suspense," not anxiety, but it's the same emotional process.) We can't help it. It's the way our brain is wired.

This is incredibly relevant to investors because, like a movie, the market is a series of unfolding events. It has its ups and its downs. We have to constantly fight to maintain a healthy, big-picture perspective. How do we do that?

Consider for a moment the mechanisms we use to protect ourselves when the "suspense" gets to be too much. During the direst moments, we may remind ourselves that it's too early in the movie for an important character to die. We may note that there are sequels coming up in which the character must appear. Sometimes we simply cover our eyes altogether.

In the former cases, we're attempting to get out of the short-term focus and into a long-term, big-picture focus where we can feel safe again. In the latter case, it's an attempt to shut out the short term completely. Whether the events we're watching are in movies or markets, it's an uphill fight. Our brains are literally wired so that when we are experiencing moments of great anxiety—or for that matter euphoria—the long-term decision-making centers of the brain are essentially powered down, forcing us to think short term. It's an adaptive mechanism and part of our evolutionary biology. (Who needs power diverted to the long-term planning sector when you're being chased by a saber-toothed tiger?)

But short-termism stacks the deck against us on an emotional level as well. We invest (and sacrifice) so that 5, 10, even 30-plus years from now we will reap the benefits in the form of security and comfort. The financial payoff is, primarily, in the future.

But we do not live in the future. Barring a wormhole in the time-space continuum, we have no choice but to live in the present. So although we have emotional goals for our future, we also have emotions exerting pressure on us now. And often they are in direct competition with our better interests (see Chapter 2 on EROI).

Short-termism is the triumph of a present focus over a future focus. How important (and how difficult) is it to keep our present-centered emotional goals from subverting our future emotional goals? The answers can be found in a famous psychological experiment consisting of a bunch of 4-year-olds . . . and a marshmallow.

The famous "Marshmallow Test" is the work of Stanford University psychologist Walter Mischel, who conducted a study using children at Stanford University's Day Care Center as participants.[3] The little kids sat at a table with a marshmallow placed in front of them. They were given a choice. They could eat the marshmallow any time they wanted, but if they waited 15 to 20 minutes for the researcher to return from "running a few errands," they would be given two marshmallows.

After explaining these instructions, the researcher would then leave the room. Follow-up research with the study's participants found that marshmallow resisters (approximately one-third of the group) performed better on standardized tests and went on to have longer-lasting marriages, higher incomes, better health, and higher life satisfaction than the marshmallow eaters. You can bet that if the researchers accounted for investing performance, the marshmallow resisters would have outpaced their peers in that as well.

The children knew that it would be better for them to wait and get the extra treat. (Even toddlers know two is more than one). But for most of the participants the prospect of getting twice the pleasure did not provide the leverage to overcome the immediate enjoyment of one delicious, fluffy marshmallow.

The ability to fully appreciate and *emotionally access* the future payoff of investing is crucial as a point of influence to keep investors in the all-important long-term, goal-based investing focus.

Short-termism causes us to eat the marshmallow. That marshmallow comes in different forms with different appeals for investors. But in all cases it involves the inability to focus on the long term. Once in a short-term perspective, investors are vulnerable to making bad decisions that not only sidetrack them from their intended investing paths, but make it difficult to find their way back to the trail.

Avoiding Trap #7

- Remember that the market is our enemy, constantly pulling us into an emotional, short-term outlook based on recent price action and events. Fight it. Successful investing is based on a rational, long-term outlook based on life goals. Whenever the market has a period of rapid rise or fall, consciously shift your focus to your long-term goals (the Slide Show Method, Chapter 2, is a great means of doing so). This will break the hold the market has on you and automatically reset the proper outlook.

- The market exerts a relentless force on our psyches. It takes a certain vigilance on our parts to resist this force. Make conscious your personal stress triggers and stress reactions. What are the types of events that provoke you into impulsivity (e.g., scary geopolitical events, all-time lows, sudden drops)? How does your body react when it is experiencing this stress (e.g., tight neck, headaches, sleeplessness)? Write these triggers and reactions down (see the section "Being Triggered" in Chapter 4). Keep them handy. It may be useful to build them into a Financial Stress Management Plan—more on that in the next chapter.

- Think of the market as a thriller and employ the same tactics you would watching any scary story unfold. Use rational data to pull you back to a long-term perspective. Remind yourself that you've seen this before. And when necessary, take a cue from the successful marshmallow resisters: Avert your eyes, sit on your hands, whistle a tune.

Trap #8: Overconfidence

Are you a good person (above average)? Would you say you have a better-than-average sense of humor? Do you consider yourself a good driver? If you answered "yes," then you can be sure of two things: You have something in common with 4 out of 5 people, and some of you are wrong.

It's a phenomenon that behavioral finance researchers cheekily call "The Lake Wobegon Effect," named after the fictional town created by humorist Garrison Keillor in which all the school children "test above average."

There is nothing inherently wrong about this tendency to hold ourselves in high regard. Having positive self-opinions is a good thing. It's not only normal, it's healthy for our general functioning. But there's no score for "general functioning." There is score-keeping in the markets. And being wrong has immediate and serious consequences.

There is a distinction worth making here. The trap of overconfidence does not pertain to what we believe to be our own sense of financial knowledge. The vast majority of the people invested in stocks could not read a balance sheet or explain what a "cup and handle" chart pattern means. Most of them will readily admit that they are "no experts" when it comes to investing. Nonetheless, those very same investors do make decisions, and those decisions are based on judgments.

Novices and experts alike form opinions constantly (e.g., "the dollar is going down," "oil prices are going up," or "China is the future"). Whether they have MBAs in finance from Wharton does not deter the forming of such opinions, nor from having the conviction that those opinions are right. And it is at this much more general level—belief in our own judgment (our "rightness"), regardless of our perceived level of sophistication—that overconfidence undermines our investing.

So although novice investors make many fewer judgments than professional traders, they tend to be no less confident in them. In fact, their certainty may even be buffeted by their selectivity (e.g., "I never do this, but . . .").

When it comes to predicting market moves, when people believe their predictions will be right 90 percent of the time, they're actually wrong half the time. And when people believe they are 99 percent likely to be right about a prediction, they're still wrong 30 percent of the time.[4]

In many areas of life such overconfidence is inconsequential. But consider the implications of such miscalibration when it comes to investing. When people say "I'm 99 percent sure," what they're saying is, "I'm as sure as I can be without literally knowing it"—and they're still wrong 3 out of 10 times. If you were to base investing decisions every year on this type of certainty, you are essentially guaranteeing that several times a decade you are going to suffer shocking losses.

This phenomenon is in no way limited to investing. To see the tragic results of such miscalibration you need look no further than the disastrous flooding of New Orleans after Hurricane Katrina in 2005. The levee holding back the water of Lake Ponchartrain from spilling into the bowl of New Orleans was considered safe. It was built to withstand a "200-year storm" (i.e., the type of storm that would come once every 200 years). The Army Corps of Engineers reckoned such a storm to be a Category 5 hurricane. Considering how many storms hit the Gulf of Mexico; what were the odds it would happen? If five hurricanes a year typically reached New Orleans and the levee should withstand a "200-year storm," the odds one of them would breach the levee would be roughly 1 in 1,000 (5 times 200). But what are the *chances* it would happen . . . it was inevitable.

Avoiding Trap #8

- Never buy into a position without hearing and digesting the best arguments against buying that position. Because this is difficult to do on your own, you should have a friend/

partner/investing professional available to you to perform this invaluable service.

- Remember the times you've been wrong. Of course you don't *think* you need to do your usual due diligence this time, but isn't that also what you thought *last* time?

- Look at your estimate of the worst possible outcome, and triple it.

- Cultivate humility. The most profitable personality trait in the MarketPsych Investing Personality test is Openness. Interestingly, investors who score highly in Openness are most likely to disagree with the question, "Compared to others, I am an excellent investor." Perhaps open people are good investors because they are flexible and humble.

Trap #9: Herding

There is safety in numbers. It's a concept so simple even sheep can relate to it. And that's part of the problem. We know that "the herd" tends to underperform.

How is this so? Because it always feels safer to invest when the market is up, and scarier when the market is down. Mutual fund managers are a bright lot, but they are not immune to this hard-wired phenomenon, so they are more likely to buy into positions at higher than optimal points (thus diminishing potential gains) and to sell at lower than optimal points (thus increasing losses). The common investor is even more susceptible to this. As more people want to buy a stock or fund, their buying pressure drives the price up, which in turn causes more people to want to buy it. The action of the herd creates the self-perpetuating "buy low, sell high" cycle we call "Whack-a-Mole" syndrome.

In fact, high fund inflows into the markets generally means a plateau or top is forming. The phenomenon is similar to the world of music from your younger days: If your mom knows the name of the band, then they're probably not that cool anymore.

When times are good, the market is a party, and we don't want to be left out. An oft-cited motivation for investing is "keeping up with the Joneses." But our desire to follow the crowd need not be considered covetous or vain. When we see others participating in a market and doing well, our most prudent selves see the potential for an opportunity that it would be foolish to miss. And each day the market rises, the 'gnawing sensation that we are letting a good opportunity pass us by becomes stronger. It is a difficult force to resist.

When times are bad, we follow the crowd to protect ourselves. There is a concept in social psychology called the *diffusion of responsibility*. It may be best thought of this way: Responsibility is a burden; the more people we have lifting that burden (e.g., joining us in our opinions, our actions), the less we feel its weight. (See "But everybody was doing it!" in Chapter 1.)

Herding is a natural way we defend ourselves from negative feelings. It is far easier to console ourselves knowing that we invested in something widely held (and thus respected) than in an obscure holding. There is an old expression among money managers, "No one ever got fired for buying General Electric." But you need not be a professional with his job on the line to appreciate the benefits of herding. It is a lot easier to tell your in-laws, "I took a big loss in IBM this year," than, "I took a big loss on McKenzie-Butterworth Applied Metallurgy, a small family-operated zinc mining operation based in Moose Jaw, Saskatchewan." The former elicits a knowing nod, the latter, a quizzical look and possibly a chuckle.

In either case herding is a trap. Its lure is that it protects us from feeling regret. Nobody wants to feel pain. But perhaps the only thing worse than external pain (e.g., the financial loss) is the internal pain of knowing it was your fault. That's the nature of regret—the emotional insult from financial injury.

Avoiding Trap #9

- While the concept of a strong investor identity is an antidote to every manner of investing poison, it may be most plainly so in the case of herding. The best way to overcome peer pressure is to feel secure enough about who we are and what we do so that we don't worry about others' opinions. Build this strength of identity by working through the chapters and insights in this book.
- Look past money as an end in and of itself and focus at every turn on your personal goals. Other people's actions are irrelevant to yours. How could they know what your vision is for the future, what you want out of life?
- We know a couple of things when it comes to investing in the markets. Individual investors reliably underperform the

market in their own portfolios. They do so because they tend to follow one another's lead (money flowing into mutual funds often indicate market tops, money flowing out of mutual funds often precedes market gains. Yet it is still hard to resist—unless you adopt a nonconformist streak as part of your investing persona. So nurture the part of you that is a rebel, the part of you that says, "If everyone's doing it, then it's no longer in style."

Trap #10: Hindsight Bias

We work with a lot of financial advisors, and one of their greatest sources of frustration is working with clients who have "20/20 hindsight." The hindsight bias is the tendency to see past events as more predictable than actually were. It is underlaid by regret and the belief that things would have been different *if only* . . . (e.g., for a market decline, "Why didn't I take profits? I knew we should have sold last year." For a market rally, "Why am I in cash? I knew the market was going to come back. Don't you remember me saying so?").

Many investors are looking back with regret on the investment decisions they made during the financial crisis—both their panicked selling and the missed opportunities to buy at the bottom. When we feel such strong regret, we look for explanations in order to "normalize" those feelings. With the hindsight bias we "rationalize" that we knew what to do all along, in order to feel a greater sense of control and expertise.

The problem is, if we "knew it all along," then we don't need to make any changes to do it better next time. We don't learn from our mistakes. The hindsight bias creates a false sense that you missed out on something you "should" have had, which can lead to overly aggressive response to the next perceived opportunity.

One point worth noting about the hindsight bias is that it isn't a case of lying. We sincerely believe we "knew better" at the time. When you really, truly "know better," you act on that thought. But it seems that way to investors because *part* of them really did believe the move was going to happen. But that part was outvoted by a stronger voice that didn't.

If you've ever mitigated a dispute between two people, you will find that if you only listen to one side of the story, that person seems right. You need to hear from both parties to make an informed judgment. The hindsight bias is like an argument in which, at the time of decision, there are two sides to the story, but after the "outcome" only one side gets a voice. And once the "winner" has the microphone, you'll never hear "I got lucky," or "We could do that 10 more times and get the opposite result." All you'll hear is, "See? I told you so!"

Investor thinking distorted by the hindsight bias often includes blame—typically toward a financial advisor or negligent spouse (who failed to be available for emotional baby-sitting during the crisis), which is why it is important to challenge such thinking. It leads to frustration, recklessness, and the deterioration of relationships (and spontaneously subscribing to Mr. X's amazing market forecasting machine) when not resolved.

Avoiding Trap #10

- Remember that it was a confusing time during the crisis (as it was during any crisis). We recall hearing opinions in every direction, from impending Armageddon to the best time to buy in our lifetimes. There was serious conversation about the benefits of stockpiling ammunition and gold in the mountains.
- On March 9, 2009, the *Wall Street Journal* ran a headline stating, "Dow 5000? A Bearish Possibility—Strategists Still See Rally, but Earnings Point to 1995 Levels for Stocks." When the *Journal* headlines are as ambivalent as that, it's bound to drive people to sell. Get real with yourself about the decisions you made—some were good and some not so much.
- It's essential to create a plan to guide your investment actions during times when the markets are at extremes. The Financial Stress Management Plan is introduced for this purpose in Chapter 7.
- Remember, we're all human. We do our best with the information we have. Doctors prescribe medicine knowing there are potential side effects, and they hope that the medicines will do more good than harm, but sometimes it just doesn't turn out that way. Same with your investments. Be humble.

MarketPsych's Investing Traps Worksheet

This checklist is intended to help investors detect the presence of 10 different investment traps (a.k.a blind spots or biases) that hurt performance. Read the questions and check off the statements that accurately describe your behavior or preferences. Do you recognize any of the following warning signs? Do you . . .

Trap #1: Win/Lose Mentality

❑ Use personal "winning/losing" language when speaking of your investments (e.g., "I don't want to give back any of my winnings")?

❑ Feel tempted to trade in and out of stocks after quick moves?

❑ Think the expression "I can't stand to lose" applies to your investing style?

❑ Notice small gains (e.g., "Company X is up 3 percent this week")?

❑ Make moves to capitalize on short-term trends in order to get more "winners" in your portfolio?

❑ When sitting on a short-term 20 percent gain, tempted to set up new profit-taking rules to lock it in (e.g., "If it drops to 15 percent I'm going to sell")?

❑ Express concern that you've made "too much" in too short a time?

❑ Feel that a 10 percent correction probably heralds a bigger change in the markets?

Total check marks for Trap # 1: _____

Trap #2: Down with the Ship Syndrome

❑ Frequently find yourself thinking/hoping that losing positions will come back "eventually"?

❑ Have difficulty recognizing/admitting errors in judgment?

❑ Think in terms of wanting to redeem yourself for past investing mistakes?

❑ Find yourself wanting to "just break even" or get your money back before selling a position?

❑ Think in terms of sunk costs (e.g., "It's down X . . . no point in selling it now")?

❑ Have a habit of avoiding looking at or mentioning underperforming assets?

❑ Ever find yourself paralyzed or unable to make a sell decision?

Total check marks for Trap # 2: _____

Trap #3: Anchoring

- ❑ Often label a stock by a historic price (e.g., "It was a $90 stock," "It's a $35 stock")?
- ❑ Often refer to your purchase price when discussing your positions?
- ❑ Find your mind-set being influenced when people make big, bold predictions (e.g., Dow "36,000!")?
- ❑ Like to use company forecasts or analyst price projections as reference points?
- ❑ Often think in terms of how much money you need to catch up to the amount you used to have?
- ❑ Like to consider all-time highs or lows when discussing the merits of a position?

Total check marks for Trap # 3: _____

Trap #4: Mean Reversion Bias

- ❑ Believe that if the market has gone up for two years in a row, the next year is more likely to be a negative one than a positive one?
- ❑ Believe that if the indexes have gone up for several months in a row, they are due for a bad month?
- ❑ Believe that a rally of 20 percent could be considered "overextended"?
- ❑ Ever use the phrase "It can't go down much further" in reference to a stock/fund?
- ❑ Often look to buy stocks on dips?

Total check marks for Trap # 4: _____

Trap #5: Endowment Effect

- ❑ Seem reluctant to change positions that you have inherited?
- ❑ Demonstrate an emotional attachment to investments?
- ❑ Frequently express "loving" certain companies, stocks, or products?
- ❑ Equate good companies with good stocks?
- ❑ Have trouble taking profits?
- ❑ Consistently give back gains you have made on positions, turning "big" gains into "small" gains or worse?

❑ Speak about owned investments in affectionate, possessive terms while speaking of unowned investments more analytically?

Total check marks for Trap # 5: _____

Trap #6: Media Hype Effect

❑ Watch financial news shows or read investment news articles frequently?
❑ Refer to recent news items/opinions when discussing your portfolio plans?
❑ Catch yourself using terms like "I keep hearing" or "I keep seeing" when referring to what influences your opinions?
❑ Ever think of repositioning investments due to topics recently in the news (gold rally, oil highs, biotech breakthroughs, China emergence)?
❑ Enjoy talking about popular stocks or markets with your friends/advisor?

Total check marks for Trap # 6: _____

Trap #7 Short-Termism

❑ Check the status of your portfolio on a daily basis?
❑ Ever fret about adjusting your long-term plans based on short-term events (e.g., a geopolitical event, a Fed move)?
❑ Have difficulty articulating long-term goals and visions for the future?
❑ Have significant debt (such as credit card balances or home equity borrowings) that you have trouble paying off in full?
❑ Frequently worry about current events as real threats to your long-term wealth?

Total check marks for Trap # 7: _____

Trap #8: Overconfidence

❑ Make predictions of short-term price moves with confidence?
❑ Feel comfortable predicting market moves within strict parameters or in terms of large numbers (e.g., "I think the Dow industrials will be between 13,500 and 13,700 by year end")?

❑ Say "I knew that was going to happen!" when you see market/
stock gains in positions you considered investing in, but didn't?

❑ Have difficulty recalling predictions that did not pan out?

❑ Have trouble identifying flaws or vulnerabilities in your
investing approach?

❑ Tend to attribute wins to your being right, but losses to bad
luck?

❑ Rate your investing ability to be in the top 20 percent?

Total check marks for Trap # 8: _____

Trap #9: Herding

❑ Use absolute terms such as "everybody" or "nobody" when
referring to what the market at large is doing?

❑ Regularly refer to the opinions of others when discussing
what you should do?

❑ Tend to dismiss investing options if you don't know anyone
who has invested in that way?

❑ Reference the opinions of media "experts" or sources when
suggesting preferred investments?

❑ Feel eager to invest in market trends?

❑ Believe in the "wisdom of crowds"?

❑ Find the thought of being left out of a market upswing a lot
more painful if you think your acquaintances or colleagues
made money from it?

Total check marks for Trap # 9: _____

Trap #10: Hindsight Bias

❑ Reminisce about a conversation in which you called a recent
bottom accurately?

❑ Use phrases like "it was obvious" in reference to predicting
past market moves?

❑ Enjoy making predictions in both the financial markets and
in other areas (e.g., sports, politics, the Oscars, etc.)?

❑ Make statements such as, "I knew I should have bought more
at the bottom. Don't you remember me telling you?"

❑ Believe that if only you had followed a guru's ("Mr. X's")
advice, then you would have made money after all

("Mr. X's software called the bottom. I knew I should have been following his advice.")?

❑ Vaguely wish that things had been different ("I wish someone had told me not to sell.")?

❑ Have accusatory thoughts ("I knew I shouldn't have sold. I thought it was [my advisor's, my wife's, etc.] job to keep me from panicking with my retirement savings.")?

Use the following score sheet to assess your risk levels for different traps.

What's Your Score?

For each trap, circle the number of check marks that applied to you.

	All Clear	Problem	Danger!
Trap #1: Win/Lose Mentality	0–2	3–4	5+
Trap #2: Down with the Ship	0–2	3–4	5+
Trap #3: Anchoring	0–1	2–3	4+
Trap #4: Mean Reversion Bias	0–1	2–3	4+
Trap #5: Endowment Effect	0–1	2–3	4+
Trap #6: Media Hype Effect	0–1	2–3	4+
Trap #7: Short-Termism	0–1	2–3	4+
Trap #8: Overconfidence	0–2	3–4	5+
Trap #9: Herding	0–1	2–3	4+
Trap#10: Hindsight	0–2	3–4	5+

Dangerous Profiles

Now look at the circles in the "Danger!" column only. Following is a list of dangerous profiles, archetypes of investors who consistently fall prey to market traps. Some of them may be familiar to you.

If you're in the danger zone for:

Traps #1–2, you are like **The Wicked Gardener**.

Traps #4–8, you are like **The Roulette Player**.

Traps #2–3–5, you are like **Corporal Clinger**.

Traps #6–7, you are like **Mr. Magoo**.

Traps #7–8–10, you are like **Maxwell Smart**.

Profile: The Wicked Gardener.   If you were to grow a garden, would you constantly clip your flowers and let your weeds run wild? Of course not. But that's exactly what this profile tends to do. These investors get the name Wicked Gardener because when tending to their garden (portfolio), they are quick to trim any flower that blooms (positions that post gains), but they ignore (hold on to) or worse yet, water (buy more of) their weeds (bad positions). In the end, the Wicked Gardener is doomed to owning a portfolio cluttered with bad holdings.

Ironically the reason why they find themselves bogged down with losing positions is that they hate losing so much. They find the prospect of losing so dreadful that they will go to extreme lengths to avoid it. You can see why this is so insidious. When a position has any sort of gain, the Wicked Gardener sells it to guarantee a win (and eliminate any chance of loss). But when a position drifts down, they can't bring themselves to sell it and realize the loss. They would rather convince themselves the position will eventually come back. It is usually a long and lonely wait. During bull markets Wicked Gardeners get very excited and look to repeatedly cash in. They may even be euphoric. But in bear markets losing positions collect like dust in a corner, becoming eternal reminders of their mistakes. They use denial as a defense mechanism. It may not seem so outwardly, but a Wicked Gardener's investing identity is fraught with self-esteem issues. After all, people with strong egos can handle losses and feel okay about themselves. It's fragile people who cannot.

Actions to Take: If you find that you're in the danger zone (or nearly so) on this profile scale, consider these actions:

- Have clear goals. Set hard and inviolable rules about stop losses, for example, "If a position loses 10 percent I will sell, no matter what, even though I won't want to."
- Install a system of rewards and punishments. If you stick to your rules, do something nice for yourself (e.g., buy yourself a book, pick up some good steaks, get a pedicure—whatever works). If you do not follow the rules, censure yourself (send a $20 check to someone, write "Next time I will follow the

rules" on a piece of paper 100 times, agree to clean out the garage on Saturday afternoon).

- Work with a partner/advisor who will hold you accountable. This tip is important to ensure the last tip gets followed. Involving/reporting to another person is the best way to ensure we will be held accountable. We love to let ourselves off the hook. But our partners love enforcing the rules even more.
- Cultivate the philosophy that what separates great investors from the rest is their ability to take smaller losses and avoid big ones.

Profile: Corporal Clinger.   The original Corporal Klinger was a character on the television show *M*A*S*H*. He was known for trying to get himself declared "Section 8" (insane) so that he could get a discharge from the army. Corporal Clingers are afflicted by a lesser madness—the inability to change their portfolios for the better. Corporal Clingers, as the name suggests, cling to their holdings. They may seem to be apathetic or even lazy investors (and perhaps they are), but often these qualities mask a fear of change. The status quo feels safer to them because change means embracing the unknown. The devil you know is better than the devil you don't. Subsequently, Corporal Clingers form strong attachments to what they possess, the better to justify their inaction.

Corporal Clingers also have a difficult time taking profits. They often allow a position to give back all its gains and more. If they have inherited a position, they will likely accept it as is, regardless of whether it is appropriate for their goals. Changing to the status quo also creates the potential for regret, and regret is felt strongest when it is associated with action, rather than inaction. Regret is feeling responsible for one's pain (e.g., "What if I'm wrong?" "I did this to myself!" "It's all my fault!"). This may be their greatest fear of all.

Actions to Take

- Because actively doing something is hard, install "autopilot" functions with your portfolio. Often a person can't commit to taking an action today, but he or she can commit to doing so in the future. Agree to set up a schedule of change for future buying/selling/reweighting that is done automatically.

- Structure a portfolio that plays to your strengths. The ability to stay the course is a good thing. Invest in vehicles that you consider steady, long-term holdings, which you never should feel compelled to sell.
- Start off small. Part of the problem with this archetype is that they tend to view investments in terms of black and white. It may be intimidating to them to relinquish a large position. That's okay. Agree to changing only a small—even comically small, 2 percent—part of an existing position to break the status quo.

Profile: Mr. Magoo.   "Oh, Magoo! You've done it again!" Many of us remember this cartoon character and his signature catch phrase from our youth. Mr. Magoo could hardly see two feet in front of himself, and his stubborn refusal to wear his eyeglasses brought him to the brink of disaster in every episode—all without his realizing it. The Mr. Magoo investing profile has "financial myopia." This profile can only focus on what's directly in front of them, what's happening *now*. Mr. Magoos have a very difficult time thinking about the future, let alone imagining how they will feel in the future. They may keep up on all the news and even be able to tell you the value of their portfolio to the dollar on any given day. This also means they get drawn into today's drama, worrying about the crisis du jour.

Actions to Take

- Create visions for the future. Develop vivid dreams and goals that you can not only articulate, but actually visualize. Use them as beacons that can lead your focus out of the foggy present and into the future. (The Slide Show Method in Chapter 2 may be useful in this regard.)
- Continually draw your focus to the long term. Relentlessly frame conversations in terms of what decisions will mean 10, 20, 30 years from now.
- Pay less attention to the financial news. Give yourself time outs, if need be. Devote time instead to hobbies or other projects.
- Keep handy examples that demonstrate how even after the worst disasters in history, the market has rewarded those with the courage to be in it.

Profile: The Roulette Player.   This profile gets its name from the casino game that most exploits what behavioral finance researchers call "the gambler's fallacy"; that past events independent of one another can somehow yield useful information about future events. Nowhere is this fallacy illustrated more clearly than in roulette. A roulette wheel has 18 numbers in black and 18 in red, so the chance of getting a red number is the same as the chance of getting a black number—1 to 1 odds. But imagine the roulette wheel comes up red for seven consecutive spins. Is the roulette wheel "due" to yield a black number, or is the roulette wheel more likely to continue its remarkable streak? The answer is "neither." The odds of the next number coming up red vs. black haven't changed. It's still 50/50. But many gamblers are inclined to place their next bet based on what they've just witnessed.

The Roulette Player investor profile falls into a version of this trap by witnessing random (usually recent) price action or market movements and using it to forecast the immediate future. The genesis of the problem is the same: an inability to grasp probability and randomness in the face of events that don't conform to our expectations. The Roulette Player doesn't appreciate that independent events (e.g., coin flips) give no indication of what will happen next. Instead, they peer into the data as a mystic peers into a cup of tea leaves, seeing meaningful patterns where none exist. Then they base their decisions on those imagined patterns, often overreaching or veering off plan in the process.

Actions to Take

- Education on the actual effect of regression to the mean. It is a widely misunderstood concept, but there are certain examples that explain its true nature. (For example, the baseball home run example. If a player has a track record of averaging 30 home runs a year, and at the midpoint he has 0 home runs, does this mean your best guess should be that he will hit 30 home runs in the second half? No. The best guess is that he will hit 15 home runs. That's his expected average for half a season.) Maintain a future focus. The problem with the Roulette Player is they love to look backwards at irrelevant data.
- Cultivate a "positive uncertainty," that is, you don't know what will happen next, but you are optimistic and prepared for whatever it is.

- Broaden your time perspective. The only trends that matter are long-term trends. Concentrate instead on time-tested market movement such as the rolling 20-year data that indicate the markets are reliable over sufficient time frames.

Profile: Maxwell Smart.   The would-be superspy Maxwell Smart is a true television icon. He was well-known for the humorous catch phrases that he'd use to demonstrate his competence: "Missed it by *that* much!" "Ah, the old *(insert comically unlikely series of events here)* trick, I knew it all along!" Of course, the joke was that he always "missed it" by a mile and never saw trouble coming.

The eponymous character from the show *Get Smart!* was always good for a laugh. But the investor profile named after him is decidedly less funny. The Maxwell Smart profile demonstrates a dangerous mixture of short-term focus and overconfidence. The short-term focus leads to micromanaging and overtrading, and the overconfidence leads to stubbornness in the face of failure.

Maxwell Smarts are convinced not only that they possesses rare gifts for spotting investing opportunities, but also that they are well equipped to get in early and out at the right time. They are often active traders who take a sizable chunk of their portfolio to invest for this reason. Maxwell Smarts enjoy sharing their numerous trading successes. They tend not to share, or even acknowledge, their many failures.

Part of the reason they indulge themselves to such an extent is what's known as the hindsight bias, a distortion in which we look back at information and are convinced we "saw it coming" or, at the very least, should have. It wouldn't be so bad a flaw, hindsight being 20/20 and all, except that it makes it very difficult for us to learn from our mistakes. It also means that we want so badly to be right that we will distort, cherry-pick, and rationalize in order to feel right, a phenomenon behavioral finance researchers call the confirmation bias.

Actions to Take

- One way to humble Maxwell Smart is to keep score. Maxwell Smarts tend to discount their failures and play up successes. Keeping a journal of both performance and predictions is a great way to generate a more accurate portrait of their trading and forecasting abilities.

- Active trading works out poorly for most who attempt it. But the impulse to do so is a strong one for many people, akin to a gambling compulsion. Carving off a small, very manageable portion of a portfolio that is dedicated to keeping score is a way to indulge competitive impulses and the desire to be involved. By all means, keep score. It may even be fun to form a club with friends and turn it into a friendly competition. The key is that in trading this dedicated portion of the portfolio, you can limit the potential for damage and create the structure necessary so that you will not be tempted to borrow from the nest egg.

Conclusion

One of the most important tasks you've undertaken in this book is learning to identify your weaknesses. That attention to danger is how we keep ourselves safe. But your weaknesses exist precisely for the reason that they are so hard to recognize. Investing is a little like driving. When driving, we know that the most dangerous place another car can be is in our "blind spot." But what applies to automobile crashes applies to portfolio and market crashes as well. It behooves all investors to become well acquainted with their own blind spots, those places most likely to lead to wealth-sapping mistakes.

Behavioral finance has done a great job of bringing these various, usually systematic, biases to light. The next step is recognizing how and when they apply to us, and further, determining the ways we can overcome them.

This chapter detailed 10 of the most common (and fiendish) investor traps that bedevil our attempts to accumulate wealth. Many may already be familiar to you, others entirely new. We encourage you to take the self-assessment in this chapter to see the ways these biases may be present in you—to probe for your blind spots. If you find that you fit one of the archetypical profiles, don't worry. They are meant to be illustrative of the concepts and colorful enough for you to remember them. What they are not meant to be is a certification of incompetence guaranteeing investing failure. In fact, it is far better to learn of your susceptibility to these investor traps than it is to carry on unaware that you may be engaging in them. This latter state captures the vast majority of the investing population.

Lastly, we hope you'll consider some of the prescriptions detailed in response to the profiles. They go a long way toward righting, mitigating, and preventing the effects of the afore-mentioned pitfalls. One such prescription that has appeared numerous times throughout the book has been the value of working with a financial advisor/trusted partner. Sometimes the easiest way to avoid or recover from a destructive behavior is for someone to tell us, "You're doing it again." The task of the remaining chapters in this book is to help you create structures and habits that prevent the financial damage of reactive emotions, misaligned values, and thought traps. As you'll see in the next chapter, stress predisposes investors to make emotion-driven mistakes and succumb to mental traps. Setting up a long-term stress management plan and learning exercises to reduce short-term stress are essential for long-term financial stability.

CHAPTER

Your Investor Stress: Smoothing Out the Ups and Downs

Brain cells create ideas. Stress kills brain cells. Stress is not a good idea.

—Frederick Saunders

Dan came to see Dr. Peterson at his coaching practice for an unusual—and improbable—complaint: He had lost money in each of his last 17 investments He was deeply concerned because he loved to manage his own money.

Being familiar with statistics, Dan understood that it's rare to be wrong by a substantial margin 17 times in a row. To put this in perspective, the odds of losing 10 coin flips in a row is 1 in 1,024. And though investing is not the same as flipping a coin, Dan had blown through 17 consecutive risk/reward scenarios without winning. And the streak was still going. Confounding matters was that his investments were scattered across different asset classes and were made during both bull and bear markets. It didn't seem to matter when and where he put his money, he still lost.

Dan was a rational person, but these losses had affected him to the extent that he was beginning to believe "God hates me," and he felt dejected and depressed most days.

So what was Dan's approach? He told Dr. Peterson that he was a fundamental investor who bought stocks and commodities cheaply and sold them for a profit as the market appreciated their true value. Dan enjoyed investing in "penny stocks" trading under $1 per share, because that was where he often saw good value.

As Dan was explaining his buy and sell techniques, it became clear that he wasn't actually using the discipline he was describing. Dr. Peterson dug a bit deeper, and this is what Dan related: "I buy when a potential investment I'm watching starts to take off." And when did he sell? "Well, I guess I sell if it reverses." And why did he invest like this? "Well, I guess the losses are changing me. I'm just reacting to the markets now. I've kind of lost focus."

Dan's problem was not statistically outrageous "bad luck." Nor did God "hate" him (as far anyone can tell). And for the record, he had not been cursed by a voodoo priestess nor recently built a home on a sacred burial ground. There was a much simpler explanation for his troubles: stress. Stress that manifested itself in predictable, consistent reactions to price moves that virtually guaranteed losses. When short-term stress arises, usually suddenly and without warning, its mental effects are such that we have great difficulty taking action to relieve it *internally* without taking some action *externally*. Yet too often, those stress-relieving external actions are extreme behaviors such as rapid-fire trading or avoidance of the problem entirely. The most challenging aspect of short-term stress is the inability to *see outside* of it—to gain *perspective*. Stress hormones focus our attention in the short term, which makes sense biologically. Our minds want us to be attentive to potential threats *right now*. Ironically, in the financial markets, it's stressful short-term "price fakes" that often shake us out of our long-term plans

In general, there are three ways of addressing and reducing the impact of stress on investment decisions:

1. Inoculate yourself from the mental effects of stress with a preventive lifestyle.
2. Learn and utilize immediate stress-relief techniques when stress or tension are present.
3. Plan ahead for stressful periods using a Financial Stress Management Plan.

Theoretically, it should be straightforward to manage stress and anxiety. Unfortunately, anxiety is like an iceberg. Ninety percent of it lies beneath conscious awareness.

As you go through this chapter, consider the ways that stress affects you and how you could reduce its effects on your life. In this chapter we offer techniques for minimizing stress and worry. An entire chapter is needed about these emotions because they are the leading cause of investing mistakes. On the other hand, frightened traders create some of the best opportunities for courageous long-term investors.

Stress: An Overview

Stress is the condition that results when person-environment transactions lead the individual to perceive a discrepancy—whether real or not—between the demands of a situation and the resources of the person's biological, psychological or social systems.

—Edward P. Sarafino[1]

Stress arises out of a conflict between expectations and reality. It's stressful if we expect a result that we just can't achieve, and it's stressful if we're stuck in a situation that is becoming worse by the day. It's also stressful if we feel that we can't control our financial future, which is the uncomfortable feeling most investors have when markets are volatile.

At low levels stress can be motivating: It stimulates activity, sharpens attention, and drives positive action. Even brief episodes of high or moderate stress, such as experienced during an amusement park roller-coaster ride or during competition, can be exhilarating. For most people, moderate stress, over a short period, feels good. Successfully coping with moderate stress can have beneficial physical and emotional effects.

At extreme levels, stress can induce an overwhelming fight or flight urge (panic). Even worse is prolonged high stress, which leads to a number of negative physical and mental consequences. Such chronic stress impairs short-term memory and concentration, contributes to accelerated aging, decreases immune function, disrupts sleep cycles, raises blood pressure, depresses mood, induces apathy, and diminishes energy. Eventually, chronic stress results in "burnout."

Every investor experiences stress at some point during his or her career. Stress would be of little consequence if it weren't for two important facts:

1. Stress alters how we think.
2. Many of the most important decisions of our lives are made while we are stressed.

Make no mistake, many choices that alter the courses of our financial lives—entering large investments, enduring major panic selling, and the decision to forgo adequate due diligence on an investment—are often driven by stress. Outside of investing, life-changing decisions such as whom to marry, when to have children, what city to live in, and what university major to choose are often made when we're feeling stress and uncertainty.

Physical Effects of Stress

"Traders age in dog years."

The above saying, heard on many trading floors, gets to the essence of what chronic stress does to the body and brain.

Investors dwell in a state of continual short-term uncertainty. And for most investors, worry is a constant companion. Yet worry about what you cannot control not only wears you down, it keeps your attention riveted on the negative. You could say that worrying is like praying for what you don't want. And stressing about what you cannot control only impairs your ability to make solid plans for overcoming it.

For example, researchers found that dogs who were given electric shocks that they could terminate by making body motions got fewer ulcers than "yoked" dogs who were given identical but uncontrollable sequences of shocks.[2] (And no, we're not fans of that study either.) Our perceived ability to exert some control over a noxious event reduces the amount of worry and distress we experience.

Another danger of stress and worry is that it induces passivity. Chronic stress decreases motivation and saps the drive to take effective action. All the more reason to plan ahead now for those future times when investment stress softens your willpower.

Importantly, researchers have found that many people are willing to suffer immediate adverse consequences now, such as a higher-voltage electric shock, rather than wait patiently for a lower-voltage electric shock up to a minute later.[3] Apparently the anxiety they suffer while waiting for the lower-voltage shock is so painful that they simply choose to "get it over with" with the more painful shock now. This is how investor panic functions in the markets. Panic relieves stress, tension, and anxiety, regardless of the fact that its long-term consequences are significantly more damaging to one's long-term wealth.

To manage investment stress, control must be exerted where it will have an effect, such as in designing consistent money management systems, performing superior research, establishing a solid investment philosophy, creating a financial stress management plan, and communicating appropriately with one's advisor. As we have noted throughout this book, successful investors orient their investing in terms of a consistent process-oriented frame as opposed to a short-term outcome-orientation. Yet worry and stress draw us into short-term thinking. Keep in mind that we generally cannot control our short-term results in the markets, but we can successfully manage our long-term investment process by planning ahead and keeping a long-term life-focused frame of mind.

Choking

In the financial markets, there is no room to "choke"—to let anxiety interfere with optimal performance. Yet choking always becomes a threat when the stakes (and one's performance anxiety) are high.

Duke University professor Dan Ariely, author of the best-selling book *Predictably Irrational* (Harper Perennial, 2010), performed experiments on the nature of "choking" in high-pressure situations. He set up a scenario in which individuals performed athletic and mathematical tasks for financial rewards several times their average monthly salaries. He found that financial incentives were motivating and improved performance, up to a point. Beyond a certain level of potential gain (approximately one month's salary) individuals could not manage their anxiety, and their performance deteriorated.[4]

Such high-stakes scenarios often occur among investment bankers trying to clinch an unprecedented deal or when people are competing for a large windfall.

With 14 gold medals, Michael Phelps is considered one of the best athletes in history. Even he uses anxiety management techniques to prevent "choking" in response to performance anxiety. For Phelps, the techniques he uses have become integrated into his daily life.

"Phelps's coach, Bob Bowman, says 'structured relaxation' has been a part of Phelps's prerace routine since he was 12 and is instrumental to his success."[5]

Bowman introduced Phelps to a progressive relaxation program based on the recitation of cues. Every night before Phelps went to sleep, his mother, Debbie, would sit with him in his dimly lighted bedroom and work with him to relax different parts of his body.

After a while, Phelps could relax without his mother's cues, and he became expert at placing himself in a meditative state in the ready room before a race. Once he had cleared his mind and loosened his limbs, Phelps would swim each race over and over in his mind.

It is not just the perfect race that Phelps pictured. He saw himself overcoming every conceivable obstacle to achieve his ideal time. As a result, when he stood on the starting blocks he felt as if nothing could stand in the way of his success.

"I do go through everything from a best-case scenario to the worst-case scenario just so I'm ready for anything that comes my way," Phelps said.[6]

Phelps has internalized structured relaxation exercises because the ability to relax under pressure is one key to his success.

How might performance anxiety trip you up as an investor? If it has been problematic for you, or you anticipate that it could be, it's important to set up a structured relaxation program. The next section contains several structured exercises for managing anxiety.

Managing Short-Term Investment Stress

Bill Gross manages the world's largest bond fund, PIMCO, with over $1 trillion in assets under management. In the run-up to the credit crisis of 2008, due to several warning signals about the economy's overheating and advice from a PIMCO trader, Scott Simon, Gross readjusted his fund's holdings into more conservative Treasury bonds and small positions in CDS mortgage bond insurance.

Gross positioned himself conservatively well in advance of the crisis. In 2006 PIMCO's performance trailed that of its peers. "It made Gross so miserable that he had to take an unplanned nine-day vacation midway through the year; it made Gross so miserable that he spent most of the vacation sitting around the house, sulking to his wife."[7]

"I couldn't turn on the business television; I couldn't pick up the paper. It was just devastating. You can't sleep at night."[8]

The markets are rarely predictable in the short-term, yet investors are almost inevitably drawn into a win/lose, short-term performance game, especially if they have clients who track their daily performance relative to their peers, as did Bill Gross.

Certain types of financial feedback predisposes investors to stress. Traders who watch price quotes tick by tick, or minute by minute, are particularly susceptible to chronic stress and burnout. The more one checks stock quotes, the more likely they are to see volatility. Because the brain, on average, experiences the pain of every downtick with twice as much intensity as the joy of every uptick, the brain undergoes a slow stress erosion. Fortunately, experienced traders have decreased stress responses to market volatility.[9]

To prevent stress when opening your latest account statement or hearing about recent financial calamities on CNBC, plan ahead by instituting predetermined alarm levels (most brokers offer such alarms). Additionally, it can be very helpful to reduce investment "noise" by avoiding financial news that isn't relevant to your investment strategy, and if you're a "buy-and-hold" investor, then essentially all the financial news is irrelevant. Also try to avoid multitasking when researching an investment. That is, determine the three or four pieces of information that matter to your strategy, and don't look at the rest.

Social support diminishes the stress response, and attendance at professional investors groups, such as AAII (American Association of Individual Investors), angel investor groups, CFA Society meetings, the Market Technicians Association, or other organizations can be an excellent source of social support from others dealing with similar challenges in the markets.

Many great investors report that constant information monitoring, although isolating them, helps them identify developing opportunities before others. Yet this type of monitoring is not possible for casual investors. Nonetheless, many part-time investors try to monitor markets frequently, which only increases stress. It's helpful to set strict boundaries on the information you monitor, otherwise it's easy to be pulled into reading excess import into random "noise."

As we've explained in this chapter, as stress levels rise, the brain becomes cognitively inflexible and unable to think of solutions to increasing losses. Suddenly panicking out of bleeding positions may appear the only viable option to reduce tension. As a result, it's important to develop habits that inoculate against stress, thus preventing short-term stress from derailing your long-term plans.

Simple Stress Reduction Techniques

A "short-squeeze" happens when a stock increases rapidly in price, leaving investors with short positions (i.e., bets that the stock will go lower) feeling "squeezed." The desperate buying of "squeezed" shorts itself generates a positive feedback effect, driving a security's price higher. Short-holding veterans of short-squeezes can easily recall the mental mush their brain becomes while witnessing rapidly escalating losses.

The inability to think clearly during a short-squeeze is due to the effects of stress hormones on the brain. Thinking clearly can only occur when stress hormone levels decline. "So how," you ask, "can I reduce stress hormone levels when I'm freaking out, because of a short-squeeze or otherwise?" Excellent question.

Stress and anxiety management techniques that are "preventive"— essentially inoculating you to stress such as meditation, yoga, and exercise routines—require self-discipline and a commitment to practice. Even without such discipline, however, there are immediate stress-reduction techniques that can be used anytime, anywhere, as needed.

The easiest and most immediate technique for relaxation is deep breathing. At Stanford University Dr. Peterson participated in an experiment with facial EMG equipment. This equipment measures arousal in facial muscle tone and skin conductance. At the time of the experiment, after being hooked up to the skin and muscle monitors, Dr. Peterson felt relaxed. He could see a slow-moving pattern of muscle activity languidly tracing across the computer screen. But after taking a deep breath at the request of his instructor, he was amazed that the tracing dropped to the bottom of the graph. He had been extremely tense at baseline, without realizing it. One long deep breath relieved the underlying tension.

Try the following breathing technique. As you inhale, silently count "1-1,000, 2-1,000, 3-1,000," as you smoothly and evenly draw in the breath. Then pause for one second. Then as you exhale, silently countdown "3-1,000, 2-1,000, 1-1,000" breathing out slowly and evenly. After a one-count pause, repeat the cycle. You can repeat this breath-work over a period of as little as five minutes and experience significant stress relief. Remember to do it in a quiet location.

Another way to reduce immediate stress is to consciously reframe your thoughts by putting your current troubles into a long-term, big-picture perspective. Imagine yourself on a mountaintop, and then contemplate the view out over the plains and mountains to the horizon. Or see in your mind the ocean stretching into the distance. Alternatively, imagine yourself looking up at the stars at night while hearing the crackle of a campfire. Slowly feel yourself expanding into the space and sky all around you.

As described previously, Michael Phelps practices structured muscular relaxation. That technique involves sequentially tensing and relaxing the muscles in your body from lower to upper. For example, tighten your feet, hold the tension for a breath, and then slowly relax the muscles. Then tighten your calves, hold the tension for a breath, and then release. Move upward, breath by breath, contracting and releasing your thighs, buttocks, abdomen, hands, arms, chest, shoulders, neck, face, and scalp. When finished sit silently, eyes closed, breathing slowly and evenly, for three to five minutes.

To relax specific tense muscles, such as tight shoulders or neck muscles, try contracting the tense muscles intentionally and holding them firm for several seconds. Then release.

Some aromatherapy scents such as lavender relax the mind. Burning incense and playing soft music have also been shown to reduce stress. Walks in nature and warm baths are usually helpful. Exercise, play, and dance are also methods of short-term stress relief that can become supportive lifetime habits.

Following is a full list of immediate anxiety-reduction techniques:

- Breathing exercises
- Vigorous exercise
- Laughing
- Meditating
- Scheduling a time to "worry"
- Prayer
- Contemplating mystery or the universality of uncertainty
- Psychotherapy techniques, such as cognitive-behavioral therapy
- Herbal remedies such as chamomile tea (a sedative) and lavender aromatherapy
- For clinical anxiety disorders, medications such as selective serotonin reuptake inhibitors (SSRIs), benzodiazepines, and beta blockers can be helpful

While the preceding are short-term stress fixes, it is long-term changes in lifestyle, such as regular exercise, regular sleep habits, meditation, religious practice, cultivating faith, self-analysis, abstinence from alcohol and caffeine, and social affiliation, that cultivate the best long-term stress resilience.

Exercise and diet are the cornerstones of every doctor's recommendations for optimal health. Eating whole grains, lots of fresh vegetables and nuts, and cold-water fish (and other high omega-3 foods containing DHA) all have benefits. Exercise includes anything from strolling to mountain climbing. The general idea with exercise is that you are gradually increasing (or maintaining) the limits of your endurance—exercise should be somewhat challenging, but not painful. Cardiovascular exercise is particularly beneficial for longevity and mental acuity. Exercise releases growth factors, both in the tissues and also in the brain, which enhances new neuronal growth and repair. Along those lines, a varying routine of exercise, in a playful or challenging context such as competitive sports, is especially healthy for the brain. Some forms of moving meditation, such as yoga, include a physical exercise component and so merge the benefits of exercise and meditation.

Meditation, Yoga, and Lifestyle

Meditation refers to a variety of practices that intentionally focus attention, helping the practitioner disengage from unconscious absorption in repetitive and habitual thoughts and feelings. Studies have shown that meditation practice can lead to improved emotional health. There are several styles of meditation. Mindfulness meditation teaches practitioners to nonjudgmentally cultivate present-centered awareness. Such awareness is that in which each thought, feeling, or sensation that arises into consciousness is acknowledged and accepted as it is. Mindfulness meditation has been shown to increase life satisfaction and bolster the immune system (increasing the antibody response to cold viruses).[10]

Concentrative meditation is a second broad type of meditation. It involves focusing on a mantra (phrase or word), image, or object. In various studies of concentrative meditation, such as Vedic meditation and transcendental meditation, it has been shown to improve mood,[11] decrease anxiety,[12] lengthen attention span,[13] and enhance feelings of connectedness, gratitude, and compassion.[14] It makes sense—if we assume that the mind is like a muscle, and we are practicing sustained attention on a daily basis, then the neurons that support concentration and impulse—control will be strengthened. Please see the instruction guide for meditation practice in Appendix A for more information.

Some individual exercises such as yoga train both the mind and the body. Yoga is a discipline developed to "yoke" (the literal meaning of "yoga") the mind. Yoga teaches breathing and meditation skills while simultaneously toning the musculature. Psychological research indicates that yoga reduces the signs and symptoms of anxiety,[15] depression,[16] attention deficit–hyperactivity disorder (ADHD),[17] addiction,[18] and obsessive-compulsive disorder (OCD).[19] Additionally, emotional stability and patience increase during a regular yoga practice.

One of the most taken-for-granted factors in emotional well-being is social connection. Positive social interactions, including in one's work environment, are essential to long-term well-being. For many people, social connections can be easily put aside while work responsibilities dominate, but this is a mistake. Intimate friendships (in which outside problems can be vented) and family support significantly promote mental health.

Tend Your Garden Regularly

Most investors enjoy the rush of trading. They like taking risk and savoring the thrills of the market roller coaster. Does this describe you? If so, you should consider setting aside a small percentage of your total capital for recreational trading ("play money"). This will allow you to get a thrill using a small portion of your total assets without jeopardizing your long-term financial security.

To prevent short-term derailments with your investments, both due to taking excessively high-risk positions or panic selling, it is useful to set up a consistent and regular schedule for monitoring them. If you aren't a short-term trader who can assess the meaning of every bit of breaking news, then it's important to use a long-term scheduled approach to monitoring and adjusting your investments.

For example, many people set aside one weekend during the winter and one during the summer to sit down with family and investing professionals. Such investment review weekends are spent educating children, revisiting current investments, discussing fundamental economic changes, and reallocating investment capital for the next six-month period. In some ways, families who follow such a protocol are teaching their children how to grow capital as if it had been planted in a garden. They are investment farmers, taking their time to review each "plant" and ensure it has adequate sunlight and soil to grow and produce the expected yield. If not, it is pared back and a new plant is grown in its place.

Cognitive-Behavioral Techniques for Long-Term Stress Management

This section is devoted to cognitive-behavioral psychotherapy and stress management techniques. Now, I realize that in the opening of this book we promised to be psychology-jargon-free so we could reconcile with our financier readers. Well, we didn't exactly lie, but we think that some of the jargon is useful and descriptive. That's the case with cognitive-behavioral therapy.

Cognitive-behavioral therapy (CBT) is a popular and effective form of psychotherapy used for everything from getting high-performers out of a slump to the clinical treatment of anxiety, depression, and obsessive-compulsive disorder. CBT therapists help clients develop concrete coping skills and strategies. They use such techniques as:

1. Challenging self-defeating beliefs
2. Teaching positive self-talk skills
3. Replacing negative thoughts with supportive ones
4. Desensitization and conditioning to stressful events
5. Education about symptoms
6. Teaching coping skills such as relaxation breathing

CBT therapists believe that one's thoughts and feelings during stress are often repeating patterns, and they may be leading to habitual, and counterproductive, coping behaviors. If the stressful pattern can be mentally broken, then the unhelpful stress response is halted.

Individuals who use the following guide can more easily learn to identify the maladaptive, stress-inducing thoughts they habitually experience. You can use the following exercises for assistance in challenging your negative or unhelpful thoughts and consciously replacing them with more adaptive ones. If you do conscious thought replacement exercises daily and keep track of the changes you notice in your daily life, you're likely to discover subtle improvements such as milder reactions to usually stressful events, people, and circumstances.

Ask yourself these questions to disrupt negative patterns of thinking that aren't serving you:

- Is there an alternate explanation to the negative one running through my mind for why things aren't working out?
- What is the evidence that my negative thoughts and assumptions are actually true?
- What will be the effect of continuing to think this way (will I not take new opportunities, or assume the worst excessively)?
- Given the bad situation I think I'm in, what is the best outcome, worst outcome, and most realistic outcome?
- What is the likelihood that the worst (best) outcome will happen?[20]

Record your responses to stressful events in a table like Table 7.1 in order to develop a clearer comprehension of how they affect you. The example is from the journal of a professional money manager.

The core skills learned in stress management programs are self-observation, cognitive restructuring (as noted in Table 7.1), relaxation training, time management, and problem solving. Self-observation is often practiced using a daily diary or journal (Table 7.1 can serve this purpose). In the journal, people write down stressful moments of their day in the first column. In the next column, they write down antecedents to the stressful event. In the third column, they document their behavioral reaction, and in the fourth column, they describe the consequences of their behavior. Investors using this strategy can gain awareness of their automatic behavioral patterns, learn to identify the precursors (eventually, they may see repeating patterns), and reduce stress-related biases. Consciously addressing the triggers, reactions, and consequences encourages interruption and eventual prevention of one's usual (and unhelpful) patterns.

Table 7.1 Journal Format for Recording Stress-Related Events

Antecedents (the stressful event and preceding triggers)	Stress Rating (0 to 100)	Behavioral Responses	Consequences (outcome)	Rational response (reframing options)
Example: A series of financial losses	80	*Thoughts:* "My year is ruined. I'm going to lose my best clients. Maybe I'm doing this all wrong." *Feelings:* Frustrated, angry, upset. *Physiological response:* Distractible, tension headache, craving alcohol and sweets, clenching teeth, stomach churning, tight chest. *Behaviors:* Started shouting at an analyst employee for a minor infraction, frequently looking away when in conversation, driving recklessly.	As soon as I realized I was off my plan, I immediately closed out the position. I'll have to work with the loss from here, but at least it's not bleeding anymore. Since closing the position, I've been able to generate a plan for the future. I'm nicer to my family and friends now.	*Rational thought:* "My quarter is what it is. I have strong relationships with my clients, and they trust me. This is the first time anything like this has happened. The markets are inherently uncertain, and I followed the best decision process I am aware of."

Getting Out of a Slump

Many investors, at one time or another, find themselves making consistently bad decisions. Often, a losing streak is simply bad luck, but many investors begin to believe it reflects problems with their strategy or personality. This is one reason why back-testing one's strategy (with the appropriate caveats) is so important—it supports confidence in the strategy during a series of draw-downs. As slumps weaken one's decision making, they may fuel a vicious cycle. In order to psychologically get through a slump, try the following cognitive techniques (many were adapted from trading coach Doug Hirschhorn and Shane Murphy's excellent book, *The Trading Athlete*[21]):

1. Recognize that slumps happen to everyone.
2. A slump is a statistical reality—go over a similar market history to what you're dealing with now. Determine the length and breadth of the worst draw-downs over that time period. Chances are you aren't doing any worse now than you would have during some similar historical periods.
3. Remember that slumps are temporary. Slumps always reverse, though they may need some time. For example, many long-term buy-and-hold investors had trouble staying invested through the 2008 market crash, but in 2009 their patience was partially redeemed.
4. Don't fight the slump. Cultivate patience and use this opportunity to do more research on your investment style.
5. View the slump as a time to rest and regenerate. When the markets turn in your favor, be sure to reemerge even stronger.
6. Remember: It's not about you. The markets aren't personal.

There is a saying in psychotherapy that every session with the therapist begins at the same subconscious point where the last one left off. The same could be said of one's dealings with the markets. Psychologically, you will begin reinvesting in the state of mind induced by your last experience in the markets. It is very helpful to stay in the game and keep learning so that personal doubts don't overwhelm your ability to grow and maintain perspective.

The ability to successfully climb out of a slump results from one's innate level of resilience. Psychologists have developed an entire field of study about resilience, understanding why some people are more resilient than others and studying techniques that can be used to reinforce resilience.

Cultivating Resilience

In life, everyone is knocked down occasionally. Resilience allows us to spring up faster and with more enthusiasm. Resilience is cultivated when we're exposed to stress and we stay in the challenge, learning what we can do to grow, adapt, and thrive.

The process of building resilience begins with a stressful event or dislocation. Identify what is stressful about the event—for example, is it the feeling of letting down your family or clients? Is it the uncertainty or ambiguity around the economy's future? Are you beginning to suspect that your investment philosophy may need a comprehensive overhaul?

1. Identify how you are responding to the stress. Do you withdraw? Work harder? Focus on what you know rather than looking for new sources of information? These are common reactions.
2. Now, consider what you can control about the situation. In most cases, your behavior and your reactions are the only aspects that can be managed. Focus on your actions and yours alone. What steps can you take to give yourself the best chance at success?
3. Identify others who will support you as you work through this challenge—who is in your network of colleagues, friends, family, or professionals who can help you with problem solving? Don't assume someone won't assist you if you've never asked. A big part of developing resilience is gaining the courage to ask for help. Learn whom you can count on and receive their assistance, so you don't feel alone in fashioning a plan.
4. Take time for breaks. No one can work constantly, responding to emergencies every day, and still develop a coherent game plan for going forward. Stop to take time to listen to yourself and the world around you. First, stop the information flow (turn off your BlackBerry and the TV). Then do what works for you—take a walk in nature, exercise, do yoga, meditate, pray, and so on.

5. Write down what you are grateful for. Every day add at least three new items to a gratitude list (see Appendix B). This will keep you positive and thinking about what you have (instead of what you don't have).

6. Visualize your "best possible self" every morning. Resilient people imagine themselves overcoming challenges with grace and alacrity. If you can't imagine yourself succeeding, then visualize that you are your role model. What would he or she do? This visualization process puts you in a can-do state of mind, which accelerates problem solving.

7. Once you have survived, focus on thriving. What can you do to make and consolidate gains? Schedule a time each day to identify advantages you can bring into your business. Then execute and use those techniques that are working in the new environment.

There are solid biological reasons why this seven-step plan can help cultivate resilience. For example, hormones such as vasopressin and oxytocin (the "trust hormone") appear to be higher in resilient individuals. You can raise your own levels of oxytocin by having more physical contact and loving/trusting interactions with others. Mistakenly, many people under stress spend more time in their offices, working longer and isolated hours, and thus avoiding contact with and support from their partners, friends, and families.

Taking Care of Yourself

In order to personalize what you've learned so far about immediate stress relief, stress-inoculation, and resilience, please answer the following questions:

- What types of investing situations are most stressful for you?
- How do you act differently after a stressful event (a loss, bad news, etc.)?
- How do you successfully decompress?
- How can you incorporate constructive, *immediate* stress-relief activities into your schedule?
- Which long-term stress-inoculation lifestyle changes make sense for you to begin?

So far in the chapter we've covered techniques for managing immediate stress and preparing for future stress through changes in your lifestyle and habits. In the next section we introduce a written plan, called the Financial Stress Management Plan, which will provide you with a plan in case of crisis. While most people have emergency disaster kits in their cars or at home, they rarely prepare emergency plans for the storms that pass over the financial markets (and their portfolios). And it's often the panicked actions we take during these storms that does the most damage.

Financial Stress Management Plan (F-SMaP™)

Decisions made under stress are impaired decisions. The impulsive, emotion-driven choices we make under duress are designed to provide immediate relief—and they often do. But that relief typically comes at the cost of long-term performance.

It takes surprisingly little to torpedo an investing plan—just a moment of distorted thinking and impulsiveness. We are most vulnerable when our investing stress-level has exceeded our ability to cope. It behooves every investor to have a plan to manage that stress. We call it a Financial Stress Management Plan™—F-SMaP™ for short. The F-SMaP is a risk management plan, with a kick—it requires a personal commitment to follow through.

There are a number of reasons why every investor should create an F-SMaP. Consider a scene in the movie *Analyze This*, starring Robert DeNiro as Paul Vitti, a mafia boss with a violent temper, and Billy Crystal as Dr. Ben Sobel, his reluctant psychotherapist.

In one scene, Paul is in the midst of a psychotherapy session with Dr. Sobel. Paul has tried, unsuccessfully, to resolve a conflict with a rival gangster. His rage has boiled over, virtually to the point of being homicidal. Dr. Sobel intervenes, and he attempts to teach Paul better coping skills.

Dr. Sobel: "You know what I do when I'm angry? I hit a pillow. Just hit the pillow, see how you feel."
(DeNiro's character pauses for a moment, thinking. Then he shrugs, pulls a handgun out of his pocket, and fires it into the pillow next to him six times. An uncomfortable silence ensues.)

Dr. Sobel: "Feel better?"

Paul Vitti: "Yeah. I do."
Dr. Sobel: "Good."

This scene is played for laughs. But the concept behind Dr. Sobel's suggestion is psychologically sound; if you feel the need to act out, do so in the least destructive way possible. Remember, if you are experiencing a strong emotion, it's important to discharge it (safely) so that you can think more rationally going forward.

Having healthy coping alternatives as an investor is so important for this reason. As we like to say, you're not paranoid, "The Market" really is out to get you. And one of its cruelest tricks is to compel us to take actions (make decisions) when we are least equipped to do so. Here is where the F-SMaP comes in.

The F-SMaP is a device that helps us regulate our stress level so that (1) we do not feel forced into making inopportune choices, and (2) the choices we do make will be constructive rather than destructive.

Fear vs. Panic

An F-SMaP is a truly personal exercise, and there are a lot of right ways to construct one. While it can be done on one's own, we encourage investors to enlist the help of a partner or trusted financial advisor. Having another person present to ask us good questions fosters self-reflection and moves the process along past stubborn emotional defenses. A rudimentary F-SMaP can be constructed in about 20 minutes, but it is best to put more thought into it than that. Ideally, it should be constructed over several sessions, and periodically revisited afterwards.

Following is a six-step process for setting up an F-SMaP.

Step 1: Acknowledge the Bad Times—Past, Present, and Future

Review a list of market declines and what drove them both in the past and in today's climate. For an example of why this is so effective, let's look at an example that has nothing (and everything) to do with investing.

Mithridates was an ancient king in what is modern-day Turkey in the first century B.C. Being a king back then was a dangerous job. People were constantly trying to kill you. One of the favorite methods was through poisoning. And indeed, his enemies attempted to kill him on multiple occasions by slipping arsenic and other deadly poisons into his wine and food. But Mithridates had great wisdom. Recognizing the precariousness of his position, he prepared for the inevitable assassination attempts years in advance by sampling small bits of every poison in the land. He had literally made himself poison-proof. (So much so that when he tried to commit suicide by poisoning himself to avoid the shame of being captured by the Romans, he was unable to drink enough to do the job!)

Back to the present century. The wisdom of Mithridates is relevant to the modern-day investor. We know "The Market" is going to launch its attacks on our net worth, and those attacks will be emotional in nature (e.g., fear, shock, confusion). One of its chief weapons is surprise. We can inoculate ourselves emotionally, literally building up our resistance to the emotional threats by taking small tastes of the market's bitter poison along the way. We do this by reminding ourselves, especially in good and stable times, that it will not last. (Take a small sip of poison.) It sounds like a downer, I know. But the goal here is not to make you more popular at cocktail parties. It's to keep conscious the inevitability of market declines so that when they come, they do not catch us off guard and we can make good, preconsidered decisions.

Yes, the market has trended up over the years and we believe it to be a safe place to have your money in the long term. But the market also reacts to itself. If there is a party, there's going to be a hangover. Failure to recognize this truth while dancing with the lampshade on your head results in headaches, literally and figuratively.

Take some time to hypothesize about the future. Brainstorm a bit. Think you can't predict the next crisis? Sure, you can. Some likely events include:

- Elections
- Monetary crises
- Commodity/energy problems
- Health scares and pandemics
- Terrorist attacks
- Border dispute
- A coup d'etat
- Natural disasters
- Internet or communications freeze

- War
- Credit defaults (et tu, Greece?)
- Banking panics

There is no way to pinpoint the exact timing or all the details of a crisis, and as such, there is no sense in fretting about it. But predicting an event is tantamount to controlling it. You cannot be blindsided by something you see coming. And this method has the virtue of instilling the investor with the sense that "I knew this was going to happen." It's a great way to maintain our emotional equilibrium.

Go ahead and make some predictions. Get in touch with your inner wet blanket. Then write them down. You can use them later as part of your own F-SMaP.

Step 2: Maintain a Rational Anchor

The emotional currents will move investors, but having a rock-solid anchor of rationality is still a great way to maintain your ground. That's why it's useful to include a phrase or a motto that keeps conscious why most investors fail. Some favorites include:

> "The greatest destroyer of wealth is short-term circumstances frightening people out of their long-term plans."
>
> The four most dangerous words in investing are "This Time It's Different."
>
> "Investing is a marathon, not a sprint."

Whatever works for you is what's best. What's important is that you keep this anchor conscious, and preferably visible. When the market is in decline, your outlook becomes foggy. Having a mantra, a place you can turn to reset your focus, is a light in that fog.

Step 3: Determine Your Personal Stress Reactions

Often we are not aware that we are experiencing stress at all. The symptoms and early warning signs (George Soros is famous for reversing his weakening positions when he felt his lower back stiffening up) provide clues that we have wandered into an unhealthy place from which to make decisions. Take some time to think about and record your physical/mental reactions to stress.

Some common reactions include:

- Aches/pains
- Disruptions in sleeping
- Eating too much/too little
- Strange dreams
- Tenseness/headaches
- Dyspepsia (upset stomach)
- Irritability
- Recurring worries (rumination)

Also pay attention to your triggers. What events tend to bring on these investing stress reactions?

Step 4: Engage In Healthy Coping Mechanisms (i.e., "Hit the Pillow")

We all do things instinctively to reduce our stress level. Sometimes those things are constructive, but they can also be maladaptive and serve to compound our problems. Things like exercise, meditation, organizing and cleaning, and hobbies are all constructive stress relievers that can be added to the program. They should be viewed as healthy activities to engage in when you are feeling market stress—or even to maintain a healthy mind-set during bad markets in general.

Much of investing stress comes from getting drawn into a short-term focus. It can be useful to engage in stress-reduction techniques that specifically target this problem. Doing so gets the investor back into a healthy mind-set, or even just buys time to get through a bad day or two. Some suggestions include:

- **Take a market "time out"** in which you simply agree not to pay attention for a set period of time (two days? a week? a month?). Often the best way to avoid making a bad decision is to give yourself enough time to regain your perspective. (This works quite well with arguments with your spouse as well.)
- **Review a list of market disasters and subsequent market performance.** The broad market indexes have been remarkably resilient through some of the worst disasters imaginable—let alone those that never materialized. It is reassuring to keep handy a collection of panic-inducing events that proved to be temporary setbacks (versus Japanese stagnation).

- **Reread an article that restores the proper mind-set.** Having some convincing articles handy on the long-term performance of equities is a good idea. Reading the article also has the added benefit of a 15–20-minute time out in cases when market emotions become overwhelming.
- **Write down on a piece of paper a predetermined list of reasons to maintain your plan.** Short-term emotions skew our perspective and often cause investors to become momentarily disoriented and abandon sound plans. Getting that rational perspective down on paper, in the form of a list of "reasons we need to stay invested for the long term" or "reasons why we have to stick to the plan," and reviewing it during difficult times is a powerful tool that brings people back to a rational state of mind.
- **Review a 100-year chart of market performance.** For more visual learners the ability to see with their own eyes the remarkable history of market returns is a particularly powerful tool for overcoming jitters in volatile/bear markets.

Step 5: Do Something!

While sticking to a good plan is of course important, it can be necessary and advisable to take some action with our investments to help us feel better. Sometimes even a symbolic step is enough to mitigate our fears and increase a sense of control. As part of the F-SMaP, include small measures that you will take to relieve the mental pressure, such as selling a small fraction of a losing position, or moving from cash to a money market fund. Investing works on the same principle as steam pipes; a predetermined pressure release that does not meaningfully affect the system is what prevents the big explosion down the road. Let off some steam. Take an action to make yourself feel better.

Another point to consider is that volatile markets present the best opportunities to boost performance for those who are prepared. The ability to reframe a negative ("bad" market) into a positive (buying opportunity) is an essential part of the F-SMaP.

Revisit some of the good businesses you considered before that just seemed too expensive. Even if the previous plans are no longer appropriate, down markets inherently provide opportunities to buy at good prices.

Step 6: Commit to the Plan

This final step is subtle, but important. Verbal agreements are good, but are rarely enough to ensure follow through in forging new habits. There needs to be some ceremony to the procedure, some overt sign of commitment, if the plan is going to retain its impact.

One of the best ways to increase this impact is to sign and date the plan and have a witness (e.g., a partner or, your financial advisor) do so as well. Our innate instinct to have our actions match our words is a powerful one. It is amazing how signing your name to an agreement increases commitment and compliance.

It also adds an air of ceremony to the agreement that makes it feel more "official." In this vein, care and respect for the presentation is also of genuine importance. A hastily printed up Microsoft Word document may command attention. But a crisp document pulled from a designated folder that says, "F-SMaP—Emergency Protocol" (or some such) in raised lettering commands much more respect. (Remember, the content of the plan is a tool, but *the process* of using the plan is also a tool.)

Involving another person in the process of creating an F-SMaP is highly advisable because it is always easier to keep our word when we are accountable to someone else.

Remember, the F-SMaP is a tool to be periodically revisited. So it may pay to go over it once a year to ensure that it is still as applicable as it was when it was created.

How do you typically cope with stress?

If you have good, healthy coping mechanisms already, then great. It's a matter of employing them. But if you don't, it's important to identify sound practices that can blow off steam, and reset your perspective back to the way it needs to be.

Creating a Crisis Plan

We know that fear is the dominant investing emotion and that combating it is essential for long-term investing success. But fear is what's called an "anticipatory" emotion. When we feel fear, we may be worried by our present circumstances, but the emotion is future-focused. To be fearful is to be afraid something bad is *going to* happen. I'm *going to* fail the test. The plane is *going to* crash. My net worth is *going to* get slammed.

As such, fear is often a healthy and appropriate emotional reaction. If you were living on a small island and suddenly learned that a seismic event had put you in the path of a massive tsunami, or if you were enjoying an afternoon at the zoo and were informed that a 600 lb. tiger had escaped its cage, you *should be* afraid. In both cases that fear would lead you to a highly adaptive behavior, namely, to escape. With all the emphasis on the dangers of fear, its value is often underappreciated. Without the emotion of fear, our *species*—let alone our portfolios—would have died out long ago.

But while fear can be adaptive and manageable, its subsequent emotion—panic—is not. Panic is a state of utter confusion compounded by a crushing sense of immediacy. Fear can lead to good decisions. Panic will not. Think of it this way: Fear is being afraid of falling overboard; panic is the sensation of drowning.

Part of the value of a good F-SMaP is its role in preventing fear from turning into panic. Let's use another scenario as an analog to illustrate the concept.

In New York City, in the weeks after the 9/11 attack, there was an increased fear of terrorist attacks, particularly attacks with weapons of mass destruction (WMDs). In an effort to combat that fear, there was a movement toward preparedness. One such recommendation that gained popularity was to assemble an "emergency kit" that could be broken out in case such an attack took place. And so a number of New Yorkers bought emergency kits or assembled their own out of readily available supplies such as food, water, radios, breathing aids, and so on.

Cynics, many of whom were in the media, scoffed at the idea. "A gas mask? Bottled water? Batteries? A map? You've got to be kidding?" they asked. "If the city were hit with WMDs, none of those things is likely to save you!" Some called it not only a pointless exercise, but a silly one.

Those people were wrong. Maybe an emergency kit would not save your life. (Then again, maybe it would.) But perhaps the greatest value of the emergency kit is that those who have one are *much less likely to panic.* Not only would they have some emotional preparedness through their anticipation of the catastrophic event, they also equipped themselves with some supplies, as well as a basic plan on how to survive. (Similarly, people like to make fun of the old "duck and cover" campaign that taught kids to sit under their desks should there be an aerial bombardment. Would they prefer a school full of kids running around screaming like banshees?)

It's important to remember what happens in a crisis; people panic, and panic causes irrational, impulsive decisions, often with a herd mentality. In such situations there is great psychological stress placed on us. Our brains are not operating at 100 percent efficiency and mental energy is in precious supply. It is incredibly valuable not to waste that mental energy answering the question, "Holy crap! What do I do now?" Having a sense of control, having a plan allows you to make good decisions, resist the mob mentality, and keep your head. That is, at its core, the difference between panicking or not.

Part of your F-SMaP should include a crisis kit, the functional equivalent of a little supply box kept in a handy location that says "In the event of an emergency, break glass and remove contents." It should contain information and instructions in the form of defensive maneuvers to be taken.

The following items should be included:

- Website information on how to access accounts (Note: For those who do not want to write down sensitive information such as passwords, make sure you provide very clear clues so that you can easily recall log-in information.)
- Phone numbers of key people to call, including financial institutions and personal advisors (financial, legal, etc.)
- Statistics. It can be difficult in the moment to get an accurate reading of "how bad it is." Having handy the percentage drop and recovery figures for past market moves will give you a better handle on the situation and lead to clearer thinking.
- Specific plans of action (e.g., in the event of an increase in interest rates over 10 percent, I will withdraw X dollars and put them into a utility stock fund).

A plan is the antidote to confusion. It provides direction and a sense of control. Please see Figure 7.1 to begin formulating your financial stress management plan.

> *"The greatest destroyer of wealth is short-term cirumstances*
> *frightening people out of their long-term plans."*

When I experience stress that threatens to affect my long-term investment strategy, I will:

1) _____

2) _____

3) _____

> *"Crisis = Opportunity"*
> *The Four Most Dangerous Words in Investing: "This Time It's Different"*

When markets decline we're going to take steps to take advantage of the current climate:

1) _____

2) _____

3) _____

Client's Name: Francis Client   Advisor's Name: Jean Advisor

Signature: Signature:

Date: Date:

Figure 7.1 Financial Stress Management Plan

Conclusion

We hope you've learned some causes of investment stress and techniques for preventing or overcoming them. We've shared some techniques for combating financial stress that we hope you'll find useful:

- Immediate stress relief: Consider breathing techniques, vigorous exercise, or some of the other tools suggested on page 159.
- Long-term stress inoculation: Develop lifestyle habits that reduce your sensitivity to stress. Limit news and information

overload; practice regular prayer, meditation, or yoga; exercise; good sleeping habits; and eat a healthy diet.

- Prepare in advance for stress: Create an FSMaP and schedule periodic meetings to review your investments, various contingencies, and your plan for dealing with them.
- Consider using a professional financial advisor or coach to run ideas by and to help you "offload" investment stress. For example, recent neuroeconomics research demonstrates that receiving financial advice can relieve the mental and emotional burden of investment decision making.[22]

In the next chapter we weave together the material you've learned thus far to help you design a plan for moving forward with confidence and clarity.

CHAPTER 8

Being Your Best Self

To change one's life: Start immediately. Do it flamboyantly.
— William James

Probably the most widely known performance coach in the investment industry is the late Ari Kiev. Dr. Kiev, a psychiatrist who was formerly employed by the United States Olympic Team, coached traders and analysts at SAC Capital Advisors LLC. SAC has one of the best performance records among hedge funds, and as a result SAC charges among the highest fees of any hedge fund: 3 percent of assets and 50 percent of performance.[1] Dr. Kiev worked at SAC for over a decade and presumably made a significant contribution toward the firm's profitability. Performance coaches such as Dr. Kiev typically draw from a common set of techniques: goal setting, structured relaxation training, visualizations, self-talk skills, concentration training, and the use of positive mental rituals.

In the previous chapters, we've given you tools and exercises to understand your unique investor identity. In this chapter we'll help you create a plan for cultivating your strengths and identifying your "best self." The exercises in this chapter are derived from the field of performance psychology. In the wake of Dr. Kiev's apparent success, more and more performance psychologists have joined hedge funds and investment firms to help improve investment decision-making and, consequently, returns.

Establishing a high-performance environment and positive rituals supports long-term success. While this chapter opens with techniques for enhancing your physical and psychological well-being, it closes with a series of worksheets, exercises, and action plans that will support and reinforce the learning you've undertaken in your reading.

Achieving excellence in investing is a lifelong endeavor, and it touches on every aspect of your life. As a result, this chapter may seem like others, it's pushing you to consider changes in your lifestyle that, on the surface, seem to have nothing to do with investing. Yet the skills underlying excellent investing are similar to those needed for success in everyday life.

It's also time we fess up to an important challenge in our approach—we're presenting specific behavioral changes in this chapter. Too often, when you consciously try to reach a goal or make a specific change you're in an outcome-oriented frame of mind. As a result, you will be more emotionally reactive to small daily achievements and setbacks along the way, thus clouding your judgment going forward. So as you go through this chapter and the suggested exercises, stay lighthearted, make it fun, and keep a broad vision of how these activities will enhance your life in the long-term.

Psychological Foundations

> *I wanted to change the world. But I have found that the only thing one can be sure of changing is oneself.*
> —Aldous Huxley

There are numerous techniques for building a stronger psychological foundation for your investing decisions. We begin with a description of the performance-impairing effects of multitasking. We then go on to describe the use of daily affirmations for motivating performance. We address several core psychological techniques used by athletes including working with one's "inner dialogue," the use of visualization, and identifying and cultivating your "best possible self." From there we move to a discussion of motivation and resilience. We describe techniques from the fields of positive psychology and behavioral economics for maintaining motivation during difficult periods and for recovering quickly from the inevitable slumps.

The Value of Mono-Tasking

If you've ever tried to remember too many facts at once—maybe phone numbers, directions, addresses—you've probably noticed that they eventually become jumbled. Our short-term memory has a limited capacity; it can store only a certain number of facts (for example, seven digits, for most people). Trying to keep several priorities in mind is even more challenging than remembering facts, and productivity suffers when we try to do so. This is the curse of multitasking.

There is a cultural respect for the ability to multitask, to the point where those with difficulty multitasking are considered inept in some professions. In fact, multitasking is the function of the brain's prefrontal cortex, a region involved in prioritization, focus, short-term memory, planning for the future, and solving abstract problems. One side effect of extensive multitasking can be mental exhaustion.

Think of the brain like a muscle. When you use a muscle too hard or too long, it becomes tired. The same thing happens with the brain. If we demand too much effort of it or put too much "load" on it, fatigue sets in. *Cognitive load* refers to the demands we put on the prefrontal cortex by attending to disparate facts, figures, and "to-do's." The higher the cognitive load, the more inefficient our executive functioning becomes.

The lack of productivity that results from multitasking has many companies advising their employees to "mono-task." Each day should be dedicated to one do-able goal. If working on several smaller goals, individuals should pursue goals of the same type—within the same domain—over the course of one day. In general, many experts believe that solid blocks of four hours without interruption are required to achieve optimal focus toward any one goal.

Trading coach Denise Shull endorses identifying the bits of information that are essential to your investing decision process and turning off the extras. For example, most investment decisions are not based on entertainment sources such as CNBC, but nonetheless, many investors keep financial news on in the background, catching collateral spray from the information fire hose all day long. When Ms. Shull asks clients to identify how many interesting bits of information they receive during a trading day, from every source they monitor, the answers often run into the hundreds. When she asks clients how many of these hundreds are directly useful for their decisions, they typically report, around four. Her observations are consistent with psychological studies that have found the optimal mental performance during complex decision-making to occur when three pieces of information are used. More than three introduces too much complexity and cognitive load, leading to deteriorating decision quality. Consider mono-tasking in your investment approach. Clear some time, find a quiet place to work, eliminate distractions, and give yourself the ability to focus exclusively on your financial strategy. It will generate a clarity of thought you will find rewarding.

Self-Affirmations Work (As Long As You Don't Need Them)

I set goals, I am positive, and I achieve!

I choose to be a winner!

I am the best investor I can possibly be!

Right now, say to yourself, "I'm an excellent investor," with conviction, five times. Say each iteration louder.

Did that self-affirmation make you a better investor? Studies say that on average, it didn't.

Repeating the affirmations above won't make you any smarter or wealthier. If achieving success were as easy as looking in the mirror every morning and repeating 20 times with conviction: "I am a success, I am a leader, I am wealthy," then we'd all be billionaire presidents of our own countries. The billionaire presidents we can think of—Sebastian Pinera (Chile), Silvio Berlusconi (Italy), Asif Zardari (Pakistan), the late Mobutu Sese Seko (Zaire)—don't seem the types to need self-affirmation. They tend to be extraordinarily confident, charismatic, and even narcissistic. And that speaks to a broader issue: If you already deeply believe you are going to be a billionaire president, then you probably don't need affirmations to get you there.

Before he was elected to the United States Senate, Al Franken was a comedian. As such, he created the character Stuart Smalley for the television comedy *Saturday Night Live* where he hosted a mock self-help show called "Daily Affirmation with Stuart Smalley." The show usually began with Smalley affirming himself: "I'm good enough, I'm smart enough, and doggone it, people like me." But Smalley couldn't maintain his fragile self-esteem during the show.

Often by the conclusion of a program Smalley would break down emotionally and need comfort from one of his guests. Sometimes, after unsuccessfully trying to bolster his fragile confidence, he would descend into despair and self-loathing on camera.

Smalley's delicate self-esteem is funny, in part, because it is so difficult to maintain. Often it is people temporarily plagued by self-doubt who use affirmations to bolster their self-esteem. Unfortunately, some studies show that people who think they need affirmations—the insecure and the doubtful—typically have a *negative* response to affirmations.[2] The people who benefit from daily affirmations are positive, confident, optimistic people—exactly those whom you wouldn't expect to need them.

If you plan to use affirmations, ensure that you are already confident in your goals, your ability to achieve them, and demonstrate to yourself every day that you are committed to those goals through concrete actions.

The Inner Dialogue

> *The soul becomes dyed with the color of its thoughts.*
> —Marcus Aurelius (Roman Emperor,
> 161–180 C.E.)

What did you say to yourself when you started the day today? What were you thinking as you brushed your teeth this morning? Do you remember?

The thoughts that run through our minds during the day are called our "inner dialogue" or "self-talk." Your inner dialogue usually does not consist of sentences or complete concepts. In fact, the running commentary often takes the form of subtle feelings, judgments, or phrases (e.g., "don't do that," "watch out!" "yuck," or "you lookin' at me?!").

The inner dialogue is often running before we wake up in the morning and it is usually benign. However, there are times when it spirals out of control, fed by and feeding into anxieties. Importantly, the moments when the inner dialogue fails us are usually during high-pressure situations as we are attempting to exercise poise, concentration, or disciplined execution.

The best way to understand the power of inner dialogue is to bring to mind two common events: waking up from a good dream and waking up in a foul mood. Have you ever woken up to your alarm from a great dream? And how did your day go after that? Probably you had a good day. However, if you've ever "woken up on the wrong side of the bed," irritable and pessimistic, then you probably experienced a bad day.

The events of our day are heavily influenced by morning moods. Fortunately, there are simple techniques we can practice to change the tone of our days. One technique involves repeating key words and phrases that reset one's inner dialogue and focus the mind. The second technique uses a mental visualization to energize dormant neural pathways.

Olympic athletes often internalize positive inner dialogues before competition. They repeat certain phrases or words like mantras, for example, "fast, clean, strong" chanted over and over. Such mantras reduce nervousness and distractions and lead to improved performance. Consider what words describe your experience during an ideal day. Could these be your mantra?

Visualization

Wayne State University psychologist L. Verdelle Clark ran a training experiment in which three groups of students taking a basketball class were assigned at random to one of three basketball free-throw exercises for 20 days.[3] The first group practiced free throws every day for 20 days. The second group practiced free throws on the first day and the twentieth day, as did the third group of students. Members of the third group also spent 20 minutes every day visualizing free throws. If they mentally "missed," then they "practiced" getting the next shot right.

On the twentieth day the percentage of improvement in each group was measured. The first group practiced daily and improved their accuracy by 24 percent. The second group did not improve. The third group, which had not physically practiced more than the second, showed 23 percent improvement—essentially as much as the physical practice group.

Interestingly, at one school the students assigned to visual imagery practice were ridiculed by their basketball coach. When the data for this group were removed from the result data for all four participating schools, the average percentage improvement in the third group increased further.

The most successful visualizations are those in which the visualizer "feels," "sees," "hears," and is emotionally invested in the practice. Presumably the best visualizers in the basketball experiment "felt" the ball in their hands, "heard" it bounce off the backboard, "saw" it go through the hoop, and believed they could improve using visualization.

Trading coach Van K. Tharp advises clients to mentally model great investors. Imagine the state of mind a "super investor" would be in to deal with your current situation. Role-play that you are that super investor and imagine the actions you would take and how you would feel. Such a mental rehearsal prepares you to act with confidence when facing important investing decisions.

Regular visualization of your "best possible self" leads to the creation of new neural pathways that support higher achievement and resilience in the face of losses. In such a visualization you can mentally play through challenges. Imagine the situation clearly, feel your reactions and intentions, and listen for new information. As you internalize coping skills and performance habits through repeated mental rehearsals, challenges will become easier to work through in real-time.

Identifying Your Best Possible Self

It may sound inconsistent, but your "peak performance mind-set" isn't fixed. Different peaks suit different situations and different roles, which changes the nature of our visualization. A casual investor might imagine finding a "hidden gem"—a stock that easily meets all of his investment criteria and has excellent potential. His or her state of mind might be described as "effective," "focused," and "consistent." A financial advisor might identify with peak mental traits at work including "serenity, connectedness, optimism, and confidence." Meanwhile, a portfolio manager might identify personal peak characteristics of "insight, flow, balance, and equanimity."

One technique for identifying your personal peak performance traits is to imagine someone you admire, perhaps a role model, performing at his or her best. Then imagine yourself in a similar situation, performing up to your role model's standards. What were you feeling when performing at your best—for example, did you feel confident, accurate, disciplined, or effective?

Please take a few minutes to consider the following questions about common situations. Personalize the scenario, and then please write your responses on the following blank lines.

Using as many adjectives as possible, describe what it is like to be in a peak mental state:

1. When I am at my best in my primary relationship (spouse, partner, best friend, or family member), I feel . . . (For example: "fun," "happy," "free," "secure," "trusting," "playful")

   _____

2. When I excel in my profession, I feel . . . (For example: "productive," "creative," "active," "energized," "learning")

   _____

3. When I perform at my best in investing, I feel . . . (For example: "analytical," "in the zone," "responding with skill," "competent," "confident")

   _____

The above adjectives reflect your target "peak mind-set" in these different situations. If you don't feel curious to explore this further, then come back to continue this exercise when you're ready. It's important to go through the exercises that follow in a restful and open state of mind.

For the remainder of this exercise, we will dig deeper into your peak mind-set in investing (#3 above).

Think of the role models, mentors, advisors, colleagues, and acquaintances who epitomize the traits you listed in #3. On your own paper or in a journal (now is a good time to start one), please list their names (or initials) and several adjectives describing their peak performance traits that you can identify with and would like to cultivate in yourself. For example, "Warren Buffett: Equanimity, humor, strategic thinking, patience."

Now perform a visualization. Imagine yourself during the investment process while embodying the peak performance characteristics you listed in your journal. See yourself in a scenario involving controllable aspects of the investment process that you are performing well. Take on the peak performance attributes listed above. Close your eyes and visualize yourself with those characteristics for 30 seconds before reading on.

Now see yourself in a situation involving a challenge that you have overcome in investing. Take on the peak performance attributes you listed previously as you tackle and overcome that challenge. Close your eyes and visualize yourself with those characteristics for 30 seconds before reading on.

Now answer the following questions about the visualizations you completed:

- How did you feel in the envisioned scenario (e.g, energized, serene, masterful, etc.)?
- How did you communicate (confidently, calmly, etc.)?
- What was your state of mind?
- What were you wearing?
- How did you behave?
- How would you have reacted to losses? Big gains?
- Which feelings were most genuine and real for you during the visualization experience (i.e., what felt right)?

Holding a positive image of ourselves literally changes our brain chemistry. You are "priming" yourself for positive action when you do this exercise. In order to create a single, memorable vision for yourself, identify a mental image that signifies the best of what you just experienced. Examples of images include the face of a role model, an image of a memento, a past experience, or a specific location. Assigning these desired qualities to a mental picture is called creating a mental tag. Mental tags remind us of our best possible selves, and they are useful for quickly summoning the most important qualities we want to embody. These come in handy for quickly priming us in situations where we need to perform.

My tag (peak mental image) is: _____

Practice calling to mind your best possible self by holding your mental tag in mind.

If you imagine you are your best possible self every day for 30 seconds—bringing the traits and qualities of your mental tag to mind—you will find yourself gradually taking on those positive characteristics and making them a part of who you are in day-to-day life.

We have all been told by the dental profession that we should take several minutes, several times a day to brush and to floss. If you're willing to take that much time each day to take care of your teeth, then in that same spirit you should be willing to take 30 seconds each morning to summon your best possible self, in order to promote the health of something much more important, your mind. Consider it your daily "Mental Floss."

Brain Boosting

In addition to the psychological techniques we've discussed so far in this book, simple physical habits such as eating a balanced diet, exercising regularly, maintaining good sleep hygiene, and dietary supplements, spices, and nutritious foods have been found to support optimal brain function. But don't worry—we're suggesting lifestyle prescriptions that are easy and enjoyable. The goal of these prescriptions are not short-term—to lose weight, eliminate wrinkles, or build muscle mass—it's to help you feel better, think more clearly, and tackle life with enthusiasm.

Exercise Regularly

> *It is exercise alone that supports the spirits, and keeps the mind in vigor.*
>
> —Marcus Tullius Cicero

Exercise is typically defined as sustained challenging or vigorous movement. In general, researchers have found several characteristics of "good" exercise routines. For one thing, exercise shouldn't be a boring routine. Mix it up in a way that keeps you challenged and interested.

Researchers have also found that when starting exercise after a hiatus or for the first time, it's essential to start slowly with a do-able routine. It can be as simple as daily walking or stretching for five minutes. Start small and build up. Overly vigorous exercise weakens the immune system and can lead to injuries.

The ideal workout combines both strength exercises and cardiovascular exercises. Both types fight depression and decrease anxiety, with slightly better benefits seen from cardiovascular exercise. The mental benefits of exercise include improved learning and memory and increased resilience to stress. In fact, exercise is so potent that a consistent routine can eliminate the cognitive effects of eating a poor diet.

Some people, for better or worse, see exercise as the enemy. If you're in that camp, you may as well consider cartoonist Charles

Shultz's defense: "Exercise is a dirty word. Every time I hear it, I wash my mouth out with chocolate."

Sleep in the Dark

Every important mistake I've made in my life, I've made because I was too tired.

—Bill Clinton

While the average American adult sleeps 6.5–7 hours nightly, most need 7.5–8.5 hours on average (there is a large range of individual sleep needs). Sleep deprivation leads to a decreased ability to learn and to retain new information, and it reduces cognitive flexibility, creativity, and problem solving.

In order to ensure good sleep habits, it's important to maintain consistency in your schedule (awaken at the same time every day, regardless of how much you've slept), take intraday power naps (usually not more than 20 minutes), and ensure that your sleeping space is dark and noise-proofed. Avoid watching TV in bed or looking at computer screens after 8 PM. (the blue light from the screens stops melatonin production, leading to lighter sleeping). Avoid caffeine after 2 PM. Some people should not use caffeine at all, especially if they have sleep difficulties. Alcohol drunk before bedtime impairs sleep quality and leads to decreased nocturnal learning and memory consolidation (not to mention next-day fatigue).

At this point you've probably realized that we're completely unhinged from your reality. We're bombarding you with sleep and exercise rules while you're laying in bed reading this on your electronic reader and wondering if you will *ever* get seven hours of continuous sleep again. We get it. Of course you can't follow most of these recommendations. That's normal. If you're planning to jump right in and change your life all at once, then that's simply not sustainable. Keep in mind that this chapter guides you in an exploration, and commit to what you can, when you can, because all-in-all, at the end of this road, is a healthier, happier, and longer life for you.

Medications

Some chemicals—medications, supplements, and illicit drugs—have been shown to alter financial decision making. So your short-term use of these may actually affect your long-term investing outcomes. In this section we discuss the roles of these chemicals in inhibiting and improving mental performance. We don't discuss nootropics ("brain boosters") due to conflicting evidence about the benefits of these substances.

Medication effects on cognition have been widely studied by pharmaceutical companies and researchers. Directly relevant to investing, benzodiazepine medications such as Lorazepam, Diazepam, and Clonazepam have been shown to cause increased financial risk-taking (albeit in studies involving small sums of money).[4] Alcohol and cannabis have similar effects on increasing financial risk-taking.[5]

Anticholinergic medications can impair memory and learning. Common anticholinergic chemicals include diphenhydramine (benadryl), muscle relaxant medications, medications used to treat Parkinson's disease, and even common pesticides.

Beta-blockers (-olol medications) are often used for management of hypertension (high blood pressure), but they too alter risk perceptions. Beta-blockers reduce anxiety and lead to reduced ability to discriminate between large and small potential losses.

Diet and Nutrition

Dietary and nutritional factors have also been found to alter financial decision making. The recommendations listed in Table 8.1 are along the lines of a dietary "prescription." All have been proven in scientific studies either to degrade or alter cognitive performance (learning, memory, creativity, and even IQ). It's worth going through the list to identify which ones you should avoid and which beneficial foods you could fit into your diet.

Eating regularly is itself important. The brain needs the constant availability of energy to function at its optimal level, and regular intake of food ensures that hypoglycemic periods are less likely to occur. For example, a snack such as handful of nuts, a boiled egg, or trail mix between meals will improve your mental energy and self-control throughout the day.

Interestingly, drinking artificially sweetened beverages impairs attention and focus.[6] The brain has more difficulty resisting impulses if it is not adequately supplied with energy, as occurs when artificial sweeteners or "zero-calorie" beverages are consumed or

Table 8.1   Eating Right Boosts Brain Function

Dietary Interventions	Explanation
Avoid These	
Trans and hydrogenated fats	Trans and hydrogenated fats create rigidity in neuronal cell walls. As a result, neurons have more difficulty regrowing after damage or growing more complexity when learning to deal with new challenges. We have shown that the consumption of a diet rich in saturated fat decreases learning and memory.
Excess saturated fats	The consumption of a diet rich in saturated fat decreases learning and memory capacity over time.
Include These	
Green or white tea	Numerous studies have shown a long-term benefit from green tea intake on cognition and learning. Those who drink four cups or more daily show the greatest benefits—benefits that regular coffee and black tea drinkers do not see.
Omega-3 fats	Omega-3 fats (as found in fish oil and many nuts) promote cell wall fluidity. Numerous studies show mental benefits (improved impulse control and mood) following omega-3 intake.
Tumeric (Curcumin)	Turmeric is a root from the ginger family. In its powdered form it appears in yellow curry powder (it gives curry its yellow color). Turmeric contains the compound curcumin, which has been found to improve cognitive function and neurogenesis (neuronal resilience and growth).
Yellow and orange and deep green vegetables, leafy greens	Deep yellow and orange fruits (apricots, cantaloupe, papaya, persimmons), carrots, sweet potatoes, pumpkin, leafy greens, and broccoli all contain high levels of beta-carotene, which appears to slow brain aging and improve learning when eaten in foods (but not in extract form).
Vitamin D3	Vitamin D3 insufficiency is linked to higher rates of many ailments including cancers, cardiovascular disease, and several chronic diseases. On the mental level, Vitamin D supplementation of 4000IU daily (generally equivalent to 15 minutes of daily sun exposure), under a doctor's supervision, has been shown to improve mood.

meals are skipped. This decreased impulse-control is not only a problem for investors, it also affects dieters who believe that drinking diet sodas or skipping meals will help them lose weight. In fact, they have more trouble resisting the urge to binge when they next become hungry.

Caffeine. Given the ubiquity of Starbucks and other coffee retailers, it might seem that a substantial share of GDP is attributable to caffeine-fueled productivity. The average adult American consumes 200 mg per day of caffeine (far behind nervous Netherlanders, who consume 400 mg per day). Five ounces (150 ml) of coffee contain about 100 mg of caffeine, while black tea contains about 50 mg, and green tea 25 mg. In the United States, more than 80 percent of adults consume caffeine on a daily basis.[7] Although caffeine does improve mental performance in motor and cognitive tasks for most people, it can produce nervousness and decrease mental flexibility. Other short-term alertness boosters include peppermint (teas or candies) and jasmine (usually in tea).

For Short-Term Alertness

Caffeine	About 25 percent of the population feels the optimal benefits of caffeine: increased alertness and focus without negative effects. Many other users experience side effects such as sleep disruption and anxiety.
Jasmine	Jasmine flowers have been used for centuries to promote mental alertness, often as an additive to tea. Many recent studies confirm this benefit.
Peppermint	Peppermint increases focus and alertness— which is one effect of peppermint tea and candies such as Altoids. In fact, Harrison Ford is quoted as saying: "I'm addicted to Altoids. I call them 'acting pills.'"

The Economics of Behavior Change

Man needs, for his happiness, not only the enjoyment of this or that, but hope and enterprise and change.
—Bertrand Russell

Have you ever made a New Year's resolution? Did you follow through with it?

Every year 88 percent of people who make New Year's resolutions don't complete them.[8] Why such a high failure rate? As you've probably noticed so far in this book, "knowledge does not equal change." Simply thinking you can achieve a goal doesn't make it so. One mental mistake that sets New Year's resolutions up for failure is projecting one's current feelings of conviction and unwavering confidence onto one's future selves (the projection bias).

When deciding to change our behavior, we've got to (1) fundamentally want to make the change for the long-term, (2) set up smart incentives, and (3) remove the emotional blocks that have prevented us from changing in the first place.

Since we know that most people are overconfident in their ability to stick to their resolutions, it's important to be realistic. Set a resolution and then reduce it by half if necessary. With that in mind, it often helps to make only one resolution at a time. Using a weight loss analogy, if one resolves to "quit sweets" all at once, then that probably isn't a sustainable resolution. One must begin by resolving to quit a class of foods: "quit sodas" or "quit donuts." As little successes become evident, only then should larger goals be taken on.

Keep in mind that one *cannot* successfully resolve to "make 30 percent in the markets this year" or "find the next decade's Apple." Resolutions have to be within one's control. One *can* resolve to "perform a thorough due diligence process that includes all of the following checks before every investment" or "not invest capital without having completed a five-point list of the criteria that would lead me to disinvest." Those latter two factors are controllable and important but usually overlooked. In addition to our investment process, new research indicates that we can also control our *attitude*.

Learning Optimism

Very little is needed to make a happy life; it is all within yourself, in your way of thinking.

—Marcus Aurelius

Do you have a friend or colleague who is relentlessly upbeat? This person probably seems to automatically see the jugs of lemonade to be squeezed from every lemon thrown their way. There is rarely a doubt that they will succeed gloriously in whatever they do.

And guess what? An optimistic outlook can become a self-fulfilling prophecy. Studies show that optimistic people live longer, suffer from less physical and mental illness, have higher incomes, and have higher life satisfaction than others.

Not a bad deal. So how can one join the club?

Recent research demonstrates that optimism and happiness are partially learned behaviors. About 20 percent of one's sense of life satisfaction is easily within your control. And another 20 percent of happiness is developmental—a result of early life experiences. Around 60 percent of happiness is genetic, so it can't be altered. If you're constitutionally pessimistic you probably just said to yourself: "Sixty percent! I'm doomed to be pessimistic forever!" while chronically optimistic people thought, "Great, I can increase my happiness at least 40 percent more!"[9]

Learning how to be optimistic requires mental exercise. Remember, the mind is like a muscle. The parts of your mind you use—especially due to repetitive thoughts or feelings—are reinforced. The aspects of your mind that go unused atrophy.

According to positive psychologist Martin Seligman, most optimistic people deal with setbacks by attributing failures to causes that are either:

- Completely out of their control (external)
- Independent and unlikely to happen again
- Isolated and will not affect their success in other endeavors

This explanatory style is associated with better performances (academic, athletic, or work productivity), greater satisfaction in interpersonal relationships, better coping, less vulnerability to depression, and better physical health. As Roman emperor Marcus Aurelius put it, "You have power over your mind—not outside events. Realize this, and you will find strength."

In order to reframe setbacks in a more optimistic light, please complete the following exercise.

1. Identify a financial setback (e.g., a real estate foreclosure, job loss, or investment loss.)
2. Ask yourself: What are some causes of it that were outside of my control? (e.g., "The credit market collapsed so I couldn't sell the property, and I lost my job so I couldn't pay the mortgage.")

3. What are some reasons it happened that were unique; that is, reasons it is unlikely to occur again? (e.g., Real estate crashes historically occur once every two generations or more.)
4. Consider why the setback likely won't affect your success in other endeavors (e.g., I learned how to identify an asset bubble, and now I can go forward with new analytical tools. My losses in real estate have nothing to do with my job market value or my ability to learn and adapt to the new economic realities.)

Now identify aspects of the situation that you *can* control to prevent a recurrence going forward and actions you can take to regain control if it happens again:

1. Things I can do to prevent similar setbacks in the future (e.g., I won't invest in assets that don't fit my valuation model. When I invest in real estate again I will employ a hedging strategy. I will keep abreast of outside factors such as currency fluctuations and international events that may affect the value of my investments.)
2. Things I cannot control about the setback and must leave up to chance (it could happen again for these reasons, and there is nothing to prevent it) (e.g., I cannot predict government policy shifts, major credit crises, or recessions. I've got to take some risk in order to make a return on my investments.)

Changing one's perspective on past failures frees up mental energy. The mind stops dwelling on the past and begins looking forward to a brighter future. This release of mental "baggage" and reframing toward the future is itself motivating.

Committing to Your Peak Performance Routine

In this book we've made all sorts of suggestions, and now we'd like to bring it all home. We'd like you to design a "peak performance plan" for your investing going forward. But first consider how important such a plan is for you. On a scale of 1 to 5 (1 being not important and 5 being extremely important), rank your level of commitment.

1. How *important* is it to create a plan to improve your investing (and life) performance?

If you chose a level of importance of 2 or below, then consider returning to this exercise at a later time. Now on a scale of 1 to 5, please rate your likelihood of follow-through.

2. How likely is it that you will follow through with a peak performance plan? That is, how confident are you that you can execute your plan?

If your confidence level isn't 5, then what can you do to increase your confidence in execution? Think about how to modify the plan. Remember, the plan is yours—it is flexible to suit your needs but also needs to keep you on track.

3. And finally, do you believe that following through on a peak performance plan can help you achieve your long-term goals (1 equals "no way" and 5 equals "absolutely")?

If you chose 1, 2, or 3, then consider setting aside your plan and doing more research before getting started. If you don't sincerely believe that following a performance plan will make a difference in your life, it will be challenging to follow through.

If you chose 4 or 5 for each question, then please proceed in creating your plan.

In the next section, you can check off realistic goals for performance-enhancing lifestyle changes for the coming month. Please plan only one month ahead. New habits, if you find them beneficial, will form after about one month of practice.

Don't Do It Alone

At our MarketPsych trainings we ask each attendee to find an investing partner before committing to a performance plan. Being accountable to another person helps both parties stay on track. There are two excellent techniques for motivating yourself with a partner: (1) compete with your partner to see who can stick to their plan and thus achieve their goals first, and (2) make a financial commitment to your goal. Making an investment of money, even a relatively small one increases follow through dramatically.

If you have serious trouble with motivation, one of the best (and most devious) ways to encourage follow-through is to make a financial commitment—a monetary deposit—with your partner. If you stick to your performance plan, then you are "given back" your financial commitment. If not, they keep it.

An alternative involves an emotionally charged "stick" to keep you motivated. If you don't complete your regimen, then your partner will donate your deposit under your name to a cause you find offensive. That's right, you will be funding the enemy! (Common choices for such donations include disagreeable political candidates/ parties, rival sports booster clubs, appalling social campaigns, and generally disagreeable causes.) There is no better way of ensuring follow-through than to have both a positive motivation and a potential punishment. Be sure to commit a sum of money that would be painful to give. (Throwing five cents the way of a disliked organization is more of a slight than a legitimate contribution).

As we mentioned at the outset of this book, improving your investing requires work. This is your chance to commit and follow through. The MarketPsych.com website has tools and resources to help you not only make a plan, but to stay on it.

Remember to commit to goals that are *do-able*. Start small. It's okay to pick items in an area in which you are already strong, as long as you intend to follow through. In the following pages potential goals are classified in three groupings: preparing to invest, lifestyle support, and emotion management.

As you read through the lists, check off the action items you would like to perform over the next one month, starting two business days from today (so you have time to prepare). You are committing, not just "testing the waters."

Keep in mind that creating a checklist to guide your lifestyle can feel, well, artificial. So take what works, and please only choose a select few of the recommendations. And definitely don't do anything that makes you feel unhappy or disconnected. If you enjoy an evening drink or a sleepless night of work, then by all means keep it up.

Preparing to Invest

Design and implement a risk management plan

❑ Schedule an introductory meeting with a financial advisor (see our resource guide on marketpsych.com).

❑ Create a Financial Stress Management Plan (F-SMaP) or risk management plan.

❑ Schedule a regular (every year, for example) meeting with family, an advisor, colleagues, or investment buddies to review your investments and strategies going forward.

❑ Commit to diversifying a specific percentage of assets into different investment classes.

❑ Commit to asking yourself the Five Questions before each investment and the Four Questions before each asset sale. Write down your answers and keep them in an investing journal for one year.

❑ Commit to using defined price stops (stop-losses) to prevent investment losses from snowballing. (Keep in mind that such measures depend on the position in question. Warren Buffett's preferred holding time is "forever" and he doesn't use stop-losses.)

Manage investment biases and thought traps

❑ Complete the bias assessments in Chapter 6. Commit to journaling and most importantly, *reframing*, when you recognize personal biases.

Manage your investment personality

❑ Take the MarketPsych.com Investment Personality Test.
❑ Identify two personality-based strengths.
❑ Identify two personality-based vulnerabilities.
❑ Identify which markets and assets appeal to your strengths and do not touch on your weaknesses. Use the worksheet on page 62.
❑ Enroll in MarketPsych's Gene Screen to understand and plan around your biological investing tendencies at www.marketpsych.com/genescreen.php.

Determine your investment values

❑ Answer the questions in Chapter 5 to identify your financial beliefs and values and the potential limitations and advantages they may construe.

Changing Your Life

Brain Boosters
Daily foods and supplements

❑ Daily omega-3 fish oil (be sure it is heavy-metal free)
❑ Curcumin (in food such as curry or daily as a capsule)

❑ Yellow or orange fruits and vegetables, at least four servings weekly (carrots, squash, yams, papaya, apricots, etc.)

❑ Deep green vegetables, at least four times weekly (spinach, Swiss chard, kale, broccoli, Brussels sprouts)

❑ Green or white tea, at least 1 cup daily (can substitute for coffee or tea).

❑ Vitamin D3 supplementation of 4000IU daily (under a doctor's supervision).

Exercise: Consider which days, where, and at what times you anticipate exercising.

❑ Low intensity: Stretching or walking for 15 minutes at least three times weekly.

❑ Moderate intensity: Four times of 30 minutes weekly, at least two cardio (rhythmic, with deep breathing and sweating). Yoga, pilates, cycling, swimming, jogging, hiking, treadmill, and aerobics all meet this criteria.

❑ High intensity: Four times of 60 minutes weekly, at least one cardio and one strength.

Sleep

❑ Commit to waking up every day at the same time.

❑ Commit to not using caffeine after 2 PM and not exercising after 7 PM.

❑ Do a "bedroom makeover"—ensure that as little light as possible enters your bedroom at night and remove any "screens" (TV or computer) from the bedroom.

❑ Commit to not looking at "screens" after 8 PM. (including your cell phone, watching TV, or using a computer).

Health Maintenance

❑ Commit to a check-up by your doctor.

Flexing Your Mind Muscles. Select at least two of the following techniques and commit to working on them. Only pick ones that are reasonable and do-able. A practice of as little as seven minutes daily is enough to begin rewiring your brain. Consider trying most of the items on this list. And remember, if it doesn't feel right, then don't do it—simply move on to try another one.

Emotion Management (healthy habits for long-term stability)

❏ Visualize your best possible self for 30 seconds daily.
❏ Start and maintain a Gratitude List and add three new items daily (you can use the template in Appendix B).
❏ Daily meditation practice of at least 10 minutes. See Appendix A for guidelines on establishing a meditation practice.
❏ Engage in a creative activity at least once weekly such as art class, learning a new sport, cooking class, dance class, learning a musical instrument, taking voice lessons, or attending a museum event.
❏ Play at least once daily: Tell or write a joke, play a video/card/board game, play with children, or watch a comedy.

Emotion Management (immediate relief)

❏ List the short-term stress relief strategies that work for you (e.g., deep breathing, vigorous exercise, napping, or structured relaxation exercises).
❏ Use a CBT journal for recording and challenging stress-inducing events as they occur (see the template on page 164). This is also a long-term preparatory strategy.
❏ Use the Slide Show technique to set clearer goals and change your perspective to the long term.
❏ Commit to creating journal entries for self-inquiry whenever feeling "something is amiss" in your investments.

Psychological strategies

❏ For "thrill-seeking" that interferes with your long-term plans, fund a small "high-risk" trading account.
❏ Maintain a "decision" journal in which you summarize your daily feelings and thoughts around financial or investment decisions taken throughout the day or week.

Social Strategies

❏ Attend a meeting of a social club or group at least once weekly or four times monthly. This includes spiritual groups (any group, as long as you are having fun). See meetup.com for groups in your area. Remember to start with a group you have never attended before.

❑ Call an old friend you've been meaning to catch up with.

❑ Have lunch, dinner, or a drink with a friend or acquaintance.

Spiritual Strategies

❑ Engage in a faith practice at least once weekly. This includes attending religious services, regular prayer, meditation, nature walks, or taking the time to contemplate what you value most in life

Now that you've identified your intentions, put them together in a workable performance plan. An example of potential plans is in Table 8.2. To facilitate the performance planning, consider how ideal goals are set and achieved.

Setting up Goals

If you don't know where you're going, any road will get you there.
—Lewis Carroll

Goals aren't easy to set up, much less to work toward. Following is a common framework for goal-setting:

1. Define what you want. What do you want to achieve?
2. Reconcile the goal with your values. Does it fit with your time, interests, priorities, and resources?
3. Write it down. Putting it on paper facilitates commitment.
4. Take action.

There is a slight problem with the above steps. What happens *after* you begin to take action? For most people, their values shift, priorities change, or interest fades, and a goal—especially a distant one—is ultimately left unaccomplished.

An entire industry of management consultants arose to help companies and employees design and follow through in achieving their goals. With those consultants arrived a sea of acronyms to describe optimal goal setting and achievement. The most widely used acronym for these steps is SMARTER.

SMARTER goals are:

Specific: Specific refers to the what, why, and how of the SMARTER model. Including details helps us focus our efforts and best define what we are going to do. Ensure the goals you set are specific, clear, and straightforward.

Measurable: Establish concrete criteria for measuring progress toward the attainment of each goal you set. If you can't measure or control your progress toward it, then you can't manage it. For example, one usually cannot predict investment returns over the short or medium term, so using monetary outcomes as a goal is not viable, while process-oriented goals are ideal.

Attainable: A goal should stretch you slightly. It should be both workable and require a real commitment from you.

Realistic: Devise a plan or a way of getting there that makes the goal realistic. If you have other priorities that will prevent you from working toward a goal, then don't try. Wait until you have the time, resources, or energy to commit to its pursuit.

Timely: Set up a realistic time deadline for seeing progress toward your goal.

Evaluate: Set a schedule for evaluating your progress. If you're not on track, consider adjustments.

Reevaluate: Continue to reassess and readjust as necessary. As long as your original passion and interest are maintained, then the goal will remain a priority and obstacles will be surmounted.

Now that you've considered how to set goals and make changes to your lifestyle (and investment style) going forward, it's time to create a commitment. Table 8.2 encourages you to write down the items you intend to pursue to improve your understanding of your investor identity, create realistic plans to strengthen it, and set goals for the future.

Use Table 8.2 to list at least three activities or changes you intend to begin as a result of this book. Be careful not to overcommit, since a failure on one often leads to less motivation to complete the others.

Table 8.2 Peak Mental Performance Plan

What I Will Do: "I commit to . . ."	Schedule: "once," "daily,""weekly"	Start date
1.		
2.		
3.		
4.		
5.		
6.		
7.		
8.		
9.		
10.		
Sign here:	Date: My partner's e-mail and telephone number:	
	Our first follow-up is scheduled in one week on [*insert date and time*].	

Conclusion

Investing successfully is deceptively hard—and is often an illusion. That most people underperform the market is a given. Some merely come up short of their financial goals, which is unfortunate. Others lose sickening sums of money and end up with a lifetime of financial hardship. It doesn't have to be this way.

Investors fail not because they are foolish or incompetent, but simply because they're *human*. We're not designed to be good at this. It's just the nature of our wiring. You need to use every weapon in your arsenal to win the battle. There are a number at your disposal, but the greatest one is a strong sense of *who you are* as investor. Only by honestly knowing yourself and learning to prepare against your vulnerabilities will you be able to withstand the psychological forces that bully the less well-grounded into bad decisions.

We designed this book so that reading through it would improve your investing self-knowledge, clarify your goals, increase your stress resistance, and help build your investor identity. Believe it or not, there were many psychological tools and techniques left out of this book. MarketPsych provides individual consultations, keynotes, workshops, and trainings. If you are interested in any of these services for you or your organization, please contact us. In such contexts we're able to help investors move forward through the learning process with inspiration and conviction.

We hope you have a brilliant journey through your life and in the markets. Of course, it's not always an easy path, and there is always work to be done. We hope we've shared with you enough tools and insights to equip you for your journey and ease your travel. We'd like to extend the invitation to get in touch with us any time. We can be found through our website, www.marketpsych.com. We wish you tremendous prosperity and lifelong happiness.

Summary of Meditation Techniques

Meditation is an ancient technique practiced for spiritual, mental, and physical growth. There are many styles of meditation. The general idea behind meditation is that most people are somewhat alienated from a direct experience of their "self," their feelings, and the world. We often live without ever truly stopping to examine our feelings and thoughts, much less the expectations and hopes and fears that underlie them. By observing our mental life, we can gain insights into *why* we do what we do, and we can begin to feel more authentic and present in daily life. The unity of your sense of self with your experience, achieved by constantly pulling your attention back to the present moment, is the core of most meditation practices.

Many meditation techniques combine awareness of the breath with an erect seated posture. There are many styles of meditation. Osho and transcendental meditation techniques are not discussed here. Following are some common meditation styles with simple instructions.

Introductory Meditation (For Rapid "Letting Go")

I know my body. (inhaling)

I am not my body. (exhaling)

I know my mind. (inhaling)

I am not my mind. (exhaling)

I know my witness. (inhaling)

I am not my witness. (exhaling)

Mindfulness Meditation (Vipassana)

Pay attention to your breathing—the inward and outward motion of the breath. As you are feeling the breath moving in and out evenly, observe and label your thoughts, feelings, and judgments as they arise, and then let them go. For example, when a thought arises, label it "thought" and then return your full attention to your breathing. Thoughts should glide in and out of your mind like the reflections of geese flying over a still pond. There is no attachment to the reflections, and the surface of the lake (your mind) remains still.

Mantra-Based Meditation

Focus on an object, vision, phrase, or word (a "mantra") and maintain your full awareness there. Sometimes a verbal phrase, such as "om mani padme hum" (in Tibetan Buddhism) or a single word is repeated. Others will visualize the Buddha or a perfect being. Some practitioners watch a candle flame or single point, others listen with full attention to the sound of Tibetan "singing bowls." Roger Walsh, M.D., has suggested visualizing a white circle with a white dot in the middle on a black background—continuously hold your full attention and awareness on the vision while labeling and letting go of thoughts and feelings that arise and interfere with your concentration.

You can cultivate awareness with any one of these repetition or focus-based mantras. Notice what thoughts, feelings, and experiences come up during the meditation, let them go, and return your full attention to the mantra.

Thich Nhat Hanh

(In sync with your breathing, repeat silently)

I am a mountain. (inhaling)

I feel solid. (exhaling)

I am a flower.

I feel fresh.

I am a still pool.

My mind feels clear.

I am empty space.

I feel free.

I am a mountain lake.

I reflect everything.

Loving Kindness (Metta)

For all the wrongs others have committed against me, knowingly or unknowingly, I forgive them.

For all the wrongs I have committed against others, knowingly or unknowingly, I forgive myself.

For all the wrongs I have committed against myself, knowingly or unknowingly, I forgive myself.

Repeat the following phrases first for yourself, then for a trusted companion, then for a neutral person, and finally for a disliked person. Try to really *feel* the blessings.

May I be filled with loving-kindness.

May I be well.

May I be peaceful and at ease.

May I be happy.

May my road be easy and my burden be light.

May I be liberated.

Cultivating Compassion (Tonglen)

In tonglen practice, when we see or feel suffering, we breathe in with the notion of completely feeling it, accepting it, and owning it. Then we breathe out, radiating compassion, loving-kindness, freshness; anything that encourages relaxation and openness. This is repeated and "inoculates" one against suffering—creating equanimity in the midst of troubles.

There is no "right" way to meditate. Please enjoy trying out different types of meditation to see which ones resonate with you.

Gratitude List

Instructions: Every day list three unique experiences, people, or events for which you feel grateful. You may continue the list on your own paper indefinitely—many people have thousands of items on their lists.

Date	I am grateful for . . .
	1.
	2.
	3.
	4.
	5.
	6.
	7.
	8.
	9.
	10.
	11.
	12.

(Continued)

(Continued)

Date	I am grateful for . . .
	13.
	14.
	15.
	16.
	17.
	18.
	19.
	20.
	21.
	22.
	23.
	24.
	25.
	26.
	27.
	28.
	29.
	30.
	31.
	32.
	33.
	34.
	35.
	36.
	37.
	38.

Date	I am grateful for . . .
	39.
	40.
	41.
	42.
	43.
	44.
	45.
	46.
	47.
	48.
	49.
	50.
	51.
	52.
	53.
	54.
	55.
	56.
	57.
	58.
	59.
	60.

Notes

Chapter 1   Your Investor Identity: And Why You Need One

1. *Beyond Behavior: Why Boomers Underfund Retirement,* Guardian Life Insurance Company, 2004.
2. Weber, E.U., A-R.E. Blais, and N.E. Betz. 2002. "A Domain-Specific Risk-Attitude Scale: Measuring Risk Perceptions and Risk Behaviors." *Journal of Behavioral Decision Making,* 15: 263–290.
3. *Dalbar Quantitative Analysis of Investor Behavior* (QAIB), Dalbar Inc., 2009.
4. Bonner, W. 2007. "Goldman Sachs fund loses 30%, Wall Street math fails to predict future." *The Daily Reckoning,* August 16. www.dailyreckoning.com .au/wall-street-math/2007/08/16/
5. Dowd, K., J. Cotter, C. Humphrey, and M. Woods. 2008. "How unlucky is 25-sigma?" Nottingham University Business School, Nottingham, UK, March 24. www.ucd.ie/bankingfinance/docs/wp/WP-08-04.pdf

Chapter 2   Investor Identity Fundamentals: Frames, Motivations and Goals

1. Maslow, A.H. 1943. "A Theory of Human Motivation." *Psychological Review,* 50: 370–396.

Chapter 3   Your Investor Personality: Your Character and Style

1. Burton, K. and A. Effinger. 2010. "Cohen Trades Secrecy for Golf With Investors Lured by 30% Gains." *Bloomberg Business,* February 26. Downloaded April 29, 2010 from www.businessweek.com/news/2010-02-26/cohen-trades-secrecy-for-golf-with-investors-lured-by-30-gains.html.
2. Hagstrom, R. 1999. *The Warren Buffett Portfolio.* Hoboken, NJ: John Wiley Sons.
3. Schwager, J. 2002. *Stock Market Wizards.* New York: HarperBusiness.
4. Dictionary.com. 2006. "Personality." http://dictionary.reference.com/search? q=personality.
5. McCrae, R.R., and P.T. Costa, Jr. 1996. "Toward a New Generation of Personality Theories: Theoretical Contexts for the Five-Factor Model." In J.S. Wiggins (ed.), *The Five-Factor Model of Personality: Theoretical Perspectives.* New York: Guilford, pp. 51–87.

6. Caspi, A. 2000. "The Child Is Father of the Man: Personality Continuities from Childhood to Adulthood." *Journal of Personality and Social Psychology* 78: 158–172.

7. Bradberry, T. and J. Greaves 2009. *Emotional Intelligence 2.0.* San Francisco: Publishers Group West.

8. Ameriks, J., T. Wranik, and P. Salovey. 2009. "Emotional Intelligence and Investor Behavior." CFA Society Research Institute.

9. See note 5.

10. Goldberg compiled these 300 responses into a new personality assessment tool, which he called the IPIP-NEO. John A. Johnson, a professor at Penn State University, posted Goldberg's phrases online in 1996. As of 2005, at least 175,000 people had answered the test items online. The five clusters remained consistent in others' research as well. Costa, P.T., Jr., and R.R. McCrae 1992. "Normal Personality Assessment in Clinical Practice: The NEO Personality Inventory." *Psychological Assessment* 4: 5–13.

11. "International Personality Item Pool: A Scientific Collaboratory for the Development of Advanced Measures of Personality Traits and Other Individual Differences," http://ipip.ori.org/.

12. Paulus, M.P., C. Rogalsky, A. Simmons, et al. 2003. "Increased Activation in the Right Insula during Risk-Taking Decision Making Is Related to Harm Avoidance and Neuroticism." *Neuroimage* 19(4) (August): 1439–1448.

13. Cohen, M.X., J. Young, J.M. Baek, et al. 2005. "Individual Differences in Extraversion and Dopamine Genetics Predict Neural Reward Responses." *Cognitive Brain Research* 25(3) (December): 851–861 (Epub November 11, 2005).

14. Barnea, A., H. Cronqvist, and S. Siegel. 2009. Working Paper, "Nature or Nurture: What Determines Investor Behavior?". Downloaded April 29, 2010 from: http://papers.ssrn.com/sol3/papers.cfm?abstract_id=1467088.

15. Sen, S., M. Burmeister, and D. Ghosh. 2004. "Meta-analysis of the Association between a Serotonin Transporter Promoter Polymorphism (5-HTTLPR) and Anxiety-Related Personality Traits." *American Journal of Medical Genetics. Part B, Neuropsychiatric Genetics.* 127(1) (May 15): 85–89.

16. Zuckerman, M., and D.M. Kuhlman. 2000. "Personality and Risk-Taking: Common Biosocial Factors." *Journal of Personality* 68: 999–1029.

17. Grinblatt, M., and M. Keloharju. 2006. "Sensation Seeking, Overconfidence, and Trading Activity." (September 14). Working Paper. http://icf.som.yale.edu/pdf/seminar06–07/Grinblatt.pdf.

18. Kuhnen C., and Chiao, J. 2009. "Genetic determinants of financial risk taking." *PLoS ONE* 4(2): e4362.

19. Cook, M. 2006. "What Makes a Trader Successful?" Handout at the Technical Securities Analysts of San Francisco Annual Conference.

Chapter 4   Your Investor Emotions: The Hidden Drivers of Behavior

1. Damasio, A. 1999. *The Feeling of What Happens: Body and Emotion in the Making of Consciousness.* New York: Harcourt Brace.

2. Beer, J.S., R.T. Knight, and M. D'Esposito. 2006. "Controlling the Integration of Emotion and Cognition: The Role of Frontal Cortex in Distinguishing Helpful from Hurtful Emotional Information." *Psychological Science* 17 (May): 448–453.

3. Bechara, A., A.R. Damasio, H. Damasio, and S.W. Anderson. 1994. "Insensitivity to Future Consequences Following Damage to Human Prefrontal Cortex." *Cognition* 50: 7–15.

4. Bechara, A., H. Damasio, D. Tranel, and A.R. Damasio. 2005. "The Iowa Gambling Task and the Somatic Marker Hypothesis: Some Questions and Answers." *Trends in Cognitive Sciences* 9(4) (April).

5. Bechara, A., H. Damasio, D. Tranel, and A.R. Damasio. 1997. "Deciding Advantageously before Knowing the Advantageous Strategy." *Science* 275: 1293–1295.

6. Trujillo, J.T., B. Knutson, M.P. Paulus, and P. Winkielman. *Taking gambles at face value: Effects of emotional expressions on risky decisions.* Manuscript under review.

7. Isen, A.M., T.E. Nygren, and F.G. Ashby. 1988. "Influence of Positive Affect on the Subjective Utility of Gains and Losses: It Is Just Not Worth the Risk." *Journal of Personality and Social Psychology* 55(5) (November): 710–717.

8. Isen, A. 1999. "Positive Affect." *Handbook of Cognition and Emotion*, ed. T. Dalgleish and M. Power. Chichester, England: John Wiley & Sons.

9. Lyubomirsky, S., and S. Nolen-Hoeksema. 1995. "Effects of Self-Focused Rumination on Negative Thinking and Interpersonal Problem-Solving." *Journal of Personality and Social Psychology* 69: 176–190.

10. Mellers, B.A., A. Schwartz, and I. Ritov. 1999. "Emotion-Based Choice." *Journal of Experimental Psychology* 128: 332–345.

11. Fogel, S.O., and T. Berry. 2006. "The Disposition Effect and Individual Investor Decisions: The Roles of Regret and Counterfactual Alternatives." *Journal of Behavioral Finance* 7(2): 107–116.

12. Lerner, J.S., D.A. Small, and G. Loewenstein. 2004. "Heart Strings and Purse Strings: Carry-over Effects of Emotions on Economic Transactions." *Psychological Science* 15: 337–341.

13. Ibid.

14. Lerner, J.S., and D. Keltner. 2001. "Fear, Anger, and Risk." *Journal of Personality and Social Psychology* 81: 146–159.

15. Bodenhausen, D., L. Sheppard, and G. Kramer. 1994. "Negative Affect and Social Judgment: The Differential Impact of Anger and Sadness." *European Journal of Social Psychology* 24(1): 45–62.

16. Ibid.

17. Malmendier, U. and G. Tate. 2009. "Superstar CEOs." *Quarterly Journal of Economics* 124, no. 4 (November 1, 2009): 1593–1638.

18. Drobny, S. 2006. *Inside the House of Money.* Hoboken, NJ: John Wiley & Sons, p. 78.

19. Ibid.

20. Lieberman, M.D., N.I. Eisenberger, M.J. Crockett, S.M. Tom, J.H. Pfeifer, and B.M. Way. 2007. "Putting Feelings into Words: Affect Labeling Disrupts Amygdala Activity in Response to Affective Stimuli." 18(5) (May): 421–8.

21. Kunda, Z. 1990. "The Case for Motivated Reasoning." *Psychological Bulletin* 108(3) (November): 480–498.

22. Ditto, P.H., G.D. Munro, A.M. Apanovitch, et al. 2003. "Spontaneous Skepticism: The Interplay of Motivation and Expectation in Responses to Favorable and Unfavorable Medical Diagnoses." *Personality and Social Psychology Bulletin* 29(9): 1120–1132.

23. Dawson, E., T. Gilovich, and D. Regan. 2002. "Motivated Reasoning and Performance on the Wason Selection Task." *Personality Social Psychology Bulletin* 28: 1379–1387.
24. Van Boven, L., and G. Loewenstein. 2003. "Social Projection of Transient Drive States." *Personality and Social Psychology Bulletin* 29: 1159–1168. 27.
25. Torre, P.S. "How (and Why) Athletes Go Broke," *Sports Illustrated* online. http://vault.sportsillustrated.cnn.com/vault/article/magazine/MAG1153364/1/index.htm.

Chapter 5   Your Investor Values: What's Most Important to You?

1. "Depression Babies: Do Macroeconomic Experiences Affect Risk-Taking?" Ulrike Malmendier (UC Berkeley and NBER) and Stefan Nagel (Stanford University and NBER), February 2009.
2. Roth, J.D. "George Kinder: Three Questions About Life Planning," Get Rich Slowly website, www.getrichslowly.org/blog/2009/02/15/george-kinder-three-questions-about-life-planning/, February 15, 2009.

Chapter 6   Your Investor Blind Spots: Identifying (and Avoiding) Mental Traps

1. Kahneman, D. and A. Tversky. 1979. "Prospect Theory: An Analysis of Decision under Risk." *Econometrica*, XLVII, 263–291.
2. Andreassen, Paul. 1990. "Judgmental Extrapolation and Market Overreaction: On the Use and Disuse of News." *Journal of Behavioral Decision Making* 3: 153–174.
3. Shoda, Y., W. Mischel, and P.K. Peake. 1990. "Predicting Adolescent Cognitive and Self-Regulatory Competencies from Preschool Delay of Gratification: Identifying diagnostic conditions." *Developmental Psychology*, 26(6), 978–986.
4. Tversky, A. and D. Kahneman. 1974. "Judgment under Uncertainty: Heuristics and Biases." *Science*, New Series, 185 (4157) (September 27): 1124–1131.

Chapter 7   Your Investor Stress: Smoothing Out the Ups and Downs

1. Sarafino, E.P. 1998. *Health Psychology: Biopsychosocial Interactions*, 3rd ed. New York: John Wiley & Sons.
2. Seligman, M., and S. Maier. 1967. "Failure to Escape Traumatic Shock." *Journal of Experimental Psychology* 74: 1–9.
3. Berns, G.S., J. Chappelow, M. Cekic, C.F. Zink, G. Pagnoni, and M.E. Martin-Skurski. 2006. "Neurobiologic Substrates of Dread." *Science*, 312:754–758.
4. Ariely, D., Gneezy, U., G. Loewnstein, and N. Mazar. 2009. "Large Stakes, Big Mistakes." *Review of Economic Studies* 75, 1–19.
5. Crouse, K. "Avoiding the Deep End When It Comes to Jitters," *The New York Times*, July 25, 2009, www.nytimes.com/2009/07/26/sports/26swim.html?_r=1&scp=13&sq=optimal%20work%20schedule&st=cse.
6. Ibid.

7. Zuckerman, G. 2009. *The Greatest Trade Ever.* New York: Broadway Books. p. 118.
8. Gregory Zuckerman, "A Bond Star's Plays Turn Riskier," *Wall Street Journal,* August 23, 2006.
9. Lo, A., and D. Repin. 2002. "The Psychophysiology of Real-Time Financial Risk Processing." *Journal of Cognitive Neuroscience* 14: 323–339.
10. Davidson, R.J., J. Kabat-Zinn, J. Schumacher, et al. 2003. "Alterations in Brain and Immune Function Produced by Mindfulness Meditation." *Psychosomatic Medicine* 65: 564–570.
11. Speca, M., L. Carlson, E. Goodey, and M. Angen. 2000. "A Randomized, Wait-List Controlled Clinical Trial: The Effect of a Mindfulness Meditation-Based Stress Reduction Program on Mood and Symptoms of Stress in Cancer Outpatients." *Psychosomatic Medicine* 62: 613–622.
12. Schwartz, G.E., R.J. Davidson, and D.J. Goleman. 1978. "Patterning of Cognitive and Somatic Processes in the Self-Regulation of Anxiety: Effects of Meditation versus Exercise." *Psychosomatic Medicine* 40: 321–328.
13. Arnold, L.E. 2001. "Alternative Treatments for Adults with Attention-Deficit Hyperactivity Disorder (ADHD)." *Annals of the New York Academy of Sciences* 931 (June): 310–341.
14. Kristeller, J., and T. Johnson. 2003. "Cultivating Loving-Kindness: A Two-Stage Model for the Effects of Meditation on Compassion, Altruism and Spirituality. Portions presented at the conference: Works of Love: Scientific and Religious Perspectives on Altruism." Villanova University, Villanova, Pennsylvania, June 3.
15. Shannahoff-Khalsa, D.S. 2004. "An Introduction to Kundalini Yoga Meditation Techniques That Are Specific for the Treatment of Psychiatric Disorders." *Journal of Alternative and Complementary Medicine* 10(1) (February): 91–101.
16. Woolery, A., H. Myers, B. Sternlieb, and L. Zeltzer. 2004. "A Yoga Intervention for Young Adults with Elevated Symptoms of Depression." *Alternative Therapies in Health and Medicine* 10(2) (March–April): 60–63.
17. Jensen, P.S., and D.T. Kenny. 2004. "The Effects of Yoga on the Attention and Behavior of Boys with Attention-Deficit/Hyperactivity Disorder (ADHD)." *Journal of Attention Disorders* 7(4) (May): 205–216.
18. Sharma, K., and V. Shukla. 1988. "Rehabilitation of Drug-Addicted Persons: The Experience of the Nav-Chetna Center in India." *Bulletin on Narcotics* 40(1): 43–49.
19. See note 16.
20. Beck, J.S. 1995. *Cognitive Therapy: Basics and Beyond.* New York: Guilford Press.
21. Murphy, S., and D. Hirschhorn. 2001. *The Trading Athlete: Winning the Mental Game of Online Trading.* New York: John Wiley & Sons, p. 52.
22. Engelmann, J.B., C. Capra, N. Monica, C. Noussair, and G.S. Berns. 2009. "Expert Financial Advice Neurobiologically 'Offloads' Financial Decision-Making under Risk." *PLoS One* 4:e4957.

Chapter 8 Being Your Best Self

1. "The Most Powerful Trader on Wall Street You've Never Heard Of," *BusinessWeek.* July 21, 2003. Retrieved March 15, 2010. www.businessweek.com/magazine/content/03_29/b3842001_mz001.htm.

2. Wood, J., Perunovic, W.Q. E., and J.W. Lee (2009). "Positive Self-Statements: Power for Some, Peril for Others." *Psychological Science*, 20(7), 860–866.

3. Verdelle, C.L. "Effect of Mental practice on the Development of a Certain Motor Skill." *Research Quarterly of the American Association for Health, Physical Education, & Recreation.* Vol. 31,1960, 560–569.

4. Lane, S.D., O.V. Tcheremissine, L.M. Lieving, et al. 2005. "Acute Effects of Alprazolam on Risky Decision Making in Humans." *Psychopharmacology* (Berlin), April 14.

5. Lane, S.D., D.R. Cherek, C.J. Pietras, and O.V. Tcheremissine. 2004. "Alcohol Effects on Human Risk Taking." *Psychopharmacology* (Berlin) 172(1) (February): 68–77; and Lane, S.D., D.R. Cherek, O.V. Tcheremissine, et al. 2005. "Acute Marijuana Effects on Human RiskTaking." *Neuropsychopharmacology* 30(4) (April): 800–809.

6. Baumeister, R.F., K.D. Vohs, and D.M. Tice. 2007. "The Strength Model of Self-Control." *Current Directions in Psychological Science* 16 (6), 351–355.

7. Weinberg, B.A., and B.K. Bealer. 2001. *The World of Caffeine. The Science and Culture of the World's Most Popular Drug.* New York: Routledge.

8. Lehrer, J., "Blame It On the Brain: The Latest Neuroscience Research Suggests Spreading Resolutions Out Over Time Is the Best Approach." *Wall Street Journal* W2, Saturday/Sunday, December 26–27, 2009.

9. Lykken, D.T. (1999). *Happiness: What Studies on Twins Show Us about Nature, Nurture, and the Happiness Set Point.* New York: Golden Books.

About the Authors

Richard L. Peterson, MD, works at the intersection of psychology and the markets. He is a co-founder of MarketPsych LLC (with Dr. Murtha), where he trains financial advisors, portfolio managers, traders, and executives in emotion management and intuitive decision skills. He is also Managing Director of MarketPsy Capital LLC, a psychology-based asset-management firm. Additionally he operates MarketPsychAdvisor.com, which offers investors psychological research on individual stocks, ETFs, and markets. Dr. Peterson received *cum laude* degrees in electrical engineering and Plan II Arts at the University of Texas in 1995. In 2000 he received a *cum laude* Doctor of Medicine degree from the University of Texas Medical Branch. He performed post-doctoral neuroeconomics research at Stanford University, and he is Board-certified in psychiatry.

Dr. Peterson has published scientific research in finance, psychology, and neuroscience journals and textbooks. He is the author of the 2007 Wiley title *Inside the Investor's Brain,* which was praised as "exceptionally well-written" and "outstanding" by *Barron's.* Dr. Peterson frequently appears in the financial press including NPR, BBC, Bloomberg, and CNBC.

He is an associate editor of the *Journal of Behavioral Finance* and is on the board of advisors of several organizations including the Social Science Research Network (SSRN) in the experimental and behavioral finance area, the CFA Society of Los Angeles Applied Behavioral Finance Group, and the Market Technicians Association Educational Advisory Board. His long-term fascination with the markets grew out of his early investing (since age 12). His primary professional interest is the role of emotion in investment decision making, both to help investors avoid making common mistakes and to identify and profit from emotion-related patterns in financial markets, and he has led top-rated seminars and workshops globally.

Dr. Peterson enjoys hiking, yoga, surfing, and family, and he lives in Los Angeles with his wife and two daughters.

Frank F. Murtha, PhD, received his doctorate in counseling psychology from the State University of New York at Buffalo in February 2001. A recognized gambling expert, his groundbreaking dissertation was the first to explore the effect of cognitive errors in gambling behavior. He has taught at numerous universities and is adjunct faculty at New York University. At the New York-based consulting firm RHR International Company, Dr. Murtha developed senior executives in leadership and pioneered a specialty in the new field of behavioral finance. His clients have included investment banks, financial services companies, and day trading firms where he has coached advisors, analysts, and portfolio managers in applied investing psychology. Dr. Murtha went on to co-found MarketPsych LLC (www.MarketPsych.com) where he has led hundreds of investing psychology workshops/trainings for financial professionals. He has developed a reputation as an engaging speaker who uses humor, plain spoken language and frequent movie quotes to make academic material accessible and fun to audiences. He has been interviewed by numerous news and print media and been featured multiple times on CNBC, NPR, and on *World Business Review,* hosted by Alexander Haig.

For fun he enjoys engaging in any activity related to baseball, working on location with his brother, Loring's films, reading historical fiction and non-fiction, playing poker, or "throwing a few" with his hometown friends in his dart league.

He works as a consultant, speaker, and writer based in New York City with his wife, Lillian and his son, Francis.

Index